COOKING FOR A CROWD

COOKING FOR A CROWD

MENUS, RECIPES, AND STRATEGIES FOR ENTERTAINING 10 TO 50

SUSAN WYLER

Portions of this book were originally published as *Cooking for a Crowd* by Harmony Books © 1988.

Printed in the United States of America

Rodale Inc. makes every effort to use acid-free ♾, recycled paper ♻.

Cover photo by Ben Fink
Author photo by Michael Downend
Book design by Carol Angstadt

Library of Congress Cataloging-in-Publication Data

Wyler, Susan.
Cooking for a crowd : menus, recipes, and strategies for entertaining 10 to 50 / Susan Wyler.— [Rev. ed.]
p. cm.
"Portions of this book were originally published as Cooking for a Crowd (Harmony Books (c) 1988)."—ECIP galley.
Includes index.
ISBN-13 978–1–59486–011–9 paperback
ISBN-10 1–59486–011–4 paperback
1. Quantity cookery. 2. Menus. I. Title.
TX820.W95 2005
641.5'7—dc22 2005019534

Distributed to the trade by Holtzbrinck Publishers

2 4 6 8 10 9 7 5 3 1 paperback

We inspire and enable people to improve their lives and the world around them

For more of our products visit **rodalestore.com** or call 800-848-4735

Contents

Acknowledgments

My very sincere thanks and grateful appreciation to all those who made this new edition possible:

My great agent, Jane Dystel.

Margot Schupf, executive editor of Rodale Books, who acquired the project.

Miriam Backes, senior editor of Rodale Books, who shepherded the book through every stage with grace, humor, and attention to detail.

Carol Angstadt, art director, who created such a handsome design.

Roy Finamore, freelance editor, who is simply the best at what he does.

Kimberly Tweed, assistant editor, who was so helpful at every stage.

Photographer Ben Fink, who created such a beautiful cover.

Prop stylist Marina Malchin, whose taste is impeccable.

Food stylist Alison Attenborough, an artist in the kitchen and under camera.

To Max and Marilyn DeLaure and my darling goddaughter Naiya Claire, who help me test Thanksgiving dinner every year.

And to my wonderful friends in the Endless Mountains, who shared so many crowded parties. I love you all: Pam and Paul Kelly; Pat and Larry Robertson; Katherine Ashe and Peter Wynne; Kevin Huffman and Allan Duncan and Maddie and Isabel; Mickey and Helene Campbell; Melanie Urdang and Joe and Haley Rosado; Ed Chaplin and Susan Ensley; Bob Stark; Alison Armstrong; Jeanette Robertson and Ron Coyan; Billee and Maria Pileggi; Ken Goodie and Todd Moffett; Allan Hochberg; Barbara Remington; Karen Blomain and Michael Downend; Jan and Ginny Quackenbush; Jill Smolowe and Becky and Joe Treen; Anuraj, Ann, and Kaie Bismal; Michael Young and Randall Sobocinski. And to Greg Mowery, and especially Richard and Emily Buckingham, who made the trek.

Introduction

It's hard to believe it has been more than 15 years since I wrote the article for *Food & Wine* that launched this book. I had been food editor at the magazine for some time and had written any number of pieces. But the feature with recipes called "Cooking for a Crowd," designed for entertaining 10 or more guests, was an immediate success, garnering more fan mail than any article I had ever written. It was clear the subject warranted a book.

Many of us at that time were excellent cooks and quite sophisticated about food—having been raised on Julia Child, James Beard, and Jacques Pépin—but our dinner parties almost always maxed out at six or eight. With families growing and moving into larger homes, the number of people we began to entertain and the way we cooked for them was in the process of changing radically. New cuisines—regional as well as exotic—entered the repertoire, and many ingredients once rare became standard stock on supermarket shelves. From such lifestyle changes and culinary development, the first edition of this book evolved.

In the intervening years, the trend toward large-scale entertaining has done nothing but expand. Children appear ever more often at the adult dinner table, and sizable gatherings of friends and family call for casual parties that do not involve hours of last-minute preparation and are, in fact, frequently potluck affairs. Often Saturday night at a country house or the beach grows into big numbers, as people drop by and the telephone rings . . . and as more and more babies are born. Baby showers, wedding showers, family reunions, the celebration of holidays, and birthday parties, all involving larger groups, fill our busy calendars. For those who entertain rarely, large parties offer an occasion to repay social obligations built up over the year. And for some people, like me and many of my friends, who groove on cooking and entertaining, the challenge and excitement of a large theme party provide a delightful opportunity to show off.

Whatever your situation—whether you are a serious cook, an eager novice, a home caterer, or simply someone who wants to throw a fabulous large party—the collection of recipes and the game plan for do-ahead preparations that accompany each menu in this book will lead you through the process with guaranteed success. Whether you're in the mood for a Flavorful Dinner for Good Friends, a rollicking Mexican Grillfest, a Black and Orange Halloween Party, or an old-fashioned Italian Abbondanza, whether you are catering your own wedding or throwing a shower for a good friend, *Cooking for a Crowd* offers a tempting menu for every occasion.

While many of the original recipes have stood up over time, wherever possible I have simplified both ingredients and instructions. There's nothing like practice and repetition to point up what is essential and what can be pared away. When feasible, I've removed extraneous ingredients. Like a well-written sentence, a good recipe should contain just the essentials; extras, like too many adjectives, simply confuse matters and can be expensive. Rarely are three herbs necessary where one will do. Many times, repeated preparation of a dish has shown me an easier technique, and I've passed that along as well. But for fans of the first book, you'll notice that many of these menus are new, and some existing plans have been significantly revised.

As recipes and articles in the best food magazines evidence, trends in dining change over the years. That's why there is always room for new cookbooks. I am acutely aware that during the past decade, tastes have changed. Just as many children we know are better traveled at the age of 2 than we were at 20, so their parents have amazingly sophisticated palates, dining out regularly on regional Italian food, as well as French bistro cooking, Mexican, Thai, sushi, Greek, Spanish, Vietnamese, Chinese, and Scandinavian food. Part of the fun of cooking and eating encompasses this sort of armchair travel.

In this revised and updated edition of *Cooking for a Crowd,* you'll find different international cuisines represented as well as many of the basics—like baked beans, barbecued chicken, and potato salad—we've reclaimed and learned to love. In a nod to current nutritional guidelines, there is less butter and more olive oil. Some recipes, such as the seafood medallions once featured in the Elegant Dinner Party in the first edition of this book, have been supplanted by trendier dishes, in this case Tuna Tartare with Avocado and Ruby Grapefruit Vinaigrette. And given the hectic pace and nutritional concerns of so many people's modern lifestyles, I have approached many of the parties with a lighter, more casual touch.

The contemporary grocery shelf, not to speak of the many high-end food shops and online sources for specialty ingredients, has opened up a broad vista of new products for the creative cook to play with. Because chefs and food magazines popularize these flavors, I've tried to incorporate some of them, where appropriate, in recipes: smoked Spanish paprika *(pimentón de la Vera),* sushi-grade tuna, and a couple of slightly more unusual dried chiles. But by and large, I decided that when you are "cooking for a crowd," you have enough work to do, and shopping should be kept simple. That's why I've designed the vast majority of these recipes to work superbly with ingredients you can buy easily in your supermarket.

HOW TO USE THIS BOOK

From front to back, the menus in *Cooking for a Crowd* are arranged by the number of people they serve, moving from smaller (10 to 12) to larger (50 or more). So one way to choose what to make is to decide on your number of guests and then see what is offered. On the other hand, wherever possible, I've indicated which dishes can be divided easily; with the exception of baking recipes, this includes most of them. So another way to plan your menu is to decide what kind of party you want to throw or what kind of food you are in the mood for and adjust the amounts as necessary.

Keep this thought in mind: You need not make every recipe in a menu! Because I wrote a cookbook, I wanted to offer as many ideas to my readers as possible. But except for the main course, purchased substitutions already prepared can take the place of many appetizers and desserts. In the Indian Buffet on page 80, which serves 12 to 16, I give a recipe for Minted Cherry Chutney, made with dried cherries and fresh mint. In a blink, you could substitute your favorite purchased chutney, such as Major Grey's Mango Chutney, which is available all over. For the Italian Abbondanza, besides the beef and pork cooked ahead in the sauce, there is a recipe for homemade meatballs; purchased Italian sausages are a fine alternative, and they require no work. In most menus, a simple steamed or roasted vegetable can almost always stand in for a more complicated preparation; good bread can often substitute for a potato or rice dish. Because I've made all these parties, I know how much work it takes; so there are purposely places where I've given you easy options—a buttered green vegetable, perhaps—or suggested a bought dessert—whether baklava or a fruit pie. If you have the energy and you want to go ahead and make a recipe of your own, by all means do so. But know that these days, there are many fine options that can be purchased.

Note also that I often include appetizers to be nibbled with drinks, a first course, and a main course before the dessert. Depending upon how you like to entertain, in most cases you can omit the starter if you want to simplify the meal. The range of servings tends toward the generous side. If you're wondering why that range is sometimes a little broad—that is, serves 20 to

24—it's because cooking for a crowd is a little imprecise. By that I mean if you invite four or six people to dinner, you know exactly who's coming. On the other hand, no matter how you emphasize RSVP, when you invite a crowd of people over, there's no telling the exact number, and it's hard to decide how to count children. In most cases, if I've erred at all, it is on the high side; so you never have to worry about having enough food.

Very large parties are also places to utilize well-meaning friends. When guests offer to bring a dish, either say, "Thank you, I could use, say, another dessert," or ask them if they would mind making one of the dishes in the book. Since most of the recipes are designed to be cooked in advance, reheating or finishing something at the last minute at your house should pose no problem.

Simplifying by offering fewer choices is especially easy for the larger parties. For example, my Mexican Grillfest (see page 233), which prepares enough food for at least three dozen guests, lists four appetizers in the menu: Barbecued Carnitas, crisp marinated pork cubes served with a fresh Pineapple-Chipotle Salsa; Guacamole for a Crowd; a Mexican Shrimp and Jicama Salad with jalapeños and cilantro, which is eaten with chips like a salsa; and an easy Taco Bean Dip. But you might choose to serve just the dip, guacamole, and bowls of purchased salsa, perhaps with peeled cooked shrimp served alongside, with chips and crudités as well, for dipping.

If you adapt a menu for a smaller number of people, you can either reduce the portions of all the recipes or make fewer dishes. With the Ultimate Tailgate Party (see page 196), for example, rather than doing both the Chicken Pasta Salad with Lemon-Sesame Dressing and the Potato Salad with Sweet Sausages and Mushrooms, prepare just one. Keep in mind that the servings noted for each recipe are within the context of the menu. When several main courses are listed, set off by themselves, they would serve fewer people. By and large, two main courses for 12 will serve 20 to 24. There is, after all, only so much food people can put into their stomachs . . . even when they're trying really hard.

When approaching the daunting task of making a meal—no, more than a meal, a party—for a dozen or more people, many home cooks throw up their hands. "Oh, if only I were a chef," they exclaim. Actually, chefs have it much easier. It's not just their facility with a knife or expert knowledge of ingredients; the professional has a small brigade of helpers to do all the hard work. Plus, the restaurant boasts equipment geared to feeding lots of people that the home cook has no access to, like a large walk-in refrigerator. So you cannot duplicate at home what goes on in a restaurant kitchen, and your job is in many ways harder. On the other hand, food appropriate for cooking at home is, in general, less fussy than restaurant food, and with the right recipe choices and a schedule, you can do a great job and enjoy your own party to boot. That's why in this book, you'll find recipes that are friendly to the cook and designed for a home kitchen. "Do-Ahead Planning" schedules let you stagger the workload and produce the food for the party at a pace you can handle. Detailed instructions tell you when you can make a dish a month in advance and freeze it or cook something a few days in advance and let it mellow in the refrigerator. Because when the guests finally arrive, you should be able to greet them with confidence and a big smile.

Which is what *Cooking for a Crowd* is all about.

A Note about the Ingredients

Unless otherwise noted:

- **Eggs are grade-A "large."**
- **Salt is ordinary salt or coarse kosher salt, though sea salt, which I prefer, can be substituted.**
- **Butter is unsalted.**
- **Flour is measured with the scoop-and-sweep technique.**

Flavorful Dinner for Good Friends

FOR 10 TO 12

THREE-MUSHROOM LASAGNE WITH GORGONZOLA SAUCE

MEDITERRANEAN SEAFOOD CASSEROLE
GARLIC CROUTONS (PAGE 60)

COMPOSED SALAD OF CARROTS, BEETS, AND CUCUMBER

HAZELNUT DACQUOISE WITH CHOCOLATE CREAM

This is, quite simply, delicious food to share with your favorite people. I love the flavors that make up these recipes: wild mushrooms, blue cheese, tomatoes, garlic, fennel, seafood, and, last but not least, chocolate and hazelnuts. Maybe it's the vibrant Mediterranean flavors of these dishes and maybe it's the close friends I've shared them with, but I'm convinced this menu guarantees an extraordinarily pleasant evening, especially for the cook, since much of the dinner can be accomplished in advance. To me, this blending of modern trends with traditional tastes reflects the best of informal entertaining.

While the lasagne can certainly be made with dried noodles, the variety of mushrooms produces a subtle and complex flavor that deserves the delicacy of fresh pasta. If you don't feel like making your own, many stores sell fresh sheets of pasta for lasagne. Though the entire dish can be assembled up to a day in advance, bake it shortly before serving to preserve its subtle flavor and light texture.

I love the taste of bouillabaisse, but I'm not comfortable with soup as a main course at a company dinner, and I don't like the fishy smell that permeates the house. That's why I developed this casserole, which has all the vibrant, Mediterranean flavors of the original—olive oil, garlic, saffron, leeks—and much of the same delectable seafood but requires no fish stock; only the cooking liquid from the mussels and clams is used. Garlic toast helps to sop up the delicious juices.

Though the dishes are savory and rich, this is a relatively light meal, so I offer a more substantial salad than usual before dessert. Colorful and different, it makes a striking presentation on the plate. I prefer the salad at this point in the meal, but if it works better for you, it could be served as the first course.

Dark chocolate and toasted hazelnuts are an unbeatable combination, which are here combined in an elegant presentation that is guaranteed to draw applause from even the most sophisticated of guests. The dacquoise can be completely assembled up to 24 hours before serving. Although the nut meringue layers soften slightly, the hazelnuts remain crunchy, and as with most chocolate desserts, the flavor improves overnight.

DO-AHEAD PLANNING

UP TO 2 DAYS IN ADVANCE: Make the tomato sauce base (Step 1) for the seafood casserole.

UP TO 1 DAY IN ADVANCE: Make the pasta and assemble the lasagne. Cover and refrigerate. Cook the mussels and clams and complete the sauce for the seafood casserole (Step 2). Refrigerate separately; remove about 30 minutes before you plan to cook the seafood casserole. Cook the beets for the salad and shred them; shred the carrots. Toss both with dressing. Wash and trim the watercress. Prepare the Hazelnut Dacquoise with Chocolate Cream.

UP TO 6 HOURS BEFORE SERVING: Make the Garlic Croutons to accompany the seafood casserole. Follow the instructions in Step 2 of Roquefort Caesar Salad on page 60 but use 2 loaves of French bread and ½ cup olive oil and do not cut the slices into cubes.

ABOUT 1½ HOURS IN ADVANCE: Shred the cucumbers, toss them with dressing, and assemble the composed salads. Refrigerate.

ABOUT 30 MINUTES BEFORE SERVING: Bake the Three-Mushroom Lasagne. Assemble the Mediterranean Seafood Casserole. Finish the casserole either before you sit down to eat the lasagne or after you clear the table from the first course.

THREE-MUSHROOM LASAGNE WITH GORGONZOLA SAUCE

12 TO 16 SERVINGS

At the original book party for *Cooking for a Crowd*, which was held at New York's favorite restaurant, Union Square Cafe, this is the menu that was served. Imagine my thrill when then-chef Ali Barker, Michael Romano's predecessor, kept the lasagne on the restaurant's menu for a year. For this more formal service at the party, the chef constructed individual portions of lasagne between thin rounds of homemade pasta.

2 ounces dried porcini mushrooms

2 sticks (½ pound) plus 1 tablespoon unsalted butter

3½ tablespoons olive oil

4 large shallots, minced

2 pounds fresh white button or cremini mushrooms, minced

1½ teaspoons chopped fresh tarragon or ½ teaspoon dried

1½ teaspoons salt

½ teaspoon freshly ground black pepper

Cayenne pepper

4 tablespoons fresh lemon juice

2 small garlic cloves, minced

¾ pound fresh shiitake mushrooms, stemmed, caps sliced ¼ inch thick

½ cup all-purpose flour

2 cups milk

1 cup heavy cream

¼ pound Gorgonzola dolcelatte cheese

¾ cup freshly grated imported Parmesan cheese (about 3 ounces)

Homemade Lasagne Noodles (opposite page) or 1 package (16 ounces) lasagne noodles

1. In a medium bowl, cover the porcini with 3 cups boiling water. Let stand until softened, 20 to 30 minutes. Lift out the mushrooms; reserve the liquid. Coarsely chop the porcini. Strain the liquid through a double layer of cheesecloth and reserve 2 cups.

2. Meanwhile, in a large heavy skillet, melt 2 tablespoons of the butter in 1 tablespoon of the olive oil over moderately high heat. Add 2 tablespoons of the minced shallots and half the minced fresh mushrooms. Sauté, stirring frequently, until the mushrooms give up their liquid, it evaporates, and the mushrooms become lightly browned, 5 to 7 minutes. Season these mushroom duxelles with half the tarragon and ¼ teaspoon each salt and black pepper, a dash or two of cayenne, and 1 tablespoon of the lemon juice. Scrape into a bowl. Wipe out the skillet with a paper towel. Repeat with 2 more tablespoons of the butter and 1 tablespoon olive oil, adding 2 more tablespoons of the shallots and the remaining minced fresh mushrooms. Season as above. Add to the bowl. Wipe out the skillet.

3. In the same large skillet, melt 3 tablespoons of the butter in the remaining 1½ tablespoons oil over moderately high heat. Add the remaining minced shallots and the garlic and sauté for 30 seconds. Add the shiitake and porcini mushrooms and sauté, stirring frequently, for 3 minutes. Reduce the heat to moderately low and cook, stirring frequently, for 5 minutes. Add 1 cup of the reserved porcini liquid and simmer, partially covered, for 5 to 10 minutes, until the mushrooms are tender but still slightly chewy. Uncover and cook, stirring frequently, until the remaining liquid evaporates. Season with the remaining 2 tablespoons lemon juice and salt and pepper to taste. Add to the mushroom duxelles and set aside.

4. In a large heavy saucepan, melt 1 stick of butter over moderate heat. Add the flour and cook, stirring, for 2 to 3 minutes without letting the flour color. Whisk in the remaining 1 cup mushroom liquid, the milk, and the cream. Bring to a boil, whisking constantly, until thickened and smooth. Reduce the heat and simmer, whisking frequently, for 5 minutes. Turn off the heat. Whisk in the Gorgonzola and ½ cup of the Parmesan cheese until melted. Season with 1 teaspoon salt and several dashes of cayenne.

5. In a large pot of boiling salted water, cook the lasagne noodles until just tender, about 1 minute after the water returns to a boil for fresh noodles, about 12 minutes for the dried variety. Drain and rinse under cold running water. Place in a bowl of cold water and, one by one, lay the noodles out in a single layer on kitchen towels to dry.

6. To assemble the lasagne, generously butter 2 large baking pans, 9 × 13 × 2 inches. If the sauce has cooled, reheat it slightly over low heat. Arrange a layer of noodles in the bottom of each dish, trimming to fit, if necessary, and overlapping the edges only slightly. Spread a thin layer of mushrooms over the noodles (using one-quarter of the total amount in each pan) and drizzle about 1 cup of sauce over the mushrooms in each pan. Repeat with another layer of noodles, mushrooms, and sauce. Top with a final layer of noodles. Spread the remaining sauce over the noodles, dividing evenly, and divide the remaining ¼ cup grated Parmesan cheese evenly over the tops. Dot each with 1 tablespoon butter. (The lasagne can be assembled completely and refrigerated, covered, overnight or frozen for up to 2 weeks.)

7. Heat the oven to 375°F. Bake the lasagne (thawed, if frozen) uncovered for 20 to 30 minutes, until heated through and lightly browned on top.

HOMEMADE LASAGNE NOODLES

MAKES ABOUT ¾ POUND, ENOUGH FOR 2 PANS OF LASAGNE

Though you can roll out pasta dough by hand with a heavy rolling pin (I did it for years), it takes muscle. A food processor and an inexpensive hand-cranked pasta machine turn this process into a breeze.

3 eggs

2¼ cups all-purpose flour

1. In a food processor fitted with the metal blade, in two batches, combine the eggs and flour. Process until well blended and the mixture resembles coarse sand. Turn out the dough and knead into a ball. Cover with a sheet of plastic wrap and a kitchen towel to keep it moist.

2. Tear off lemon-size pieces of dough to work with. Keep the remaining dough covered until you are ready for it. Pass the piece of dough through the widest setting on the pasta machine. Fold the dough in thirds like a letter and pass through the same setting. Repeat two more times to complete the kneading of the dough. Then pass the dough through consecutively smaller settings until it is rolled through the thinnest setting.

3. Drape the dough over a rack (or the back of a chair) to dry for at least 20 minutes. Trim into manageable 6- to 8-inch lengths before cooking. (The noodles can be sealed in plastic bags and refrigerated for up to 2 days before using.)

MEDITERRANEAN SEAFOOD CASSEROLE

12 SERVINGS

The do-ahead trick in this recipe is to steam the clams and mussels in Step 2 until they just open. When they are reheated, they will finish cooking and taste fresh. If you cook them completely in advance, they will toughen when reheated.

Garlic croutons are a traditional accompaniment.

⅓ cup plus 2 tablespoons extra-virgin olive oil

4 medium leeks (white and tender green) or 2 large onions, chopped

6 large garlic cloves, chopped

2 cans (28 ounces each) Italian peeled tomatoes, drained and coarsely cut up

1½ teaspoons fennel seeds, lightly crushed

Pinch of saffron threads

½ teaspoon salt

2 shallots, minced

1½ cups dry white wine

½ teaspoon crushed hot red pepper

¾ cup coarsely chopped parsley

4 pounds mussels, preferably cultivated, debearded

2 dozen cherrystone clams, scrubbed

3 pounds firm-textured white fish fillets, such as scrod, red snapper, halibut, cut into 3 × 2-inch pieces

12 jumbo shrimp or langostinos in their shells, rinsed

1 pound bay scallops or quartered sea scallops

2 tablespoons Pernod, optional

1. In a large nonreactive flameproof casserole, heat ⅓ cup of the oil. Add the leeks and cook over moderate heat, stirring occasionally, until they are very soft and just begin to color, about 10 minutes. Add two-thirds of the chopped garlic and cook until fragrant, about 1 minute. Add the tomatoes, fennel seeds, saffron, and salt; simmer until the sauce thickens, about 20 minutes. (The tomato sauce can be made up to 2 days ahead and refrigerated, covered. Reheat before Step 3.)

2. In a large nonreactive saucepan, heat the remaining 2 tablespoons oil over moderately low heat. Add the shallots and remaining garlic and cook for 30 seconds. Add the wine, hot pepper, and ¼ cup of the parsley and bring to a boil over high heat. Dump in the mussels and clams, cover tightly, and steam, stirring up the shellfish from the bottom once or twice, until they just open, about 3 minutes. Immediately remove the mussels and clams from the broth and set aside in their shells; discard any that do not open. Strain the broth through a double thickness of cheesecloth and add to the tomato sauce. (The recipe can be prepared to this point up to 1 day in advance. Cover and refrigerate the shellfish and sauce separately. Let stand at room temperature for about 30 minutes before you plan to cook the casserole.)

3. Shortly before you are ready to serve the first course, arrange the fish and shrimp in a large paella pan or flameproof casserole. Scatter the scallops around the pan. Quickly bring the tomato sauce to a boil. Stir in the Pernod and pour over the seafood. Cover, bring to a simmer, and cook without stirring for 5 minutes. Uncover and tuck the mussels and clams around the other seafood. Cover and simmer until the shellfish are hot and the shrimp are cooked through, about 5 minutes longer. Sprinkle the remaining parsley over the top. Serve in shallow soup plates.

COMPOSED SALAD OF CARROTS, BEETS, AND CUCUMBER

10 TO 12 SERVINGS

Finely julienne the vegetables for this colorful salad using the julienne blade on a food processor or a mandoline or Japanese vegetable slicer. If not, use the shredding disk to grate them.

2 bunches of beets

3 long, narrow European seedless cucumbers

¾ teaspoon coarse salt

8 large carrots

1½ tablespoons fresh lemon juice

2 tablespoons balsamic vinegar

¼ cup olive oil

1 teaspoon grated orange zest

3 tablespoons fresh orange juice

2 teaspoons sugar

2 tablespoons rice wine vinegar

1½ teaspoons Asian sesame oil

1 tablespoon toasted sesame seeds

2 tablespoons minced chives or scallion greens

Watercress, for garnish

1. Heat the oven to 375°F. Trim the stems off the beets, leaving about 3 inches attached. Wash the beets and wrap in heavy-duty foil. Bake in the oven for 1 to 1¼ hours, or until just tender but still firm. Let cool; then trim and peel.

2. Julienne the cucumbers in a food processor or on a mandoline. Put in a bowl and toss with the salt. Let stand for at least 15 minutes while you prepare the other vegetables.

3. Peel the carrots and julienne them. Place in a bowl and toss with the lemon juice, 1 tablespoon of the balsamic vinegar, and 2 tablespoons of the olive oil.

4. Julienne the beets. Put them in a separate bowl and toss with the orange zest, orange juice, 1 teaspoon of the sugar, the remaining 1 tablespoon balsamic vinegar, and the remaining 2 tablespoons olive oil.

5. Drain the cucumbers; pat dry on paper towels. Put the cucumbers in another bowl and toss with the rice vinegar, sesame oil, toasted sesame seeds, chives, and the remaining 1 teaspoon sugar.

6. To assemble, arrange mounds of carrots, beets, and cucumbers on a large platter or on individual plates. Set a few sprigs of watercress in the center for garnish.

HAZELNUT DACQUOISE WITH CHOCOLATE CREAM

12 SERVINGS

An elegant but surprisingly light dessert, this is, in a word, fabulous!

1½ cups hazelnuts (6 ounces)

1¼ cups granulated sugar

¼ cup confectioners' sugar

6 egg whites

Pinch of cream of tartar

Pinch of salt

8 ounces semisweet chocolate

½ cup brewed coffee

1 tablespoon Frangelico (hazelnut liqueur), optional

1 teaspoon vanilla extract

2 cups heavy cream

Toasted hazelnuts or shaved chocolate, for garnish

1. Heat the oven to 250°F. Butter and flour 3 baking sheets. Make sure they can all fit in your oven, even if the edges of 2 overlap slightly. Trace a 10-inch circle onto each sheet.

2. In two batches in a food processor, grind the hazelnuts with ½ cup of the granulated sugar until finely ground. Transfer to a bowl.

3. Sift the confectioners' sugar over the ground hazelnuts and toss to mix.

4. In a large bowl, beat the egg whites until foamy. Add the cream of tartar and salt and beat until the whites begin to peak. Gradually beat in the remaining ¾ cup sugar, about 1 tablespoon at a time. The meringue will be very stiff.

5. Fold the ground hazelnuts, one-third at a time, into the meringue. Scoop one-third of the nut meringue onto each circle on the baking sheets and smooth to even 10-inch rounds with a spatula. (Or, if you're handy with a pastry bag, pipe into rounds.)

6. Bake for 45 minutes. Turn off the oven but leave the nut meringue layers in the warm oven for 30 additional minutes, until completely dry and crisp. Gently scrape around the edges of the rounds with a spatula to loosen them and transfer to racks to cool.

7. In a very heavy saucepan or double boiler, melt the chocolate in the coffee over low heat, stirring until smooth. Remove from the heat and let cool, whisking occasionally, until almost room temperature and slightly thickened. Whisk in the Frangelico and vanilla.

8. In a large bowl, beat the cream until fairly stiff. Fold one-third of the cream into the chocolate to lighten it. Pour the chocolate down the side of the bowl into the remaining cream and fold until no streaks remain.

9. To assemble the dacquoise, gently place 1 meringue layer on a cake stand or large round serving platter. Scoop a heaping cupful of the chocolate cream on top and spread over the meringue, leaving a ½-inch border all around. Put another meringue on top and repeat. Place the last meringue, with the smooth, flat side up, on top and frost the top and sides with the remaining chocolate cream. If the sides look a little messy, refrigerate the dacquoise for about half an hour, or until the cream begins to set up; then smooth out the sides with a long narrow spatula, packing the cream into any gaps that show. Clean off the edge of the cake stand or platter. Garnish the top with the toasted hazelnuts or shaved chocolate and refrigerate until serving time.

Easy Morning Brunch

FOR 10 TO 12

PINK GRAPEFRUIT HALVES

ARUGULA AND CHEESE BREAD PUDDING

MAPLE-GLAZED BACON

ROSEMARY-GARLIC ROAST TOMATOES

YOGURT PARFAITS WITH GRANOLA AND BERRIES

COFFEE

Morning is not my favorite time for entertaining, but frequently Sunday morning is the best chance to get together with friends and their children. This menu is particularly easy because almost everything is prepared in advance. The whole spread can be served either as a sit-down breakfast or as a very attractive buffet.

Begin with lovely pink grapefruits. Sweet, deep-flavored Ruby reds are my favorite, when they are in season. While you can always drizzle a little honey over the cut grapefruits and broil them, if you have really sweet fruit, they are awfully good and refreshing in the buff. Simply use a curved, serrated grapefruit knife to separate the sections, so they can be scooped out easily by your guests. To dress up the citrus halves for company, stick a little sprig of fresh mint in the center of each.

A savory bread pudding, in this case chock-full of peppery arugula and nutty Gruyère cheese, is really a sort of strata. Chunks of bread are layered with the main ingredients and soaked in a simple custard—eggs and half-and-half—for several hours or overnight, then baked to a lovely golden brown. I like some of the bread a little drier on top so that it turns out crisp and coated with cheese. As accompaniment, I suggest bacon, here glazed with maple syrup, and easy baked tomatoes seasoned with rosemary, garlic, and good olive oil. The combination of foods is both beautiful and delicious.

In case you want to stretch out the meal, I've added some Yogurt Parfaits for dessert, but you may not need that much food. Alternatively, you could serve the yogurt and granola first, in place of the grapefruit, with perhaps small glasses of grapefruit or orange juice. For a special breakfast like this, be sure your coffee is the best, with freshly ground beans, and offer your guests a choice of reduced-fat milk and half-and-half.

DO-AHEAD PLANNING

AT LEAST A DAY IN ADVANCE: Cut up the bread and let the chunks become stale.

THE NIGHT BEFORE: Assemble the bread pudding. Cook the bacon through Step 1, if you like; otherwise, do the preliminary cooking a couple of hours ahead. Prepare the berry puree for the Yogurt Parfaits.

A COUPLE OF HOURS BEFORE COMPANY ARRIVES: Prepare the Rosemary-Garlic Tomatoes through Step 2. Remove the Arugula and Cheese Bread Pudding from the refrigerator. Cut the grapefruits. Assemble the yogurt parfaits; refrigerate.

ABOUT 1 HOUR BEFORE SERVING: Put the Bread Pudding in the oven. Roast the tomatoes; set aside at room temperature.

SHORTLY BEFORE SERVING: Reheat the tomatoes in the oven. Finish the Maple-Glazed Bacon.

ARUGULA AND CHEESE BREAD PUDDING

10 TO 12 GENEROUS SERVINGS

My dear friend Kevin Huffman, cook and host extraordinaire, first served me this excellent strata, which is really a savory bread pudding. I find the peppery bite of arugula very pleasing with the mild custard, bread, and cheese, but you can substitute spinach. If you do so, either use thawed frozen, squeezed as dry as possible, or baby spinach leaves, blanched for just a minute, well drained, and again squeezed dry. The reason I call for organic eggs is that they tend to be much fresher, with better flavor. If you can find them, use them.

Savory bread pudding is perfect for easy entertaining, because the dish can be prepared the night before and simply popped into the oven at the last minute. To serve this many people, you'll need two large casseroles at least 2 inches deep; a 2-quart soufflé dish can serve as one of them.

This recipe halves perfectly to serve just 6.

2 large loaves (1 pound each) day-old French, Italian, or country-style bread

4 cups torn or very coarsely chopped arugula

12 ounces Gruyère or Swiss cheese, shredded (about 6 cups)

16 eggs, preferably organic

5 cups half-and-half

1 teaspoon salt

½ teaspoon freshly grated nutmeg

¼ teaspoon cayenne pepper

4 tablespoons unsalted butter

1. Trim off as much of the crust from the bread as you can easily. Cut the bread into 1- to 1½-inch cubes. Let stand for several hours or overnight to dry out.

2. Divide about one-third of the bread cubes between two 14-inch oval casseroles, 9 × 12-inch baking dishes, or 2-quart soufflé dishes. Scatter half the arugula and one-third of the cheese over the bread, dividing evenly between the two dishes. Cover with half the remaining bread. Then layer on the remaining arugula and half the remaining cheese. Top with the rest of the bread.

3. In a large bowl, beat together the eggs, half-and-half, salt, nutmeg, and cayenne. Pour over the bread in the casseroles; tip the dishes gently to allow the custard to penetrate all over. Sprinkle the remaining cheese on top and dot with the butter. The recipe should be prepared in advance to this point. Cover with foil and refrigerate at least 3 hours or overnight.

4. Heat the oven to 325°F. Bake the pudding, covered, for 30 minutes. Remove the foil and continue baking until set throughout and light brown on top, about 30 minutes longer. The pudding is best served hot or warm, but it holds up at room temperature.

MAPLE-GLAZED BACON

10 TO 12 SERVINGS

The easiest way to cook enough bacon for this many people is to roast it. If you have a sheet pan or half-sheet pan, that's your best choice; otherwise a couple of large, rimmed baking sheets will do. Cracked black pepper adds a subtle spark of heat in contrast to the sweetness of the maple syrup.

2 pounds thick-sliced bacon

⅔ cup pure maple syrup, preferably amber

1 teaspoon black peppercorns, preferably Tellicherry, coarsely cracked

1. Heat the oven to 375°F. Arrange the bacon in a single layer on baking sheets and roast for 10 minutes. Turn over with tongs and roast for 8 to 10 minutes longer, until the bacon is lightly browned but slightly underdone. Carefully pour the fat out of the pan(s) and dab the bacon with paper towels. (The bacon can be cooked up to a day ahead and refrigerated.)

2. Reduce the oven temperature to 325°F. Put all the bacon in a single layer on the baking sheet. Drizzle the syrup over the slices, brushing if necessary to coat. Season with the cracked pepper. Bake for 5 to 10 minutes. You'll need the longer time if the bacon has been refrigerated.

3. Turn over, brush again with syrup, and bake another 5 minutes, or until the bacon is nicely glazed. Remove to a serving tray while still warm; the bacon will firm up in a couple of minutes. If it cools first, the syrup will make the bacon stick to the pan; if it does harden, simply rewarm for 5 minutes and the slices will come loose.

ROSEMARY-GARLIC ROAST TOMATOES

12 SERVINGS

A traditional English breakfast, which includes broiled tomatoes and sautéed mushrooms, inspired me to include this recipe in the brunch. It really dresses up the plate. Think of these tomatoes also anytime you are serving roast lamb or chicken.

12 plum tomatoes

Sea salt and freshly ground pepper

½ cup extra-virgin olive oil

1 teaspoon minced fresh rosemary or crumbled dried

1 garlic clove, finely minced

1. Heat the oven to 325°F. Cut the tomatoes in half lengthwise. Season them with salt and pepper. Arrange them in a single layer in a large baking dish brushed with olive oil.

2. Put the olive oil into a small bowl and stir in the rosemary and garlic. If you have time, wait 15 minutes. Drizzle the oil with the bits of rosemary and garlic over the tomatoes. (The tomatoes can be prepared to this point up to 2 hours in advance; set aside at room temperature.)

3. Roast the tomatoes until they are softened but still hold their shape, about 25 minutes.

YOGURT PARFAITS WITH GRANOLA AND BERRIES

10 TO 12 SERVINGS

Tall, narrow parfait glasses make the prettiest presentation for this dish, but you can use wine glasses or even glass dessert dishes and mix and match if you are short. Note that while the yogurt can be mixed with the berries and jam well in advance, the texture will be best if you assemble the parfaits not too long before serving. That will save refrigerator space as well.

1 quart plain or lemon yogurt

2 pints strawberries

½ cup seedless raspberry jam, or more to taste

2 cups granola

1 pint blueberries

½ pint raspberries

1. Stir the yogurt in a bowl to smooth it out. Puree the strawberries with the raspberry jam in a food processor. Swirl the berry puree into the yogurt.

2. Spoon half the berry yogurt into 10 to 12 parfait glasses, wine glasses, or dessert dishes. Sprinkle about 2 tablespoons granola into each glass.

3. Mix the blueberries and raspberries. Scatter a few berries into each glass over the granola. Add another layer of the remaining yogurt and then the remaining granola. Garnish with the remaining berries.

Goose for Thanksgiving

FOR 10 TO 12

OYSTERS WITH GINGER BEURRE BLANC

SLOW-ROASTED GOOSE WITH PORK AND PRUNE DRESSING AND PORT WINE SAUCE

CREAMED BRUSSELS SPROUTS AND CHESTNUTS

POTATO AND RUTABAGA PUREE

CRANBERRY CHUTNEY

LEMON MOUSSE MERINGUES WITH RASPBERRY SAUCE

CHOCOLATE TRUFFLES

This holiday menu happens to be one of my favorites. The juxtaposition of flavors is perfect, and almost all the dishes can be prepared in advance. Goose is a wonderful bird—all dark meat and flavorful without tasting gamy. Roasted to a rich mahogany brown, it makes a glorious centerpiece to the holiday table, and every part can be put to good use. The fat can be rendered to make the world's best fried potatoes, the neck and giblets can be browned for an easy stock, and the liver—rich and mild—makes an excellent addition to almost any stuffing. Even the carcass can be hacked up, thrown into a pot with some aromatic vegetables and herbs, and made into goose soup.

Go for goose if you are planning a relatively small Thanksgiving. A 12- to 14-pound bird will serve only 10 to 12 people. That's assuming there are a lot of side dishes and trimmings and you don't plan on leftovers. If you're expecting a larger crowd, you could cook two geese, but it becomes such a chore to drain off all the fat, you're better off with a big turkey (see page 127).

This elegant oyster recipe for a first course is also geared to a smaller crowd. Lightly poaching the oysters a day ahead keeps them fresh tasting and minimizes last-minute work. They stay moist and plump and, after being gratinéed with the sauce, are indistinguishable from fresh. If you prefer a different sort of starter, or if you want to include a soup as well, either the Curried Carrot-Ginger Soup (page 126), whose humble vegetable base belies its extraordinary character, or the Maple-Butternut Bisque (page 138) would be lovely.

The goose's Pork and Prune Dressing is a meaty and substantial stuffing. About half of it will fit inside the goose; the remainder is baked in a separate dish during the last half hour the goose roasts.

Both the Creamed Brussels Sprouts and Chestnuts and the Potato and Rutabaga Puree have a mild, subtle sweetness that complements the rich goose beautifully. If your family can't imagine Thanksgiving without sweet potatoes, substitute the Gratin of Sweet Potatoes Flambéed with Bourbon (page 132) for the pureed potatoes. The tangy, spiced Cranberry Chutney can be prepared weeks in advance.

After so much food, I like a light, refreshing dessert with just enough sweetness to satisfy. These stunning meringue shells, filled with tart lemon mousse and topped with intense raspberry sauce, qualify perfectly. My dinners usually include only one dessert, because I try to match it to the entire menu, but I know that many people enjoy presenting a dazzling variety, especially during the holidays. Chocolate truffles, available both in local chocolate shops and by mail, are my concession to the multiple dessert table here, but, if you like, include your family's favorite pumpkin pie, chocolate cake, or fruit tart.

DO-AHEAD PLANNING

UP TO 3 WEEKS IN ADVANCE: Make the Cranberry Chutney; store in the refrigerator.

UP TO 5 DAYS IN ADVANCE: Make the Meringue Shells; store them in an airtight container at room temperature.

UP TO 3 DAYS IN ADVANCE: Make the Lemon Mousse and the Raspberry Sauce.

THE DAY BEFORE THANKSGIVING (THE BUSIEST DAY): Poach the oysters; reduce and reserve the cooking liquid. Boil the shells. Make the goose stock. Prepare the bread cubes and pork and prune mixture for the dressing. Make the Creamed Brussels Sprouts and Chestnuts. Make the Potato and Rutabaga Puree.

THANKSGIVING DAY—ABOUT 6 HOURS BEFORE SERVING: Finish the dressing. Stuff and truss the goose and put it in to roast.

ABOUT 30 MINUTES BEFORE THE GOOSE IS READY: Put the extra dressing in the oven to bake. Reheat the Creamed Brussels Sprouts and Chestnuts in the oven (or reheat at the last minute in a microwave oven). Make the Ginger Beurre Blanc; set over warm water.

AS SOON AS THE GOOSE COMES OUT OF THE OVEN: Make the Port Sauce; keep warm. Broil and serve the oysters. Reheat the Potato and Rutabaga Puree.

SHORTLY BEFORE DESSERT: Assemble the Lemon Mousse Meringues.

OYSTERS WITH GINGER BEURRE BLANC

12 SERVINGS

Poaching the oysters a day ahead gives you a triple boon: There is no mess before serving, the poaching liquid makes a delicious base for your sauce, and the shellfish remain as fresh tasting as if they were just opened.

As part of a multi-course meal, I feel that 4 large oysters are a perfect serving to start. If you must offer 6 oysters to each guest, increase the proportions accordingly. By the way, beurre blanc is a tricky sauce, and if yours ever breaks, simply retitle the dish "Oysters with Ginger Butter." No one will be any wiser, and the dish will be just as delicious. I speak from experience.

4 dozen large oysters on the half-shell, 1 cup liquor reserved

2 sticks (½ pound) plus 2 tablespoons unsalted butter

2 medium shallots, minced

¼ cup dry white wine

3 tablespoons Champagne vinegar or white wine vinegar

½ cup chopped fresh ginger

Dash of cayenne pepper

1. Unless you are very handy with an oyster knife, ask the fish market to open the oysters for you. Have them pack them on the half-shell on ice and reserve the oyster liquor separately. (Preopened oysters that come in containers are often mushy and unpleasant.) Just before you cook the oysters, take them out of their shells. Rinse them briefly under cold running water only if there is grit or pieces of shell on them. Reserve the shells.

2. In a large skillet, melt 2 tablespoons of the butter. Add the shallots and cook over moderate heat until softened and translucent but not browned, 1 to 2 minutes. Add the wine, vinegar, and reserved oyster liquor. Bring just to a simmer. Add the oysters and poach, turning once, until the edges just begin to curl, about 1 minute. If in doubt, remove the oysters earlier rather than later (they will be cooked again). Put them in a covered container and refrigerate at once.

3. Add the ginger to the poaching liquid in the skillet and boil until the liquid is reduced to 3 tablespoons. Strain into a small bowl, pressing on the ginger to extract as much flavor as possible. Cover and refrigerate.

4. Boil the oyster shells in a large pot of water for at least 15 minutes; drain. When they are cool enough to handle, rinse them well under running water, rubbing off any pieces of muscle that cling to the shell. Drain well; then refrigerate in a plastic bag. (The recipe can be prepared to this point up to a day ahead.)

5. Before cooking the oysters, arrange the shells in a single layer in several roasting pans. I use disposable ridged aluminum foil broiling pans; each pan will hold 16 oysters.

6. Shortly before you plan to serve the oysters, remove them from the refrigerator; drain, reserving the liquid; and set 1 in each shell. Pour any accumulated liquid into a small heavy saucepan. Add the 3 tablespoons reserved poaching liquid, bring to a boil, and cook until reduced to 2 tablespoons. Whisk in the cayenne and 2 tablespoons of the butter. Remove from the heat and beat in 2 more tablespoons butter until just blended. Return to low heat as necessary and continue whisking in the butter, 2 to 3 tablespoons at a time, making each addition after the previous one is almost incorporated, until all the butter is added and the sauce is thick and emulsified. Set over a pan of warm water (it will hold for about 20 minutes).

7. Heat the broiler. Spoon a little dab of the beurre blanc over each oyster, to coat. In batches as necessary, broil the oysters just until they are heated through, 1 to 2 minutes; do not overcook. Spoon a heaping teaspoon of the remaining sauce over each oyster and serve at once.

SLOW-ROASTED GOOSE WITH PORK AND PRUNE DRESSING AND PORT WINE SAUCE

10 TO 12 SERVINGS

The only trick to this recipe is to buy a fine fresh goose from a good butcher. If you cannot find one locally, you can order an excellent goose online from D'Artagnan. My old way of cooking goose took 3½ hours: half an hour at 425°F and the rest at 350°F. After reading Paula Wolfert's *The Slow Mediterranean Kitchen*, however, I have become an advocate of slow roasting, especially for fatty birds like goose. The technique used here takes about 4½ hours, but it is time well spent. Long, low-temperature roasting, with a blast at the end to ensure gorgeous crisp skin, yields soft, succulent meat.

1 fresh goose, 12 to 14 pounds, wing tips cut off and reserved for stock

Coarse salt and freshly ground pepper

Pork and Prune Dressing (page 16) or your favorite stuffing

2 shallots, chopped

½ cup port or Madeira

3 cups Brown Goose Stock (recipe follows) or chicken stock

2 tablespoons cornstarch

1 tablespoon fresh lemon juice

2 tablespoons unsalted butter

1. Heat the oven to 275°F. Remove any loose fat from the goose. Rinse the bird inside and out with cold running water and pat dry. Season liberally inside and out with coarse salt and pepper. Prick all over, especially in the fatty parts. Stuff loosely. The bird will hold 6 to 7 cups of stuffing; bake the remainder separately as directed. Sew up the cavity and tie the legs together.

2. Put the goose upside down on a rack in a large roasting pan and roast for 1½ hours. Remove the fat that accumulates in the bottom of the pan with a bulb baster, saving it in a heatproof container. Turn the bird right side up, prick the goose again, and baste with hot water. Continue to roast for 2 hours longer, basting with about 1 cup of hot water every 30 minutes or so to keep the fat in the roasting pan from burning and removing the accumulated fat from the roasting pan with a bulb baster as necessary to avoid smoking.

3. Raise the oven temperature to 400°F and roast the goose 45 to 60 minutes longer, until the skin is crisp and mahogany brown and the goose joints are loose.

4. Transfer the goose to a carving board and cover loosely with foil to keep warm. Pour out all but 2 tablespoons fat from the roasting pan. Add the shallots and set over moderate heat. Cook for 1 minute, or until softened. Pour in the port and bring to a boil, scraping up all the flavorful brown bits from the bottom and sides of the pan. Boil for 1 minute. Add 2½ cups of the stock and return to a boil. Pour the sauce into a saucepan.

5. Dissolve the cornstarch in the remaining ½ cup stock; stir into the sauce. Bring to a boil, stirring, until thickened and smooth. Add the lemon juice and whisk in the butter. Season with salt and pepper to taste.

Brown Goose Stock

Render about 2 tablespoons goose fat in a heavy medium saucepan over moderately low heat. Add the cut-up goose neck, giblets, and wing tips and a sliced onion and carrot. Sauté over moderately high heat until deeply browned. Add 6 cups water, 2 bruised garlic cloves, a bay leaf, several sprigs of parsley, ¼ teaspoon thyme, 8 peppercorns, and 8 to 12 mushroom stems if you have them. Reduce the heat to low and simmer, skimming occasionally, for 1½ to 2 hours; strain. Measure the stock and, if necessary, boil down to 3 cups.

PORK AND PRUNE DRESSING

MAKES 10 TO 12 CUPS

12 ounces good-quality pitted prunes, quartered

¾ cup port, such as Croft Distinction

4 tablespoons unsalted butter

2 large onions, chopped

2 celery ribs with leaves, finely diced

¼ pound thickly sliced Black Forest ham, prosciutto, or Serrano ham, finely diced

¾ pound lean ground pork

1½ teaspoons minced fresh thyme or ¾ teaspoon dried

⅛ teaspoon freshly grated nutmeg

1½ teaspoons salt

½ teaspoon freshly ground pepper

Goose or turkey liver (reserved from bird you are stuffing), diced

1 loaf (1 pound) firm-textured white bread

1 cup unsalted turkey or chicken stock

½ cup chopped parsley

1 egg, lightly beaten

1. Put the prunes in a bowl. Pour in the port and ½ cup hot water and let soak while you prepare the rest of the stuffing.

2. In a large flameproof casserole, melt the butter over moderate heat. Add the onions and celery, cover, and cook, stirring once or twice, until the vegetables are softened and translucent, about 10 minutes. Uncover, add the ham, and cook until the onions are just beginning to turn golden, about 10 minutes longer. Add the pork and season with ½ teaspoon of the thyme, the nutmeg, ½ teaspoon of the salt, and ⅛ teaspoon of the pepper. Cook, stirring occasionally, until the pork is no longer pink, about 5 minutes. Add the liver and cook, stirring frequently, for 2 minutes. Pour the port from the prunes into the pan and let cook, stirring occasionally, for 2 minutes longer to boil off the raw alcohol taste. Add the prunes, blend well, and remove from the heat.

3. Dry out the bread slices in a very low oven (200°F or less) or let stand until stale. Cut into ½-inch cubes. (The recipe can be prepared to this point up to a day ahead. Set the bread aside in a plastic bag. Transfer the prune mixture to a large bowl, cover, and refrigerate.)

4. Shortly before you stuff the bird, add the bread cubes to the prune mixture and toss to blend. Drizzle on the stock, mixing to moisten. Season with the remaining salt, pepper, and thyme. Add the parsley and egg and toss to blend well. (Pack any stuffing that does not fit into the bird into a greased baking dish, cover with foil, and bake during the last ½ hour.)

Goose

Goose is an incredible bird, so flavorful that every part of it can be used for something. I make goose only once a year, but with the renderings from that single bird, I have a jar of delicious fat that can be used year-round for special fried potatoes, soups, sauces, stews. Often just a single tablespoon can make all the difference in a dish that needs a boost of flavor.

To render goose fat, pull out all the loose firm white fat. I usually add the extra skin as well. Cut into 1½-inch pieces and put it in a saucepan with enough water to cover. Bring to a simmer over moderately low heat and cook, uncovered, stirring occasionally, until all the water is evaporated and the clear fat is bubbling away.

With a skimmer or slotted spoon, transfer the large pieces of fat, or cracklings, to paper towels to drain. Browned and sprinkled lightly with coarse salt, these make wonderful crunchy nibbles with drinks. They can be frozen until you need them, then reheated. They are also fabulous tossed in a wilted salad of bitter greens or in an omelet with chopped garlic and parsley. Let the fat in the saucepan cool; then strain it through a fine-mesh sieve or several layers of cheesecloth into a clean jar. Cover and store in the refrigerator for up to a year.

As a final bonus, I always make a delicious soup out of the roasted goose carcass and lightly browned cabbage, with an enrichment of Roquefort cheese.

CREAMED BRUSSELS SPROUTS AND CHESTNUTS

12 SERVINGS

Chestnuts are one of winter's treats, but peeling them is a chore. Luckily, you can buy jars of vacuum-packed peeled chestnuts, which are of excellent quality and all ready to use. If you do so, skip Step 2.

2 pounds Brussels sprouts

1 pound chestnuts

4 tablespoons unsalted butter

1 cup heavy cream

½ teaspoon salt

¼ teaspoon freshly ground pepper

1. Trim the Brussels sprouts. Cut a tiny X in the stem end of each with the tip of a small knife. Bring a large saucepan of salted water to a boil. Add the sprouts and cook for 7 minutes, until they are about three-quarters cooked. Drain, rinse under cold water to cool, and drain well. Chop very coarsely.

2. Heat the oven to 375°F. Cut an X into the flat side of each chestnut. Put in a shallow baking pan and roast for 15 to 20 minutes, until the ends of the cut shells curl back. As soon as they are cool enough to handle, peel and chop the chestnuts very coarsely.

3. In a large saucepan, melt the butter in the cream. Add the Brussels sprouts and chestnuts; season with the salt and pepper. Cook over moderate heat, stirring occasionally, until most of the liquid is absorbed, 5 to 10 minutes. Season with additional salt and pepper to taste, cover, and set aside for up to 3 hours or refrigerate overnight. Reheat in a saucepan over moderate heat or in a gratin dish in the oven with your roast before serving.

POTATO AND RUTABAGA PUREE

12 SERVINGS

While rutabagas may look coarse and dumpy in their natural state, when peeled and boiled until tender, they are sweet and mild. Blended with mashed potatoes and butter, with just enough cooking liquid to make them silky, they make a lovely accompaniment to roast goose, turkey, and pork.

2½ to 3 pounds rutabagas (yellow turnips)

2 pounds baking potatoes

8 tablespoons (1 stick) unsalted butter, at room temperature

¼ teaspoon freshly grated nutmeg

Salt and freshly ground pepper

1. Cut the peel off the rutabagas with a paring knife, removing any traces of green underneath. Cut them into large chunks. In a large pot of boiling salted water, cook the rutabagas for 20 minutes.

2. Peel the potatoes and cut them into chunks. Add the potatoes to the pot and continue to cook until both vegetables are very tender, 15 to 20 minutes longer. Scoop out and reserve 1½ cups of the cooking liquid; then drain the potatoes and rutabagas into a colander.

3. Pass the vegetables through the medium disk of a food mill or a ricer to mash. Beat in the butter until blended and smooth. Blend in enough of the reserved cooking liquid to thin the puree to the desired consistency. Season with the nutmeg and salt and pepper to taste. (The puree can be prepared a day ahead and reheated in a microwave oven or over moderate heat, stirring frequently.)

CRANBERRY CHUTNEY

MAKES 2 QUARTS

A pleasant relief from the standard, cloyingly sweet cranberry sauce usually served at Thanksgiving, this condiment is tangy, enhanced with apples and pears, and complexly flavored with spices and seasonings. I like it best after it has mellowed for at least 3 days in the refrigerator. If you make this in a double or triple batch and put it in pint or quart jars, it makes a great homemade Christmas gift.

1 large onion, chopped

3 tablespoons minced fresh ginger

¾ cup cider vinegar

¾ cup sugar

Juice and grated zest from 1 large navel orange

2 garlic cloves, crushed through a press

½ teaspoon ground cinnamon

½ teaspoon coarsely cracked black pepper

½ teaspoon ground coriander

¼ teaspoon ground mace or freshly grated nutmeg

¼ teaspoon ground cloves

¼ teaspoon salt

Several dashes of cayenne pepper, to taste

2 large, tart apples, such as Greening or Granny Smith, peeled and cut into ½-inch dice

2 large, firm pears, peeled and cut into ½-inch dice

2 bags (12 ounces each) fresh cranberries

2 cinnamon sticks, optional

1. In a large nonreactive saucepan or flameproof casserole, combine the onion, ginger, vinegar, sugar, orange juice and zest, garlic, ground cinnamon, black pepper, coriander, mace, cloves, salt, and cayenne. Bring to a boil and cook over moderate heat for 5 minutes.

2. Add the apples and cook for 5 minutes. Add the pears and cook, stirring occasionally, for about 5 minutes, or until the apples and pears are tender but still hold their shape. Add the cranberries, bring to a boil, and cook, stirring once or twice, until they just pop their skins, about 5 minutes. Stir in ¼ cup water and remove from the heat.

3. If you have the cinnamon sticks, put 1 in each of two 1-quart mason jars. Divide the cranberry chutney between the jars and let cool; then cover and refrigerate at least overnight and for up to 3 weeks before serving.

LEMON MOUSSE MERINGUES WITH RASPBERRY SAUCE

12 SERVINGS

A tart lemon mousse, set off with an intense raspberry sauce, contrasts pleasantly with sugary meringues in this elegant dessert. To save you work, look for meringue shells in better bakeries.

6 egg yolks

3 tablespoons sugar

⅓ cup fruity, off-dry wine, such as Vouvray (if you have only dry white wine, increase the sugar to ¼ cup)

1½ teaspoons grated lemon zest

½ cup fresh lemon juice

1 teaspoon plain gelatin, dissolved in 2 tablespoons water

½ cup heavy cream, whipped

12 Individual Meringue Shells (recipe follows)

Whipped cream for serving, optional

Raspberry Sauce (page 21)

1. Set a bowl of cold water on your counter. In a heavy medium saucepan, preferably enameled cast-iron, or in a double boiler, beat the egg yolks to break them up. Gradually whisk in the sugar and then the wine, lemon zest, and lemon juice. Set over moderate heat and cook, whisking constantly, until the mixture is hot, foamy, and thickened, 5 to 10 minutes. Beat in the dissolved gelatin and whisk over heat for about 30 seconds longer.

2. Remove from the heat. Set the bottom of your pan in the bowl of cold water and whisk for about a minute to stop the cooking. Remove from the water and whisk for 1 to 2 minutes longer, until the mixture is thick and cool. Transfer to a bowl and fold in the whipped cream. Cover and refrigerate. (The mousse mixture can be made up to 3 days in advance.)

3. To assemble the dessert, shortly before serving, use a large spoon or ice cream scoop to mound the lemon mousse neatly in the meringue shells. Top with a dollop of whipped cream and drizzle on a little raspberry sauce. Pass the remaining sauce separately.

INDIVIDUAL MERINGUE SHELLS

MAKES 12

Since these can be made up to a week in advance, they do make dessert easy on the cook. Just be sure to store in a tightly closed container and do not attempt to make them on a very humid day. Instead of the lemon mousse suggested above, the shells can be filled with ice cream before being topped with a chocolate or fruit sauce for a delightful meringue *glacée.*

6 egg whites

⅛ teaspoon cream of tartar

½ teaspoon vanilla extract

¾ cup superfine sugar

¾ cup confectioners' sugar

1. Heat the oven to 225°F. Butter and flour 2 large baking sheets or line them with parchment.

2. In a large bowl, beat the egg whites with an electric mixer until frothy. Add the cream of tartar and vanilla and beat on high speed, gradually adding the superfine sugar, 1 tablespoon at a time. Gradually beat in ¼ cup of the confectioners' sugar. The egg whites should be very stiff and stand up in spiky peaks when the beaters are lifted. If they are not that firm, continue beating a little longer.

3. Put the remaining confectioners' sugar in a sifter. In 2 batches, sift the sugar over the meringue and fold in with a rubber spatula.

4. Either put the meringue in a pastry bag with a ½-inch plain tube and pipe out a dozen 4-inch rounds with low rims on the baking sheets or scoop the meringue into 12 mounds and shape them into nests with the back of a spoon, trying to make the bottoms relatively flat, about ½ inch thick, and the sides higher all around.

5. Bake the meringues for 1 hour 15 minutes. Turn off the oven and let the meringues sit in the closed oven for at least 3 hours, or until crisp and dry throughout. Peel off the parchment, if used, or carefully remove from the baking sheet with a wide spatula. Store in an airtight container for up to 1 week.

RASPBERRY SAUCE

MAKES ABOUT 3 CUPS

2 packages (12 ounces each) individually quick-frozen raspberries without added sugar, thawed

⅓ cup red currant jelly or seedless raspberry jam

2 tablespoons framboise (raspberry eau-de-vie) or kirsch (cherry eau-de-vie)

2 teaspoons fresh lemon juice

Sugar

1. In a food processor, combine the raspberries with their juice, the jelly, framboise, and lemon juice; puree until smooth. Taste and add a little sugar only if you really feel it's necessary; the sauce should be intense.

2. Strain, if desired, to remove the seeds. Pour into a jar, cover, and refrigerate for up to 5 days before serving.

Casual Dinner

FOR 10 TO 12

SALAD—YOUR CHOICE, AND IT'S OPTIONAL

SENEGALESE CHICKEN STEW WITH PEANUT SAUCE

STEAMED RICE OR COUSCOUS

BANANAS IN RUM CREAM SAUCE

Whether you've planned dinner in advance and other duties call or you suddenly find yourself host to a dozen people about to arrive in a few hours, there are times when simplicity and cost-efficiency are paramount. For those times, you'll find this savory African stew, called *maffé*, just the ticket—especially when you're serving a mix of adults and children. With its colorful blend of chicken, sweet potatoes, sweet peppers, and pigeon peas—all bound together in a toothsome, mildly spiced peanut butter–tomato sauce—there's nothing more you need to do than put up a pot of instant couscous or rice. Maffé is truly a one-pot meal. And it's immensely appealing.

My recipe for this Senegalese dish came to me from Africa via Guadeloupe. Here's the history: My friend the writer Maximilian Delaure, whose family lives in Guadeloupe, got the recipe from his friend Joseph Dieme, who hails from Senegal. Max put his stamp on the dish with the addition of carrots and pigeon peas, Caribbean beans that are almost a cross between beans and lentils and that hold their texture beautifully in stews. I made a few tweaks to the sauce, which may or may not be authentic but which have survived numerous taste tests with flying colors.

For a casual meal, this is not a multi-course menu, but if you like, you can add your favorite salad, either alongside the stew or served as a first course. For dessert, I suggest Bananas in Rum Cream Sauce, which can be served simply with their luscious rum cream sauce or over vanilla ice cream, with or without cookies on the side.

DO-AHEAD PLANNING

UP TO 2 MONTHS IN ADVANCE: Prepare the Senegalese Chicken Stew with Peanut Sauce through Step 3; freeze in a tightly covered container or in sealed freezer bags. Or make the stew 1 to 2 days in advance and refrigerate.

UP TO 2 HOURS BEFORE SERVING: Finish the stew; set it aside at room temperature. Sauté the bananas very briefly; set them aside. Make the sauce for the bananas and set it aside in the pan.

JUST BEFORE SERVING: Make the couscous or rice. Reheat the stew. Reheat the rum cream sauce and return the bananas to it in batches just to warm through.

SENEGALESE CHICKEN STEW WITH PEANUT SAUCE

10 TO 12 SERVINGS

In Africa, there are probably as many recipes for *maffé* (also spelled *mafé*) as there are cooks. It is made with beef, lamb, and goat as well as chicken, and the vegetables included range widely, from those listed below to the addition of cabbage and eggplant. The constant is the sauce, which is always composed of peanut butter and tomatoes. Feel free to add or subtract vegetables, depending upon what is in your refrigerator or what's fresh in your market. For a good value, look for sales on jumbo packs of chicken parts.

All this one-pot dish needs is a big bowl of steamed rice or—easier yet—instant couscous to soak up plenty of that irresistible sauce. I use a skimmer to transfer the chicken and vegetables with some of the sauce to a large, wide serving bowl; it looks very attractive with the big pieces of vegetables and the peas. Pass the remaining sauce separately in a pitcher.

6 pounds skinless chicken thighs and/or breasts on the bone

Salt and freshly ground pepper

⅓ cup peanut oil or olive oil

3 medium onions, sliced

4 garlic cloves, finely chopped

1½ tablespoons minced fresh ginger

1 teaspoon crushed hot red pepper, or more to taste

2 cans (28 ounces each) Italian peeled tomatoes, with their juices

2 tablespoons brown sugar

3 large red-skinned or Yukon gold potatoes, peeled and cut into thick wedges

2 imported bay leaves

1⅓ cups smooth peanut butter

3 tablespoons fresh lemon juice

3 or 4 large carrots, peeled and sliced crosswise on an angle into thick oval slices

3 sweet potatoes, peeled and cut into 1-inch-thick slices

2 bell peppers—1 red and 1 green—seeded and cut into large wedges

2 cans (15 ounces each) green pigeon peas or black-eyed peas, drained

1. Trim any extra fat from the chicken. Hack the breasts crosswise in half. Season the pieces with salt and pepper.

2. In a very large flameproof casserole, heat the oil over moderately high heat. Add the onions, cover, and cook for 3 minutes. Uncover and sauté until golden and beginning to brown, 5 to 7 minutes. Add the garlic, ginger, and hot pepper; sauté for about 30 seconds. Add the chicken pieces and cook, turning in the oil until they are white outside and coated with oil, 8 to 10 minutes.

3. In a blender or food processor, puree the canned tomatoes with their juices and add to the pot. Stir in the brown sugar, 2 teaspoons salt, and ½ teaspoon freshly ground pepper. Add the red-skinned potatoes, bay leaves, and 3 cups of water, or enough to barely cover the chicken. Bring to a boil, reduce the heat, and simmer, partially covered, for 15 minutes. Stir in the peanut butter and lemon juice.

4. Add the carrots, sweet potatoes, bell peppers, and pigeon peas; simmer until the chicken and vegetables are tender, 10 to 15 minutes longer. It's nice if the peppers remain slightly crisp. Season again with salt and pepper, keeping in mind the sauce should be strong enough to stand up to the couscous or rice.

Note: If you wish to make this dish a day or two in advance, cook the chicken through Step 3. Let cool in the sauce, then cover and refrigerate. Finish the stew shortly before serving, so that the vegetables do not soften too much.

BANANAS IN RUM CREAM SAUCE

10 TO 12 SERVINGS

This is my last-minute dessert standby, and everyone loves it. Dark rum lends a tantalizing Caribbean flavor, and the dish cooks literally in minutes. Choose bananas that are yellow but have no trace of brown in the skin, so that they will hold together over heat. Serve the bananas alone with their rich sauce or ladle over scoops of vanilla ice cream.

10 to 12 ripe but firm bananas

12 tablespoons (1½ sticks) unsalted butter

1 cup packed dark brown sugar

⅔ cup dark rum

3 cups heavy cream

1. Peel the bananas and cut them first lengthwise in half, then crosswise in half to make 4 pieces from each banana.

2. In a large nonstick skillet, melt half the butter over moderate heat. Add about one-third of the bananas and turn them in the butter for about 1 minute to heat through. Gently transfer to individual plates or a serving dish, leaving as much butter as possible behind in the pan. Repeat 2 more times with the remaining butter and bananas.

3. Add the brown sugar to the butter remaining in the skillet and stir over heat to melt until bubbling. Pour in the rum and boil for about 30 seconds. Add the cream and bring to a boil. Boil until the cream reduces and thickens slightly, 2 to 3 minutes. Pour over the bananas and serve.

An Elegant Dinner with Fine Wines

FOR 10 TO 12

TUNA TARTARE WITH AVOCADO
AND RUBY GRAPEFRUIT VINAIGRETTE

*FULL-BODIED WHITE WINE, SUCH AS CALIFORNIA
CHARDONNAY OR FRENCH WHITE BURGUNDY*

ROAST FILLET OF BEEF

PUREE OF PEAS AND WATERCRESS

POTATO GRATIN WITH GARLIC AND THYME

*ELEGANT, HERBACEOUS RED WINE, SUCH AS
BORDEAUX OR CALIFORNIA CABERNET SAUVIGNON*

GREEN SALAD

ASSORTED CHEESES, SUCH AS EPOISSES
OR CAMEMBERT, ROQUEFORT OR MAYTAG BLUE,
AND CANTAL OR AGED SONOMA JACK

FRENCH WALNUT OR WHOLE-GRAIN BREAD

*RED WINE, PREFERABLY AN OLDER BORDEAUX,
A BIG CALIFORNIA CABERNET SAUVIGNON,
OR A FINE BURGUNDY*

PROFITEROLES

ESPRESSO

People often make a fuss about pairing food and wine. That's because on those rare occasions when the match is perfect, the effect is stunning—the whole becomes much more than the sum of its parts. When the wine is the star, keep the food simple. Avoid strong flavors and piquant spices.

I begin this meal with tuna tartare, silky with avocado, which pairs perfectly with an equally lush Chardonnay or French white Burgundy. Because the acid in the dressing is grapefruit juice rather than vinegar, the dish can take a fine wine, and it deserves to be applauded. This is a simple starter that by its presentation and taste elevates a good cook to a chef in the eye of the diners. By packing diced avocado and pink fresh tuna into a small ramekin and then unmolding it, the resulting appetizer, with its spring green cover, is beautiful. A drizzle of extra dressing and small chunks of pink grapefruit for garnish truly make this a stunning beginning to a lovely meal.

Beef is the classic match for a good Bordeaux (or its California counterpart, Cabernet Sauvignon), so I serve a simple roast fillet here. As accompaniments, I've chosen a pretty green Puree of Peas and Watercress and a creamy potato gratin, with just a hint of mellow garlic and thyme. The pepperiness of the watercress and the herbal overtones of the thyme will match the character of the wine.

After the main course is the point in the meal when the French serve salad, to refresh the palate and give new vigor to the appetite. I recommend it highly. Use a simple assortment of greens—perhaps Bibb and red oak leaf lettuces with a few leaves of arugula—and a dressing either based on lemon or with proportions of oil and vinegar no less than 4 to 1.

The cheese course is a French touch that is highly complementary to wine and has become much more popular in America in recent years. Many top restaurants now wheel cheese carts through the dining room after dinner, and cheese plates can be had as an alternative to a sweet or as an extra course. Offer a variety of artisanal cheeses; and do be sure all are at room temperature when you serve them. Even at a formal dinner, I sometimes pass the cheese plate while people are eating their salads, so that the two courses are served on one plate.

And the Profiteroles, all ready to go with just a drizzle of chocolate sauce, provide the perfect ending to this sumptuous meal. Classic and simple, with a contrast of crisp pastry and cold, creamy ice cream and warm chocolate sauce, this dessert is one of my all-time favorites, both at home and in restaurants.

I confess this menu does look intimidating, but it was carefully designed with the home cook in mind. Notice that both the first course and the dessert are cold and are prepared in advance. Except for reheating the vegetables, the only last-minute work is roasting the fillet of beef.

DO-AHEAD PLANNING

UP TO 2 MONTHS IN ADVANCE: Bake the pastry puffs for the Profiteroles. Freeze in a covered container.

UP TO A DAY IN ADVANCE: Prepare the Puree of Peas and Watercress. Prepare the Potato Gratin with Garlic and Thyme, baking it 10 to 15 minutes less than the recipe calls for; let cool, then cover and refrigerate. Rinse and dry the salad greens.

UP TO 4 HOURS BEFORE SERVING: Make the citrus vinaigrette for the Tuna Tartare. Prepare the Tuna Tartare through Step 4; cover and refrigerate. Marinate the fillet. Remove the cheeses from the refrigerator. Make the chocolate sauce for the Profiteroles.

ABOUT 20 MINUTES BEFORE YOU PLAN TO SERVE: Unmold and garnish the tuna. Bake the potatoes until tender and heated through. Roast the fillet. Finish off the puree as you reheat it. Dress and toss the salad.

JUST BEFORE SERVING DESSERT: Fill the Profiteroles using a small ice cream scoop and drizzle with sauce.

TUNA TARTARE WITH AVOCADO AND RUBY GRAPEFRUIT VINAIGRETTE

12 SERVINGS

Even people who don't eat sushi enjoy tuna tartare, which is simply raw tuna cut into small dice, usually tossed with a light citrus- or vinegar-based dressing, which helps to "cook" the fish, much like a seviche. It is a contemporary takeoff on the classic beef tartare. Practically all the fresh tuna you'll find available has been frozen at some point, so you don't need to worry about parasites. You do need to worry about flavor, though, so go to the trouble of ordering ahead and searching out the best quality you can buy. Fresh tuna should be a glistening garnet, with no trace of brown or gray, and it should have a nice sheen. Most fresh tuna sold is sushi (or sashimi) grade, which is what you want. Check the frozen food department as well, because many good supermarkets sell sashimi-grade yellowtail tuna steaks (two 4-ounce steaks per package), which is of impeccable quality if you follow the directions for thawing. Most sushi restaurants use frozen tuna, so you're not losing anything but the health risk.

For an elegant presentation, the tuna is layered like a napoleon in a straight-sided ramekin with diced avocado. Then it is unmolded and garnished with a drizzle of the vinaigrette and little chunks of red grapefruit. It's a guaranteed crowd-pleaser and looks like a chef's creation, which it is. To make this, you'll need a dozen straight-sided 6-ounce ramekins or 3-inch ring molds. Serve with crisp toasts.

Ruby Grapefruit Vinaigrette (opposite page)

Extra-virgin olive oil

1 pound sashimi-grade yellowtail tuna steaks

3 ripe but firm avocados

Diced or sectioned Ruby red or pink grapefruit

1. Make the vinaigrette just before you plan to assemble the tartare. Generously oil 12 straight-sided 6-ounce ramekins with olive oil.

2. Cut the tuna into ¼-inch dice. Place in a bowl. Stir up the vinaigrette and spoon ¾ cup of it over the tuna. Stir gently to mix.

3. Halve the avocados. Remove the pits and scoop out the flesh. Cut the avocados into ¼-inch dice. Toss in a bowl with ½ cup of the vinaigrette. Spoon into the bottom of the oiled ramekins, spreading to cover completely.

4. Spoon the tuna on top of the avocado and pack lightly. Either unmold at once or cover and refrigerate for up to 3 hours.

5. To unmold, invert each ramekin onto a salad or other medium plate. Lift the plate and, holding the ramekin in place with your thumbs, shake firmly. If the tartare does not loosen, run a dull knife around the rim and repeat. Lift off the mold. If any avocado sticks, simply pat it back into place.

6. Drizzle a couple of teaspoons of the remaining vinaigrette around each tartare and garnish with a few pieces of grapefruit.

RUBY GRAPEFRUIT VINAIGRETTE

MAKES ABOUT 1½ CUPS

If Ruby red grapefruits are in season, they make the best choice for this recipe. Pink are the next best alternative. If the grapefruit juice tastes unusually tart, add a pinch of sugar to compensate. Two large grapefruits should be enough for both the juice and the garnish.

⅔ cup fresh Ruby red or pink grapefruit juice (pulp is fine)

3 tablespoons Banyuls vinegar, Champagne vinegar, or other white wine vinegar

Coarse salt and freshly ground pepper

¾ cup extra-virgin olive oil

3 tablespoons minced chives

2½ tablespoons minced shallots

In a small bowl, whisk together the grapefruit juice, vinegar, and a pinch each of salt and pepper. Gradually whisk in the olive oil to make an emulsion. Stir in the chives and shallots. Season with additional salt and pepper to taste.

ROAST FILLET OF BEEF

12 SERVINGS

Though fillet of beef is an expensive cut, there is absolutely no waste, it cooks in 20 minutes or less, and it carves beautifully. You can increase the cooking time for more well done meat, but fillet is best when cooked to a rosy rare, as suggested here. This recipe can be multiplied exactly to accommodate as many roasts as you need. Since perfect doneness is critical here, I use a digital thermometer.

1 whole fillet of beef, about 5 pounds, trimmed and tied

2 tablespoons Cognac

2 tablespoons minced shallots

½ teaspoon salt

1 teaspoon coarsely cracked black peppercorns, preferably Tellicherry

¼ cup extra-virgin olive oil

4 strips of bacon, optional

1. About 2 hours before you plan to serve the meat, remove it from the refrigerator, unwrap it, and set it in a large glass dish or baking pan. Rub the meat all over with the Cognac, shallots, salt, pepper, and 2 tablespoons of the olive oil. Set aside at room temperature, turning once or twice.

2. Heat the oven to 450°F. About 35 minutes before you plan to serve the meat, heat the remaining 2 tablespoons oil in a large, heavy flameproof gratin dish or roasting pan over moderately high heat. Add the fillet and cook, turning, until browned all over, about 5 minutes. If you are using the bacon, lay it on top of the roast. Transfer the pan to the oven and roast the fillet for 15 to 20 minutes, or until a digital or instant-read thermometer registers 125° to 130°F for rare. (Remember, the meat will keep cooking after you remove it from the oven.)

3. Remove the bacon and transfer the roast to a carving board. Cover loosely with foil and let stand for about 10 minutes before carving.

PUREE OF PEAS AND WATERCRESS

12 SERVINGS

Peppery watercress adds a little punch as well as bright green color to mild peas, for a lovely vegetable puree that goes with just about anything. Note that there is no need to defrost the peas before cooking.

2 bags (1 pound each) frozen baby sweet peas

5 large shallots, sliced

3 cups packed watercress with tough stems removed, about 1½ large bunches

6 tablespoons unsalted butter

1 teaspoon sugar

Salt and freshly ground pepper

1. Bring a large saucepan of salted water to a boil over high heat. Add the peas and shallots; cook for 4 minutes, or until tender. Add the watercress, pushing it beneath the water. Cook for 1 minute longer; drain.

2. Puree the vegetables with the butter in a food processor, in batches if necessary, or pass through the fine blade of a food mill. Season with the sugar and salt and pepper to taste. (The puree can be made to this point up to a day in advance. Refrigerate in a covered container.)

3. Shortly before serving, reheat in a heavy medium saucepan over moderately high heat or in a microwave oven.

POTATO GRATIN WITH GARLIC AND THYME

12 SERVINGS

Whenever I am faced with more than 2 pounds of potatoes, I try to avoid peeling them. Cooking them first so that the skins slip off easily makes things much easier.

3 to 3½ pounds Yukon gold potatoes

2 garlic cloves—1 cut in half, 1 minced

4 tablespoons unsalted butter

Salt and freshly ground pepper

1 teaspoon minced fresh thyme or ½ teaspoon dried

3 cups half-and-half or light cream

1. Cook the potatoes with their skins on in a large pot of boiling salted water for 15 minutes. Drain and rinse under cold running water. (The potatoes can be prepared to this point up to a day ahead; refrigerate.)

2. Peel the potatoes and cut them crosswise into very thin slices. Use a mandoline, if you have one, or the slicing blade on a box grater.

3. Rub the cut garlic all over the inside of a large flameproof gratin or baking dish (or 2 smaller dishes). Grease the dish with 1 tablespoon of the butter.

4. Arrange one-third of the potatoes in a layer in the bottom of the dish, overlapping the slices as necessary. Season liberally with salt and pepper. Sprinkle on half the minced garlic and thyme; dot with 1 tablespoon of the butter. Repeat with half the remaining potatoes and the rest of the garlic and thyme; dot with another tablespoon of the butter. End with a top layer of the remaining potatoes. Season with salt and pepper and dot with the remaining tablespoon butter. Pour the half-and-half over the potatoes. (The recipe can be prepared to this point up to 3 hours ahead. Set aside at room temperature.)

5. Heat the oven to 375°F. Bring the gratin to a boil on top of the stove or in a microwave. Transfer to the oven and bake for 20 minutes. Increase the oven temperature to 450°F and bake for 10 minutes, or until most of the cream is absorbed and the gratin is browned on top.

PROFITEROLES

12 SERVINGS

Some classics deserve their reputation, and this irresistible dessert is one of them. Crisp puffed pastry balls filled with vanilla ice cream and drizzled with an excellent hot fudge sauce combine crisp and creamy, hot and cold, for one of the all-time great treats. Since the pastry puffs freeze so well, I always keep a cache of them in my freezer, for any time an easy but really special last-minute dessert is needed.

6 tablespoons unsalted butter, cut into tablespoons

1 teaspoon sugar

⅛ teaspoon salt

1 cup all-purpose flour

4 eggs

Egg glaze, made by beating 1 egg with 1 teaspoon water

1½ quarts rich vanilla ice cream

Rich Chocolate Sauce, preferably homemade (below)

1. Heat the oven to 425°F. In a large saucepan, bring 1 cup water, the butter, sugar, and salt to a rolling boil over moderately high heat.

2. Add the flour all at once. Beat with a wooden spoon over the heat until the flour masses together in a ball, about 2 minutes. Remove from the heat.

3. Turn the flour paste into a food processor with the metal blade. One at a time, add the 4 eggs and process until smooth and shiny (or beat them in with a wooden spoon).

4. Butter 2 large baking sheets. Using a pastry bag and a plain ½-inch tip, pipe the dough onto the baking sheets to form 18 to 20 mounds about 1 inch in diameter and ½ inch high on each sheet; leave about 2 inches in between the mounds. If you're not handy with a pastry bag, use 2 teaspoons. Brush the tops of the mounds with the egg glaze.

5. Bake for 20 minutes, or until puffed and browned. Remove from the oven and cut off the top third of each puff. Reserve the tops. Return the shells to the hot turned-off oven for 5 minutes, or until dry. Let cool, then set aside in a tightly covered container for up to 2 days or freeze for up to 2 months.

6. To assemble the profiteroles, fill each small shell with vanilla ice cream and put the tops back in place. Arrange 3 on each plate and drizzle a little hot chocolate sauce over each serving.

RICH CHOCOLATE SAUCE

MAKES ABOUT 2½ CUPS

This is the best hot chocolate sauce I've ever tasted. It can transform the simplest dessert into a grand finale.

1 cup heavy cream

8 tablespoons (1 stick) unsalted butter, cut into pieces

8 ounces bittersweet or semisweet chocolate, coarsely chopped

1. In a medium heavy saucepan, combine the cream and butter. Bring to a simmer over moderate heat, stirring to dissolve the butter.

2. Reduce the heat to low and add the chocolate. Whisk until melted and smooth. Use hot or let cool, then cover and refrigerate for up to 2 weeks before serving. Reheat gently, preferably over simmering water or in a microwave oven, stirring until smooth and warm.

BISTRO SUPPER

FOR 12

FRISÉE SALAD WITH BACON LARDONS AND BLUE CHEESE

TOASTED ROUNDS OF FRENCH BREAD

CASSOULET OF LAMB SHANKS

FRENCH RHÔNE WINE OR CALIFORNIA SYRAH

PEARS POACHED IN RED WINE

ESPRESSO

Fall and winter invite candlesticks, red wine, and jovial dinner parties for good friends who like to eat and talk. Cassoulet, that famous French casserole of beans baked with preserved goose or duck, called *confit,* sausages, and pork is a fabulous dish, as much a conversation piece as a substantial bit of sustenance. If you want to make this classic version, I refer you to Paula Wolfert's *The Cooking of South-West France*. There, the critically acclaimed "Queen of the Mediterranean" details perhaps the best recipe for cassoulet ever recorded.

The only problem is that the classic is unbelievably time consuming, and sometimes you just don't have the time . . . or the energy. My shortcut version here uses all lamb: Shank bones provide flavor and some visual interest; boneless leg adds meatiness. No stock is needed for this recipe, and the crusty top, which is a little hard to achieve without practice in the original, is here simulated with a simple bread crumb topping, added at the last minute. For relaxed entertaining, the dish is a dream, because it needs no accompaniment and can be prepared a good 2 days in advance.

To start off the meal, I suggest a tasty salad of frisée, which is a curly endive, all frilly and mildly bitter, set off with strips of crisp bacon and creamy blue cheese. Even served with toasted French bread on the side, it's light enough to leave room for the cassoulet, tasty enough to pique the appetite.

For dessert, you can always serve a purchased apple tart or other pastry. But I usually opt for a fruit dessert, especially pears, which are at their peak at this time of year. An intense spiced wine sauce is just the right note at the end of a meal like this, and you can always embellish the fruit if you like with cookies or a scoop of ice cream or sorbet.

DO-AHEAD PLANNING

UP TO 3 DAYS IN ADVANCE: Soak the beans and marinate the lamb for the Cassoulet of Lamb Shanks.

UP TO 2 DAYS IN ADVANCE: Rinse and spin-dry the frisée. Refrigerate wrapped in a kitchen towel inside an unsealed plastic bag. Prepare the Cassoulet through Step 6. Cover and refrigerate.

A DAY IN ADVANCE: Prepare the Pears Poached in Red Wine through Step 2.

THE MORNING OF THE DINNER: Finish the poached pears and return to the refrigerator. Cook the bacon and make the dressing for the Frisée Salad.

ABOUT 2 HOURS BEFORE SERVING: Remove the Cassoulet from the refrigerator.

ABOUT 15 MINUTES BEFORE DINNER BEGINS: Put the Cassoulet in the oven to reheat. Complete the Frisée Salad.

FRISÉE SALAD WITH BACON LARDONS AND BLUE CHEESE

12 SERVINGS

A bracing salad of bitter greens is just the thing to stimulate the appetite. Here, in its classic form, the frisée is adorned with snippets of bacon and lush blue cheese, moistened with a nicely tart vinaigrette. Though Roquefort is traditional, my choice for the cheese is a slightly sweeter—and less expensive—French Bleu d'Auvergne or an American Maytag blue, which is excellent.

16 cups frisée, about 1 pound

1½ pounds thick-sliced flavorful bacon

⅓ cup sherry vinegar or wine vinegar

3 tablespoons fresh lemon juice

½ teaspoon powdered mustard

½ teaspoon sugar

1 cup extra-virgin olive oil

2 medium shallots, minced

Sea salt and freshly ground pepper

10 ounces good blue cheese, such as Maytag blue or Bleu d'Auvergne

1. Separate the frisée leaves, rinse them well, and spin dry. (The greens can be prepared up to 2 days in advance, loosely wrapped in a clean kitchen towel inside an unsealed plastic bag, and stored in the refrigerator.)

2. Cut the bacon crosswise into thick strips. Sauté in a large skillet over moderate heat until the bacon is lightly browned. With a slotted spoon, remove the bacon lardons to paper towels to drain. (If you cook the bacon in advance, reheat it until hot and crisp before assembling the salads.)

3. In a very large bowl, whisk together the vinegar, lemon juice, powdered mustard, sugar, and 2 tablespoons water. Slowly whisk in the olive oil until the vinaigrette is emulsified. Stir in the shallots. Season with salt and pepper to taste. (The dressing can be made ahead. Store in a tightly covered jar. Shake well before using.)

4. Add the frisée to the bowl and toss to coat with the dressing. Add the bacon and toss to mix. Divide among 12 salad plates. Crumble the cheese over the salads and top with a grinding of pepper.

CASSOULET OF LAMB SHANKS

12 SERVINGS

Lamb shanks are combined here with lean boneless lamb from the leg, so you get a mix of the best in flavor and texture. To reduce fat, the lamb is broiled first and the drippings discarded. In place of the traditional pork rind, I thicken the gravy with the bean cooking liquid and a little flour. While this looks like a production, the entire dish can be made well in advance and baked off just before you're ready to serve. I love it for cold weather entertaining and usually serve the cassoulet with just a salad, as suggested here, or with braised greens, such as kale or chard. Drink a big, earthy red wine, such as a Châteauneuf-du-Pape, Crozes-Hermitage, or Gigondas.

2 pounds dried navy beans

2 cups dry white wine

⅔ cup extra-virgin olive oil

¼ cup fresh lemon juice

6 garlic cloves—3 crushed through a press, 3 chopped

4 teaspoons dried herbes de Provence

1 tablespoon coarse salt

1 teaspoon freshly ground pepper

6 lamb shanks, cut in half (ask your butcher to do this)

4 pounds boneless lamb from the leg, trimmed of all extra fat and cut into 1½-inch pieces

3 whole cloves

4 medium onions—1 whole, 3 finely chopped

1 imported bay leaf

1 dried chipotle or small hot red pepper

3 tablespoons all-purpose flour

¼ cup tomato paste

¼ cup chopped parsley

Garlic-Herb Crumbs (page 36)

1. Rinse the beans and pick them over to remove any grit. Put in a large heavy pot and add fresh cold water to cover by at least 2 inches. Let stand overnight.

2. Also the night before, in a large bowl, combine ½ cup of the wine, ⅓ cup of the olive oil, the lemon juice, crushed garlic, half the herbes de Provence, and half the salt and pepper. Add the lamb shanks and chunks of meat and turn to coat with the marinade. Cover tightly and refrigerate overnight. The next day, remove from the refrigerator and let stand at room temperature, turning the pieces of lamb occasionally, for 1 to 2 hours.

3. Drain and rinse the beans. Return them to the pot and add enough cold water to cover by about 1½ inches. Bring to a boil, skimming to remove all the foam that rises to the surface. Stick the cloves in the whole onion and add to the pot. Add the bay leaf and hot pepper. Reduce the heat slightly and cook the beans for 45 to 60 minutes, or until they are just tender. Season with the remaining salt and pepper and cook about 15 minutes longer, until they are tender but not falling apart. Remove from the heat. Let stand for about 10 minutes; then drain, reserving the bean liquid. There should be about 3 cups liquid. Remove and discard the bay leaf, onion, and hot pepper.

4. Meanwhile, heat the broiler. Remove the lamb from the marinade; reserve the marinade. Dry the meat with paper towels and arrange in a single layer without crowding in a shallow flameproof baking dish or roasting pan. If necessary, do the meat in 2 batches to avoid crowding. Broil the lamb, turning, until browned, 10 to 15 minutes. Remove the meat with a slotted spoon and set aside. Carefully pour off any fat or juices that collect in the pan. Pour the remaining 1½ cups wine into the hot dish and use a wooden spoon to scrape up all the brown bits from the bottom and sides of the pan into the liquid. Pour the wine into a bowl and set aside.

5. In a large flameproof casserole, heat the remaining olive oil over moderately high heat. Add the chopped onions, cover, and cook for 5 minutes. Uncover and cook, stirring, until the onions are soft and beginning to turn golden, about 5 to 7 minutes longer. Sprinkle on the flour and cook, stirring, for 1 minute. Pour in the reserved wine from the roasting pan and the marinade and bring to a boil, stirring until thickened. Stir in the tomato paste, parsley, and remaining 2 teaspoons herbes de Provence. Add the browned lamb to the casserole. Pour in enough of the bean liquid to just cover the meat; you may well need all of it. Partially cover and simmer for 45 minutes, stirring once or twice and turning the pieces of meat for even cooking. Taste the sauce and season with additional salt and pepper, if necessary.

6. To assemble the dish, turn the beans into a large shallow baking dish, ceramic or enameled cast iron, or into 2 large casseroles. Add the lamb, distributing the pieces evenly around the beans. Pour the sauce over all and stir gently to mix. Some pieces of meat will poke up from the beans, which is fine. Cover tightly with foil and let stand until cooled. (The dish can be made to this point up to 2 days in advance. Refrigerate if not baking within an hour or two.)

7. Remove the baking dish from the refrigerator at least 1 hour before baking. Heat the oven to 375°F. Remove the foil and sprinkle the Garlic-Herb Crumbs generously over the top of the dish. Bake for 25 to 35 minutes, until the cassoulet is piping hot and the crumb topping is lightly browned.

GARLIC-HERB CRUMBS

MAKES ABOUT 3 CUPS

7 slices of firm-textured white bread

2 medium shallots, chopped

5 garlic cloves, minced

½ cup loosely packed parsley sprigs

1½ teaspoons hot paprika

1 teaspoon dried herbes de Provence

1 teaspoon dried thyme leaves

2 teaspoons coarse salt

⅓ cup extra-virgin olive oil

1. In a food processor, combine all the ingredients except the olive oil. Pulse until the parsley is chopped, then run briefly to mix well.

2. In a large nonstick or cast-iron skillet, heat the olive oil over medium-high heat. Add the seasoned crumbs and cook, stirring often, until crisp and lightly browned.

PEARS POACHED IN RED WINE

12 SERVINGS

Fruit poached in a lightly spiced wine sauce performs beautifully after a substantial meal, providing just the right note of sweetness to cap off dinner while avoiding the extra heaviness of cake or pastry. Bartletts have by far the best flavor, but Bosc pears are good for poaching, too. Serve in pretty glass dessert dishes with some of the wine syrup. To dress up the dessert further, you can serve butter cookies alongside or add a dollop of crème fraîche or whipped cream or a scoop of vanilla ice cream.

6 cups dry red wine

1 cup sugar

2 tablespoons fresh lemon juice

2 wide strips of lemon zest

3 cinnamon sticks

2 imported bay leaves

2 whole cloves

1 teaspoon black peppercorns

12 flavorful pears

1. In a large enameled or stainless steel saucepan, combine the wine, sugar, lemon juice, lemon zest, cinnamon sticks, bay leaves, cloves, and peppercorns. Bring to a simmer, reduce the heat to low, and let steep for 10 minutes.

2. Meanwhile, peel the pears, leaving the stems intact. Place the pears in the simmering syrup and poach for 15 to 20 minutes, or until they are just tender but still firm. If they don't all fit, do them in 2 batches, but return all the pears to the syrup for cooling. Let the fruit cool in the syrup for several hours or overnight.

3. The next day, remove the pears; cut them in half and scoop out the cores, if desired. Place in a pretty glass serving bowl or individual dessert dishes. Strain the syrup, return it to the pan, and boil until reduced by about one-third. Taste and adjust the sugar or lemon juice if you need to. Let the syrup cool, then pour it over the pears. Serve chilled.

SPANISH DINNER

FOR 12

MARCONA ALMONDS

SPANISH OLIVES

ROMESCO SAUCE, SERVED WITH CRUDITÉS
FOR DIPPING

CHILLED FINO SHERRY

GARLIC SHRIMP WITH SMOKED SPANISH PAPRIKA

CRUSTY PEASANT BREAD

EITHER MORE SHERRY OR A CHILLED CRISP WHITE WINE, SUCH AS A SPANISH ALBARINO

SPANISH CHICKEN AND RICE WITH ARTICHOKES, SAUSAGES, AND SWEET PEPPERS

HEART OF PALM AND ORANGE SALAD
WITH SHERRY VINAIGRETTE

A SPANISH RED RIOJA, PREFERABLY AN AGED RIOJA RISERVA

FLAN

ESPRESSO

It used to be that the only Spanish celebrations you saw were composed from many tapas dishes. While these delightful tasty snacks, derived from the small plates served at wine bars, comprise a unique and extremely pleasant part of Spanish cuisine, the number required to feed a crowd can be daunting. And as many people are discovering, there is a lot more to Iberian cooking than tapas. While star chefs take Spanish flavors to new heights of creativity, sometimes in ways that are little short of conceptual art, traditional recipes from the Basque and Andalusian regions boast lively flavors and easy techniques that work well for the home cook.

Here you do get a few tapas first—roasted almonds, olives, and an amazing red pepper dip—served, as they would be in Barcelona, with a small glass of ice-cold, very dry sherry. Thanks to Foods & Wines of Spain, the marketing arm of the Spanish government, many of their finest products are now readily available in larger supermarkets. If not, two online mail-order sources, The Spanish Table and La Tienda, can sell you everything you need. I urge you to get ahold of the smoked paprika called *pimentón de la Vera,* which imparts an indescribable smoky flavor that cannot be duplicated any other way. It comes in several forms, and if you're not sure, I suggest you purchase the "bittersweet" version. Medium-hot and pungent, it is the secret ingredient in the fabulous garlic shrimp on page 40. Marcona almonds may be a bit harder to find locally. While they, too, have a unique taste, ordinary whole almonds, rolled in olive oil, toasted until pale golden brown, and sprinkled with sea salt, can be substituted.

It is guaranteed that you will receive applause for the first course. These garlicky shrimp are irresistible and unbelievably easy. Since they take less than 5 minutes after prep, you can toss them into the pan immediately before serving or cook them just before your company arrives, leaving them slightly undone, and finish them in a minute or two before bringing them to the table. Be sure to pass a basket of French or Italian bread to sop up the garlicky oil.

Absolutely glorious, the reddish-yellow mound of savory rice, studded with tomatoes, sausage, and peas, garnished with baby artichokes, olives, and sweet red pepper, all cloaking grilled chicken thighs, is one of the best meals in a single dish you will ever encounter. It needs absolutely no accompaniment, though I have included a simple but interesting salad, which features heart of palm. This salad can be served with the chicken and rice or as a separate course before dessert, or you can omit it.

Vanilla and smoky caramel are flavors married in Spanish custard, called *flan.* This recipe, which features a fairly dense vanilla custard dripping with caramel sauce, is a Cuban version, which was given to me many years ago. It is failure-proof. While small ramekins are charming when unmolded and glass custard cups are inexpensive, you can save some effort by making the flan in glass pie plates and serving it in wedges.

DO-AHEAD PLANNING

UP TO 4 DAYS IN ADVANCE: Make the Romesco Sauce; cover and refrigerate.

UP TO 2 DAYS IN ADVANCE: Make the Flan; cover, set on a baking sheet or other tray, and refrigerate.

UP TO A DAY AHEAD: Prepare the Spanish Chicken and Rice through Step 4. Prepare the Sherry Vinaigrette; refrigerate in a covered jar. Prepare the crudités for the Romesco Sauce; store them in a covered container filled with salted water.

UP TO 6 HOURS IN ADVANCE: Prepare the greens and orange segments for the salad. Prepare the Garlic Shrimp; let cool, then cover and refrigerate, making sure you do not lose any of the garlic or oil.

UP TO 3 HOURS IN ADVANCE: Prepare the sausages and rice for the chicken dish.

ABOUT 30 MINUTES BEFORE SERVING: Assemble the chicken and rice and set it in the oven.

JUST BEFORE SERVING: Reheat the shrimp and toss the salad. Unmold the flan directly onto dessert plates.

ROMESCO SAUCE

MAKES ABOUT 4 CUPS

Quite a few years ago, I predicted that this luscious Basque sauce would be the next pesto. Well, I was wrong, but every time I serve it, whether as a dip or as a thick sauce with roast lamb or vegetables, everyone raves and asks me about it. Brick red and just piquant enough to add zest, Romesco sauce contains roasted red peppers, almonds, and tomatoes, flavored with lemon juice, garlic, and cumin. For an appetizer dip, I sometimes put out crisp pita triangles along with assorted raw vegetables.

3 medium red bell peppers

3 plum tomatoes

1 cup natural whole almonds (about 5 ounces)

6 garlic cloves

⅔ cup fruity extra-virgin olive oil, preferably Spanish

1 teaspoon whole cumin seeds

¼ cup fresh lemon juice

2 teaspoons bittersweet or hot pimentón (Spanish smoked paprika) or ½ teaspoon crushed hot red pepper

2 teaspoons sea salt

1. Heat the broiler or light a hot fire in a grill. Either broil the peppers and tomatoes as close to the heat as possible or grill them or roast them over an open gas flame, turning, until blackened all over, 3 to 5 minutes for the tomatoes and 8 to 10 minutes for the peppers. (The grill or open flame will take less time than the broiler.) When the vegetables are cool enough to handle, peel off the blackened skins. Cut out the stem cores from the tomatoes; cut the tomatoes in half and add to a blender or food processor. Cut open the peppers and remove the stems, seeds, and ribs. Add the peppers to the blender.

2. Heat the oven to 375°F. Spread out the almonds on a baking sheet and toast, stirring the almonds once or twice, until they are golden brown and fragrant, 8 to 10 minutes. Check early to make sure the nuts do not burn.

3. Meanwhile, in a small, heavy saucepan, cook the garlic in the olive oil over low heat for 9 minutes. Add the cumin seeds, cook 30 seconds, remove from the heat, and let stand to cool slightly.

4. Add the lemon juice, pimentón, and salt to the blender. Puree the vegetables until coarsely chopped. Add the olive oil with the garlic and cumin seeds and puree. With the machine on, add the toasted nuts through the feed tube. Puree until as smooth as possible. Season with additional salt and hot pepper to taste. Scrape into a serving bowl, cover, and refrigerate until about half an hour before serving.

GARLIC SHRIMP WITH SMOKED SPANISH PAPRIKA

12 SERVINGS AS A FIRST COURSE, 24 SERVINGS AS TAPAS

As a first course at table, you will find that your guests scarf up these garlic shrimp like popcorn. Traditionally served in small earthenware *cazuelas*, piping hot out of the oven, the shrimp can be cooked and served in one large dish. Just be sure everyone gets a spoonful or two of the savory garlic oil.

2 pounds large shrimp (26 to 30 to a pound), shelled and deveined

¼ cup fino or pale dry sherry

1 teaspoon coarse salt

¾ cup extra-virgin olive oil, preferably Spanish

⅓ cup thinly sliced garlic (8 to 10 cloves)

½ teaspoon crushed hot red pepper

1½ teaspoons sweet or bittersweet pimentón (Spanish smoked paprika)

1. Marinate the shrimp with the sherry and salt for 15 minutes, tossing once or twice. Remove and pat dry on paper towels.

2. In a large cast-iron skillet or wok, heat the olive oil over medium-low heat. Add the garlic and cook for 2 minutes. Add the hot pepper and cook until the garlic starts to brown, 1 to 2 minutes longer.

3. Immediately add the shrimp and the pimentón. Raise the heat to medium-high and cook, stirring, until the shrimp are pink and curled, 3 to 4 minutes.

4. If making the dish ahead, undercook the shrimp by 30 to 60 seconds, or until they are just loosely curled; remove the shrimp from the heat and let cool, then cover and refrigerate. Reheat on a baking sheet under the broiler for 2 minutes, or until hot.

SPANISH CHICKEN AND RICE WITH ARTICHOKES, SAUSAGES, AND SWEET PEPPERS

12 SERVINGS

Not many one-dish meals are this beautiful or as delicious. While a medium-grain rice would be absolutely authentic, converted long-grain rice is infinitely more forgiving when you are cooking this much rice and reheating it, and I recommend it highly here. While the recipe looks long, you can prepare the dish in stages if you like, get it all ready ahead of time, and reheat it just before serving. A 16-inch metal paella pan allows you to serve this in a dramatic fashion, but if you cannot get ahold of one, use two large casseroles no more than 3 inches high.

12 large skinless chicken thighs on the bone, about 6 pounds

⅓ cup plus ¼ cup extra-virgin olive oil

2 tablespoons coarse salt

2 tablespoons bittersweet or hot pimentón (Spanish smoked paprika) or Hungarian paprika

1½ tablespoons ground cumin

1 tablespoon dried oregano

1½ teaspoons coarsely ground black pepper

5 garlic cloves—2 crushed through a press, 3 chopped

1 lemon, cut in half

12 baby artichokes or 3 large globe artichokes

2 pounds Spanish chorizo or hot Italian sausage, thickly sliced

2 large onions, chopped

1 bottle (12 ounces) lager beer, such as Corona Extra or Budweiser

2 cans (14½ ounces each) diced peeled tomatoes, with their juices

3 cups unsalted chicken stock

1 teaspoon saffron threads

3 cups converted long-grain white rice

1 package (10 ounces) frozen peas

Strips of roasted red pepper, preferably Spanish piquillo or morrones peppers, and pimiento-stuffed green olives, for garnish

1. Trim any excess fat from the chicken thighs. In a large bowl, combine ⅓ cup of the olive oil with 1 tablespoon each of the salt and pimentón, 1½ teaspoons of the cumin, 1 teaspoon each of the oregano and black pepper, and the crushed garlic. Add the chicken thighs and turn them in the marinade to coat. Let stand for about 30 minutes while you prepare the artichokes.

2. Squeeze half of the lemon into a large saucepan of salted water. Bring to a boil. If using baby artichokes, simply cut off the stems and about one-third of their tops. If any of the outer leaves look tough, bend them back and snap them off. As you trim the artichokes, rub the cut parts with the other lemon half. If using globe artichokes, cut off the stems and about half the tops. Bend back all the dark green leaves and snap them off until you have a pale center with the tiny purple leaves that hide the choke.

3. Add the artichokes to the boiling water and cook for 15 minutes. Drain and rinse under cold water to stop the cooking. Drain well. When the artichokes are cool enough to handle, cut the baby ones in half. If using globe artichokes, use a teaspoon to scoop out and remove the purple leaves and hairy choke. Cut each artichoke bottom into 6 wedges. (The artichokes can be prepared a day in advance. If prepared ahead, salt lightly, toss with a little olive oil and lemon juice, and refrigerate in a covered container.)

4. Grill the chicken thighs over medium-low heat on a gas grill or over medium coals in a charcoal grill, turning every 5 to 10 minutes, for 20 minutes, or until they are just barely cooked (they will finish cooking with the rice). Set aside on a baking sheet to cool a bit, then cover with foil and refrigerate. (The recipe can be prepared to this point up to 2 days in advance.)

5. Two to 3 hours before serving, heat the remaining ¼ cup olive oil in a very large flameproof casserole; I use a 9-quart enameled cast-iron Dutch oven. Add the chorizo and sauté over moderately high heat, stirring occasionally, until most of the pink is gone, 5 to 7 minutes. With a skimmer or slotted spoon, remove the sausage to a plate. Add the onions to the pot and cook, stirring occasionally, until they are golden, about 10 minutes. Add the chopped garlic and the remaining 1 tablespoon each pimentón and cumin, 2 teaspoons oregano, and ½ teaspoon black pepper. Cook 1 minute longer.

6. Pour in the beer and bring to a boil, scraping up any browned bits from the bottom of the pot. Add the tomatoes with their juices, chicken stock, saffron, and the remaining 1 tablespoon salt. Return the liquid in the pot to a boil. Add the rice and return the sausage to the pot. Bring to a simmer, stirring up the ingredients from the bottom to the top once or twice. Reduce the heat to low and simmer for 12 to 15 minutes, until the rice is tender but still has a bit of resistance and some liquid remains visible. Remove from the heat and let cool slightly, gently folding the rice several times to help it cool a bit.

7. About 1 hour before serving, if the chicken is ice cold, reheat it under the broiler for about 5 minutes. Arrange the thighs in the bottom of a generously oiled (use olive oil) 16-inch paella pan or 2 large shallow casseroles. Stir the frozen peas into the rice and mound the rice and sausage on top of the chicken. Set aside for up to 1 hour or refrigerate to hold longer; if chilled, let stand at room temperature for at least 1 hour before baking.

8. Heat the oven to 350°F. Heat the paella pan on top of the stove. Transfer it to the oven and bake the dish uncovered for 25 to 35 minutes, until hot throughout. (If you are using casseroles that cannot go on top of the stove, bake the rice covered with foil for 15 minutes, then uncover and bake until hot, 20 to 25 minutes longer.) Garnish with the pepper strips and olives and bring to the table.

HEART OF PALM AND ORANGE SALAD WITH SHERRY VINAIGRETTE

12 SERVINGS

Pretty and a touch unusual, this salad combines the sweet tartness of oranges with the almost meaty richness of heart of palm. It is both light and satisfying at the same time.

Tip: If your red onion smells harsh, rinse the rings under cold running water and shake them dry before adding to the salad.

12 cups mesclun or assorted baby spinach leaves

3 oranges, peeled and sectioned

2 cans (16 ounces each) hearts of palm, sliced

1 medium-small red onion, thinly sliced into rings

¼ cup sherry vinegar

1 teaspoon Dijon mustard

¼ teaspoon coarse salt

¼ teaspoon sugar

¼ teaspoon freshly ground pepper

¼ cup orange juice

½ cup extra-virgin olive oil

1. Rinse and spin dry the salad greens. In a large salad bowl, toss together the mesclun, orange sections, heart of palm slices, and red onion rings.

2. In a small bowl, whisk together the sherry vinegar, mustard, salt, sugar, and pepper. Blend in the orange juice. Slowly whisk in the olive oil in a thin stream so that the dressing emulsifies.

3. Just before serving, pour the dressing over the salad and toss to mix.

FLAN

12 SERVINGS

These days, creative pastry chefs design different flavored flans. Indeed, on page 153, I offer a Toasted Coconut Flan. But my favorite of all is still the utterly simple caramel custard presented here.

1 cup sugar

4 whole eggs

4 egg yolks

2 cans (14 ounces each) sweetened condensed milk

2 cups whole milk

2 teaspoons vanilla extract

Pinch of salt

1. Heat the oven to 350°F.

2. In a small saucepan, melt the sugar with 2 tablespoons water over moderate heat, stirring until the sugar dissolves. Boil without stirring until the syrup turns a light golden brown. Immediately remove from the heat and carefully pour or ladle the caramel into twelve 6-ounce ramekins or custard cups or into two 1½-quart shallow casseroles. Quickly tilt the cups to line with the caramel as best you can. Set the caramel-lined containers in a roasting pan filled with enough hot water to reach about halfway up the sides of the dishes.

3. In a large bowl, beat together the whole eggs and egg yolks until blended. Beat in the condensed milk, whole milk, vanilla, and salt. Pour into the caramel-lined dishes and bake for 1 to 1¼ hours, or until set. Remove the flans from the water bath and let cool, then refrigerate for at least 4 hours or overnight, until chilled.

4. When serving, if the custards do not loosen easily, run a blunt knife around the edge of the dishes, then quickly dip the bottoms in a pan of warm water and invert to unmold. Drizzle any caramel remaining in the baking dishes on top. Serve chilled.

DINNER FOR A SUMMER EVENING

FOR 12

ICED CUCUMBER SOUP WITH CHIVES AND DILL

MESQUITE-GRILLED CHICKEN

RUTH'S SPANISH RICE

GRILLED CORN ON THE COB

HEIRLOOM TOMATO AND SWEET ONION SALAD
WITH BLUE CHEESE VINAIGRETTE

GARDEN GREEN SALAD

STRAWBERRY-CHOCOLATE CHIP BREAD PUDDING

ICED COFFEE

I love entertaining on warm evenings when the red sun looks like a painting as it sets slowly in the hazy sky. As the last rays slip through the gold- and mauve-edged clouds, chances are you will find me on the terrace with friends, sipping long cool drinks and talking softly, dragging out the pleasures of summer as long as we can. It's not a time to fuss. I serve easy food, tasty enough to tempt tired appetites, light enough to be refreshing. Usually the main course is prepared on the grill while guests watch; they can even help if they want to—an iced gin and tonic in one hand, barbecue fork in the other. An artful vase of fresh-from-the-garden flowers and a crisp pastel cloth set the perfect table, with small white candles mimicking the fireflies outside the screen.

The first course is cool, waiting in the fridge: a refreshing cucumber soup, slightly tart with yogurt, piqued with snippets of fresh dill and chives. If you've never eaten cooked cucumber, you're in for a treat. A splash of buttermilk imparts its uniquely tart, nutty taste, and an extra handful of chives and thinly sliced fresh radishes make this subtle soup as pretty as it is refreshing.

Mesquite-Grilled Chicken uses a dry marinade blended with onions, garlic, and a little oil and citrus juice to produce the best barbecued chicken you've ever tasted. Experiment, if you like, with other types of woods; use regular charcoal or gas; or, in a pinch, even employ the broiler. Grilled sausages add variety and complement the Spanish-style rice. Flavorful heirloom tomatoes and sweet onion doused with a tangy blue cheese dressing is a classic steakhouse salad having a casual fling. I recommend ice-cold beer or a fruity white wine, such as a Viognier, or a subtle rosé—yes, rosé!—to quench summer thirst and wash down this zesty food. If you think rosé wine is insipid, you are in for a surprise, and a treat. Well-made ones—from both France and California—are delicate and dry. Two labels you might want to try are Bonnie Doon's Vin Gris de Cigare or a Tavel or Domaines Ott from Provence. They are delightful in summer and particularly good with grilled or spicy food. It's my wine of choice on picnics.

For dessert, I've suggested a crowd-pleaser: Strawberry–Chocolate Chip Bread Pudding, a luscious play on those chocolate, vanilla, and strawberry flavors that complement each other so well. It's one of those make-ahead recipes that can be served at any temperature. If, however, you are short of time and prefer a delightful no-work dessert, buy a good mango or raspberry sorbet. Scoop into small dessert bowls and garnish each with a few bright berries, slices of kiwi, and a couple of nut cookies. All you need to complete the perfect evening are tall glasses of iced coffee (brewed extra-strong to stand up to the melting ice) to sip late into the long, warm night.

DO-AHEAD PLANNING

UP TO 1 DAY AHEAD: Make the Iced Cucumber Soup. Marinate the chicken. Make the dressing for the tomato salad through Step 1; crumble the blue cheese and refrigerate separately.

UP TO 6 HOURS IN ADVANCE: Make the Strawberry–Chocolate Chip Bread Pudding.

UP TO 3 HOURS BEFORE SERVING: Slice the tomatoes and onions and arrange on a platter. Cover with a damp paper towel and a loose sheet of plastic wrap and set aside at room temperature. Make the dressing.

UP TO 1½ HOURS BEFORE SERVING: Make Ruth's Spanish Rice; it will hold for 30 to 45 minutes.

ABOUT 1 HOUR BEFORE SERVING: Grill the chicken.

JUST BEFORE SERVING: Ladle the cold soup into bowls and garnish. Give the salad dressing a good shake, stir in the blue cheese, and drizzle over the tomatoes and onions. Reheat the rice, if necessary, in a microwave oven.

ICED CUCUMBER SOUP WITH CHIVES AND DILL

12 SERVINGS

Nothing could be easier or more welcome in hot weather than this 15-minute soup. If you feel you need a bread to accompany it, choose something crisp, like cheese sticks or crackers. And if you have any radishes on hand, throw a few slices onto the top of each bowl of soup along with the minced chives, for a really pretty contrast.

4 large seedless European cucumbers (about 3 pounds)

3 large leeks (white and tender green) or 2 medium onions

⅓ cup olive oil

¼ cup plus 2 tablespoons all-purpose flour

6 cups unsalted or reduced-sodium chicken stock

1½ cups buttermilk

1 cup sour cream

3 tablespoons fresh lemon juice

Sea salt and cayenne pepper

1 cup minced fresh dill

¾ cup minced fresh chives

1. Using a swivel-bladed vegetable peeler, remove the cucumber skin in strips, leaving about one-third of the green intact. Thickly slice the cucumbers.

2. Thickly slice the leeks and swish them around in a large bowl of cold water. With your fingers, lift the leeks out of the water to drain in a colander, leaving any grit behind in the bowl. (If using onions, simply slice them.)

3. In a large flameproof casserole, heat the olive oil over moderate heat. Add the leeks or onions, cover, and cook for 5 minutes; don't worry if there is water on the leeks. Uncover and continue to cook until very soft but not brown, 5 to 7 minutes longer.

4. Sprinkle on the flour and cook, stirring, for 1 minute. Whisk in the chicken stock and bring to a boil over high heat, whisking until the liquid thickens. Add the cucumbers and return the liquid to a boil. Reduce the heat to moderately low and simmer, partially covered, until the cucumbers are soft, about 15 minutes. Remove from the heat and let cool slightly.

5. Whisk in the buttermilk, sour cream, and lemon juice. Season with salt and cayenne to taste. Stir in the minced dill and chives. If you have an immersion blender, you can puree the soup right in the pot. Otherwise, puree it in a blender or food processor, in batches if necessary, until smooth. Transfer to a covered container and refrigerate until ice cold. Just before serving, check the seasoning again.

MESQUITE-GRILLED CHICKEN

12 SERVINGS

Sometimes simpler is better, and that is the case with the marinade for this succulent chicken. Lime juice, oregano, and cumin provide a subtle Mexican note, with plenty of aromatics to contribute both moisture and taste. It may look like a lot of salt and pepper, but the seasoning is essential for this much food.

I like to grill some sweet Italian sausages along with the chicken. If you do that, adjust the number of people it will feed, allowing about ⅔ pound chicken on the bone plus ¼ pound sausage per person. Prick the sausages all over and simmer in a saucepan of water for 10 minutes before grilling to be sure the pork is thoroughly cooked.

8 to 9 pounds chicken—either 3 quartered chickens or an equal amount of your favorite chicken parts

2 medium onions, quartered

5 large garlic cloves, crushed

1 tablespoon sweet paprika

1 tablespoon fresh oregano or 1 teaspoon dried

1½ teaspoons ground cumin

1 to 1½ teaspoons cayenne pepper

2 tablespoons coarse salt

1½ teaspoons freshly ground black pepper

⅓ cup fresh lime juice or lemon juice

¼ cup extra-virgin olive oil or peanut oil

1. Rinse the chicken and pat dry. Put in a large bowl.

2. In a food processor, combine all the remaining ingredients. Puree until smooth. Pour over the chicken and toss to coat. Let marinate at room temperature for up to 2 hours or cover and refrigerate for up to 24 hours.

3. Light a covered charcoal or gas grill or preheat the broiler. If you are using mesquite or other wood, soak the chunks in water for at least 30 minutes. Let the charcoal or gas fire get very hot, then add the wood and splash with water if it flares up.

4. Remove the chicken from the marinade, letting any excess drip back into the bowl. Put the chicken on the grill with the heat on high or the vents wide open and sear for about 5 minutes on each side to brown the outside. Turn the heat to low or close the vents, splash the fire with water if necessary, cover the grill, and grill the chicken, turning once, for 35 minutes, or until it is no longer pink but still juicy. (The chicken can be smoked earlier in the day. Reheat, wrapped in foil, in a 300°F oven. Unwrap during the last 5 minutes.)

RUTH'S SPANISH RICE

12 SERVINGS

Less than 12 hours after her mother, Emily, polished off three helpings of this spicy rice, Ruth Buckingham entered the world, so I couldn't resist naming this dish in her honor. I use converted rice here so the recipe can be made a day ahead and reheated in a heavy covered casserole in the oven or, preferably, in a glass container in a microwave. It is also good at room temperature.

3 tablespoons extra-virgin olive oil

2 medium onions, chopped

⅓ cup slivered almonds

3 garlic cloves, minced

⅓ pound baked ham, diced

½ green bell pepper, diced

½ red bell pepper, diced

1 can (14½ ounces) diced peeled tomatoes, with their juices

1½ teaspoons dried oregano, preferably Mexican

½ teaspoon crushed hot red pepper

¼ teaspoon saffron threads, crumbled

1 can (12 ounces) lager beer, such as Budweiser

1 imported bay leaf

1¾ teaspoons salt

¾ teaspoon coarsely cracked black pepper

3 cups converted rice

⅔ cup small Spanish pimiento-stuffed olives, well drained

1. In a large saucepan or flameproof casserole, heat the oil. Add the onions and almonds and sauté over moderately high heat until the onions are softened and golden and the almonds are lightly browned, 5 to 7 minutes. Add the garlic, ham, and bell peppers and sauté until the peppers are crisp-tender, about 3 minutes.

2. Add the tomatoes and their juices, the oregano, hot pepper, saffron, beer, bay leaf, salt, black pepper, and 3 cups of water. Bring to a boil, then add the rice. Stir once. Cover and simmer over low heat for 18 to 20 minutes, until the liquid is absorbed and the rice is tender. Stir in the olives. (I like them whole, but if yours are large, you can slice them thickly.)

HEIRLOOM TOMATO AND SWEET ONION SALAD WITH BLUE CHEESE VINAIGRETTE

12 SERVINGS

While many would recognize this as a classic steak-house salad, it goes beautifully with grilled chicken. Incorporated in the light vinaigrette are chunks of blue cheese, which really makes the dish. I recommend an excellent American blue—such as Maytag, Great Hill, or Humboldt Fog—or a French Roquefort or milder Bleu d'Auvergne.

As for the tomatoes, any ripe, native tomato will do, but these days such a pretty assortment of heirlooms, in colors that range from red, orange, and purple to yellow and green, can be found both at farmers' markets and in supermarkets that carry local produce. It's worth looking for them. An assortment will make a spectacular platter.

About 3 pounds heirloom tomatoes or 4 large beefsteak tomatoes

2 large Vidalia or other sweet onions

Sea salt and freshly ground pepper

Blue Cheese Vinaigrette (page 50)

⅓ cup shredded or coarsely chopped basil or parsley

1. Trim the tomatoes to remove the stems and cut out the cores. Cut the tomatoes crosswise into ¼-inch slices. Cut each onion in half lengthwise and then thinly slice crosswise into half moons.

2. Arrange the tomatoes and onions decoratively on a platter. I like to arrange them alternating tomatoes and onions in concentric circles. Season with salt and pepper. Drizzle the vinaigrette over the salad platter. Sprinkle the basil on top.

BLUE CHEESE VINAIGRETTE

MAKES ABOUT 1 CUP

Like most vinaigrettes, this can be made days in advance and refrigerated, but it is best used when fresh. Since it takes just minutes, you could cut up the blue cheese well in advance and make the vinaigrette a couple of hours before serving. Let it stand at room temperature. When you're ready to use the dressing, give it another good shake and then stir in the cheese.

Tip: The small amount of juice or water added helps the dressing to emulsify.

3 tablespoons of your favorite vinegar: aged sherry, Banyuls, Champagne, balsamic, red wine, or white wine

½ cup excellent extra-virgin olive oil

1 tablespoon walnut oil, optional

1 tablespoon orange juice or water

¼ teaspoon sugar

Salt and freshly ground pepper

½ cup finely diced or crumbled blue cheese (about 2 ounces)

1. In a pint jar, combine the vinegar, olive oil, walnut oil, juice, and sugar. Cover tightly and shake until emulsified. Taste and season with salt and pepper, keeping in mind that the blue cheese is salty.

2. Stir in the blue cheese.

STRAWBERRY–CHOCOLATE CHIP BREAD PUDDING

12 SERVINGS

This incredibly appealing dessert is based on a recipe from Lola, a New York City restaurant that offers a great gospel brunch. It is quite simply the best bread pudding I've ever eaten—good warm, at room temperature, or cold. For warm weather, I usually opt for chilled, which makes it easy to serve as well. I wait until the pudding is cold and set, then I cut it into squares and arrange it on a platter.

1 loaf (1 pound) sliced challah or firm-textured white bread, preferably sandwich cut

5 tablespoons unsalted butter, at room temperature

1 pint strawberries

1 cup plus 2 tablespoons sugar

⅓ cup slivered blanched almonds

⅓ cup chocolate chips, preferably mini

1 quart half-and-half or light cream

4 whole eggs

5 egg yolks

1 tablespoon vanilla extract

1. Heat the oven to 350°F, with a rack set in the middle of the oven. Lightly butter one side of all the bread slices with 4 tablespoons of the softened butter. Set the bread, buttered side up, on a large baking sheet and bake for 15 minutes, or until lightly toasted.

2. Meanwhile, hull and thickly slice the strawberries. Put them in a bowl and sprinkle them with 2 tablespoons of the sugar. Toss and set aside.

3. When the bread is toasted, reduce the oven temperature to 325°F and set a large roasting pan half-filled with hot water on the middle rack to act as a water bath. Trim the crusts off the bread and cut each slice of bread diagonally in half into triangles.

4. Use the remaining 1 tablespoon butter to grease a 9 × 12-inch baking dish at least 1½ inches deep. Line the sides of the baking dish with the pieces of bread, points up. Line the bottom of the dish with more of the bread. Stand the remaining bread, points up, wedged between the bottom slices. (Don't worry if there are some spaces in between the slices or if the pieces standing up lean over a bit.)

5. Scatter the almonds and chocolate chips over the bread and between the slices. Lift the strawberries with a slotted spoon, leaving any juices behind, and scatter them around the baking dish.

6. In a large saucepan, heat the half-and-half and the remaining 1 cup sugar over moderate heat, stirring to dissolve the sugar, until the mixture is hot but not boiling.

7. In a medium bowl, beat the whole eggs and egg yolks to blend. Whisk in the vanilla. Remove the hot half-and-half from the heat and immediately whisk in the eggs. Pour the custard through a sieve into the baking dish. Set the dish in the roasting pan in the oven and bake for 35 to 40 minutes, or until the custard is just set. Remove from the water bath and serve warm, at room temperature, or chilled.

Falafel Party

FOR 12

HUMMUS

BABAGANOUSH

PITA CRISPS AND/OR CRUDITÉS FOR DIPPING

OLIVES

PISTACHIO NUTS

FALAFEL

PITA BREADS

LEMON-GARLIC TAHINA

CHOPPED SALAD WITH FETA CHEESE AND FRESH MINT

MIDDLE EASTERN HOT SAUCE
WITH TOMATOES AND CILANTRO

PURCHASED BAKLAVA OR OTHER PASTRY

STRAWBERRIES AND FRESH PINEAPPLE MARINATED
IN HONEY AND GRAND MARNIER

It was many years ago that I was introduced to the pleasures of falafel and its attendant accompaniments—some refreshing, some spicy. This initiation took place neither in the Middle East nor on the lower East Side of Manhattan but at a graduate school party at the University of Chicago. A couple had returned from a semester in Israel, and they threw a huge homecoming bash with an enormous buffet composed of all these foods I'd never tasted. To this day I remember the raucous party and the piquant flavors that were such a delight. Only later did it occur to me that this is a great choice for a big party not only because of its high spirits but for its low cost.

Both the hummus and babaganoush, a smoky eggplant spread, can easily be made in advance. I like to buy organic dried chickpeas, soak them overnight, and cook them for both the hummus and the falafel. For convenience, canned chickpeas can be used to very good effect. In either case, though, the papery outer skins should be rubbed off the chickpeas for better flavor, texture, and digestibility. While both appetizers are chilled, I take them out of the refrigerator about an hour before serving. Both evidence more flavor closer to room temperature.

If you've never had falafel before, let me explain that it is eaten as a vegetarian sandwich, tucked into a pita round along with plenty of crisp salad and dollops of tahina sauce and a fresh hot relish, whose real name is *schloog*. If you ask me, it's the hot sauce that works the magic. There's no doubt that falafel, like any fried food, is best eaten as soon as it is cooked. For a large party, however, I find last-minute frying a daunting task, so unless you have help in the kitchen, I recommend you fry all the falafel ahead of time and reheat them on a large baking sheet in the oven just before serving. With all this casual, tasty food, cold beer has to be the beverage of choice, though there are always some who will ask for white wine.

After all that tasty food, a light dessert, with the tart sweetness of strawberries and pineapple, makes a nice palate cleanser. And for die-hard sugarholics, store-bought baklava, a honey and nut pastry that originated in the eastern Mediterranean, satisfies perfectly.

DO-AHEAD PLANNING

UP TO 4 DAYS IN ADVANCE: Soak the chickpeas overnight.

UP TO 3 DAYS IN ADVANCE: Cook the chickpeas and rub off their outer papery skins. Unless you plan to fry at the last minute, make the Falafel, let cool completely, then refrigerate in a tightly closed container. Make the Hummus; cover and refrigerate.

UP TO 2 DAYS IN ADVANCE: Make the Babaganoush; cover and refrigerate.

UP TO A DAY IN ADVANCE: Cut up the pineapple; refrigerate in a covered container or sealed plastic storage bag. Make the Lemon-Garlic Tahina.

UP TO 4 HOURS BEFORE SERVING: Make the Middle Eastern Hot Sauce; cover and set aside at room temperature. Make the Chopped Salad through Step 2; cover and refrigerate. Prepare the Strawberries and Fresh Pineapple through Step 4.

ABOUT 1 HOUR BEFORE SERVING: Remove the Hummus and Babaganoush from the refrigerator. Finish the Strawberries and Fresh Pineapple.

SHORTLY BEFORE SERVING: Warm the pita breads and heat the Falafel in a 425°F oven until hot and crisp. Dress the Chopped Salad.

HUMMUS

MAKES 3 CUPS

While these days you can buy perfectly good hummus in the club stores as well as in supermarkets, homemade can be tailored to your own taste, and, of course, by volume, it's much more economical. The dip takes just minutes to whip up in a food processor or blender. Serve with pita triangles or corn tostadas. Baby carrots or other crudités can also be offered.

1 can (19 ounces) chickpeas (garbanzo beans)

½ cup tahina (Middle Eastern sesame seed paste)

¼ cup fresh lemon juice

2 tablespoons extra-virgin olive oil

4 garlic cloves, crushed through a press

1½ teaspoons ground cumin

1 teaspoon salt

⅛ teaspoon cayenne pepper

Paprika

1. Rinse the chickpeas and drain well. Pick over to remove any skins. In a blender or food processor, combine the chickpeas, tahina, lemon juice, olive oil, garlic, cumin, salt, and cayenne.

2. Add ¾ cup warm water and puree until smooth. If not serving the hummus in the next couple of hours, cover and refrigerate.

3. Spread in a shallow serving dish and garnish with a dusting of paprika. Hummus is best served at room temperature.

BABAGANOUSH

MAKES ABOUT 4½ CUPS

There's one secret to making really good babaganoush: You have to roast the eggplant until it is completely blackened and shriveled. That's the only way to add the subtle smoky flavor that makes all the difference. If you have a barbecue grill, that's ideal. Otherwise, a really hot broiler works almost as well. Be sure to choose shiny dark eggplants that are hard and have fresh green tops.

3 medium eggplants (about 1 pound each)

3 to 4 tablespoons tahina (Middle Eastern sesame seed paste), at room temperature

½ cup fresh lemon juice

3 tablespoons fruity extra-virgin olive oil

2 garlic cloves, crushed through a press

½ cup coarsely chopped parsley

Coarse salt

1. Light a hot fire in a barbecue grill or heat your broiler with the rack set about 3 inches from the heat. Pierce each eggplant in several spots with the tip of a knife to allow steam to escape; do not forget to do this or you may end up with a mess.

2. Grill the eggplants, turning, until blackened and completely soft, 20 to 25 minutes. Remove and let stand until cool enough to handle. Either peel off the skin or cut open the eggplants and scoop the flesh into a bowl, whichever is easier.

3. Mash the eggplant with a fork to retain a little texture. Blend in the tahina, lemon juice, olive oil, garlic, and parsley. Season with salt to taste.

FALAFEL

MAKES ABOUT 72; 12 SERVINGS AS A MAIN COURSE

A common street food throughout the Middle East, these tasty chickpea croquettes are traditionally served in warm pita pockets. Tahina sauce, hot sauce, and chopped salad are set out separately, and each guest assembles his or her own. While falafel are best served freshly cooked, for a party I recommend frying them a day or two ahead, refrigerating them, and reheating them in a hot oven just before serving. Because they do not absorb the oil, these are not at all greasy.

Tip: In place of dried chickpeas, you can use 4 cans (19 ounces each) of chickpeas or enough to equal 9 cups; if you do so, skip Step 1.

1½ pounds (about 3 cups) dried chickpeas

¾ cup bulgur

2 medium onions, grated

5 garlic cloves, crushed through a press

½ cup chopped parsley

½ cup all-purpose flour

2 tablespoons ground cumin

1 tablespoon ground coriander

1 tablespoon coarse salt

¾ teaspoon cayenne pepper

3 eggs, lightly beaten

1 quart peanut oil

1. Soak the chickpeas overnight in plenty of cold water to cover. Drain, place in a large pot, and add enough fresh water to cover by at least 2 inches. Boil for 1½ to 2 hours, or until the skins begin to come off.

2. Soak the bulgur in cold water to cover for 1 hour to soften. Drain in a fine-mesh sieve.

3. Drain the cooked chickpeas and rinse well under cold running water. Rub through your fingers to remove as many of the skins as possible. Drain well and let dry.

4. In batches, put the chickpeas through the shredding disk of a food processor. Transfer to a large bowl. Add the bulgur, onions, garlic, and parsley. Mix lightly to blend. Combine the flour, cumin, coriander, salt, and cayenne. Sprinkle over the chickpea mixture and toss lightly to blend evenly. Add the eggs and blend until evenly moistened.

5. Roll the chickpea paste lightly into walnut-size balls. Flatten slightly and arrange on 1 or 2 baking sheets in a single layer. Meanwhile, in a wide saucepan, heat the oil over moderately high heat to 350°F.

6. Using a mesh skimmer, lower the falafel into the hot oil. Fry in batches of 6 to 8 without crowding for 3 to 5 minutes, until deeply browned and nicely crusted. Remove with the skimmer and drain on paper towels. Serve at once or let cool, then refrigerate in covered containers. Reheat in a 400°F oven for 20 to 30 minutes, until heated through and crisp outside.

LEMON-GARLIC TAHINA

MAKES 3 CUPS

My friend and former colleague Irene Thomas, who is of Lebanese extraction, shared this recipe with me. It's good on fish and vegetables, too.

Tip: If you make this sauce in advance and it thickens too much, thin with a little hot water and adjust the seasoning so that it remains zippy.

1 cup tahina (Middle Eastern sesame seed paste)

½ cup fresh lemon juice

4 garlic cloves, crushed through a press

¾ teaspoon salt

Several dashes of cayenne pepper, or more to taste

Put the tahina, lemon juice, garlic, salt, and cayenne in a blender or food processor. Add 1¼ cups water and puree until smooth.

CHOPPED SALAD WITH FETA CHEESE AND FRESH MINT

12 SERVINGS

Amazingly refreshing, this minted salad makes a great accompaniment to any barbecue or spicy food. It's also a delightful salad to enjoy as a main course for a light lunch. If you want to prepare this in advance, cut up the cucumbers, radishes, and bell peppers and store them in the refrigerator in a covered container of salted water overnight. Chop the tomatoes, onions, and mint at the last minute and toss the whole salad together.

1½ pounds red, ripe tomatoes

1 cup finely diced mild white bunching (spring) onions with green tops or scallions

Coarse salt and cracked black pepper

4 large cucumbers, peeled, seeded, and diced

6 large radishes, trimmed and diced

2 green bell peppers, seeded and diced

2 red bell peppers, seeded and diced

¾ cup coarsely chopped fresh mint

2 cups crumbled feta cheese, preferably Israeli (about 10 ounces)

½ cup fresh lemon juice

⅔ cup fruity extra-virgin olive oil

1. Core the tomatoes and cut them into ½-inch dice. Put them in a large bowl and add the white onions. Season with 1 teaspoon coarse salt and a generous grinding of pepper. Toss and let stand for 10 to 15 minutes at room temperature.

2. Add all the other vegetables, the mint, and 1½ cups of the feta cheese to the tomatoes and onions. Toss lightly to mix.

3. Sprinkle the lemon juice and then the olive oil over the salad and toss again. Season with additional salt and pepper to taste. Sprinkle the remaining cheese over the salad.

MIDDLE EASTERN HOT SAUCE WITH TOMATOES AND CILANTRO

MAKES ABOUT 3 CUPS

Because the heat of fresh chiles varies wildly, you'll need to adjust the heat in this sauce with crushed hot red pepper, the kind you shake on pizza. Of course, you can season to your personal taste but keep in mind that traditionally this sauce is served fiery hot.

1½ pounds ripe tomatoes, quartered

¾ cup loosely packed cilantro leaves

½ cup coarsely diced white onion

⅓ to ½ cup finely diced serrano or jalapeño peppers with some seeds

¾ teaspoon salt

Crushed hot red pepper

Combine the tomatoes, cilantro, white onion, serrano peppers, and salt in a food processor. Pulse, then run until the vegetables are minced. Add enough crushed hot pepper so that the sauce is spicy hot, to your taste.

STRAWBERRIES AND FRESH PINEAPPLE MARINATED IN HONEY AND GRAND MARNIER

12 SERVINGS

Fresh fruit and orange-flavored Grand Marnier are a match made in heaven. My friend, publicist Greg Mowery, suggested the honey, which adds a mellow sweetness. The amount of honey you'll need here depends upon the sweetness of both the berries and the pineapple.

4 pints fresh strawberries

1 ripe fresh pineapple

⅓ to ½ cup honey, preferably wildflower

⅔ cup Grand Marnier liqueur

⅓ cup chopped fresh mint, plus several sprigs for garnish, optional

1. Hull the strawberries and halve or quarter them, depending upon size.

2. Cut the top and bottom off the pineapple. With a large sharp knife, cut off the thick skin and "eyes," in wide strips from top to bottom. Turn the pineapple on its side and cut it into ¾-inch rounds. If the central core is tough, cut it out; otherwise, leave it. Cut the rounds into ½-inch wedges.

3. Measure ⅓ cup of the honey into a medium bowl. Whisk in the Grand Marnier until blended.

4. In a large serving bowl, combine the strawberries and pineapple. Pour the honeyed Grand Marnier over the fruit and toss. Cover and refrigerate for 3 to 4 hours, tossing occasionally. If the fruit is not sweet enough for your taste, drizzle on the remaining honey.

5. If you have fresh mint, stir the chopped leaves into the fruit salad. Let stand at room temperature, tossing once or twice, for about 1 hour. The fruit should be chilled but not ice cold. Garnish with mint sprigs just before serving.

HEARTY WINTER MEAL

FOR 12 TO 14

ROQUEFORT CAESAR SALAD

HERBED ROAST PORK LOIN

CREAMY BUTTERMILK DO-AHEAD GRITS

OR

OVEN-ROASTED GARLIC POTATOES

GREEN BEANS WITH LEMON BUTTER

HAZELNUT ROULADE WITH BANANA CREAM AND RICH CHOCOLATE SAUCE

I'm not quite certain why a big chill and a big appetite go together, but there's no question they do. What I like about this food is that while the meal is warming and substantial, it is unquestionably sophisticated and welcome on the grandest table. Notice that both the first course and the dessert are served cold or at room temperature and the beans are cooked ahead, so you have only a couple of dishes to finish cooking once guests arrive.

If ever a recipe deserved its title, Caesar salad is it. Fresh lemon, fruity olive oil, pungent garlic, a hint of anchovy, and the tang of fine aged Parmesan cheese make this truly the king of salads. I've added rich Roquefort cheese to increase the body and creaminess and add yet another dimension of flavor. While it's served as a first course here, the two cheeses make this satisfying enough to serve as a main-course at lunch, which you'll appreciate if you love Caesar salad as much as I do.

The pork recipe is my version of a traditional Tuscan roast, or *arrosto*, the most flavorful, succulent pork you've ever tasted. Grits may seem like an odd choice with an Italian roast—but what is polenta but Italian grits? Here buttermilk adds richness and nuttiness without a lot of extra fat. If you prefer potatoes, you'll find the oven-roasted recipe presented here both easy and irresistible. Simple green beans dressed with lemon butter complete the savory portion of this meal.

After such a substantial dinner, I've chosen one of my favorite desserts, which is delectable but on the light side. Besides being absolutely scrumptious, this Hazelnut Roulade with Banana Cream and Rich Chocolate Sauce can be completely assembled up to a day ahead.

DO-AHEAD PLANNING

UP TO 1 WEEK IN ADVANCE: Make the Rich Chocolate Sauce.

UP TO 2 DAYS AHEAD: Prepare the lettuce. Grate the Parmesan cheese for the salad; refrigerate in a covered container.

UP TO 1 DAY AHEAD: Make the garlic croutons for the salad. Marinate the pork roast. Make the Hazelnut Roulade with Banana Cream. If you choose the potatoes over the grits, boil them now.

ABOUT 4 HOURS BEFORE YOU PLAN TO BEGIN SERVING: Roast the pork. Chop the anchovies and make the dressing for the salad.

ABOUT 2 HOURS BEFORE SERVING: Make the grits through Step 2. Stir in the buttermilk and set aside. Blanch the green beans. Set aside, covered, at room temperature. Roast the garlic potatoes with the pork; while the pork rests, increase the oven temperature to 425°F and finish the potatoes.

AFTER THE PORK COMES OUT OF THE OVEN AND WHILE IT RESTS: Finish the grits; set aside, covered, to keep warm. Complete and serve the Roquefort Caesar Salad.

WHILE THE ROAST IS BEING CARVED: Reheat and complete the Green Beans with Lemon Butter.

SHORTLY BEFORE SERVING DESSERT: Reheat the Rich Chocolate Sauce.

ROQUEFORT CAESAR SALAD

12 TO 14 SERVINGS

Two cheeses—Roquefort and Parmesan—make this salad quite substantial. For a richer and more authentic salad, coddle 3 eggs by dipping them into boiling water for 35 seconds, then cracking them and tossing the loose eggs with the salad.

3 large heads of romaine lettuce (about 1¼ pounds each)

2 loaves of Italian bread (8 to 12 ounces each), cut into ½-inch-thick slices

1½ cups extra-virgin olive oil

4 garlic cloves—2 cut in half, 2 crushed through a press

2 cans (2 ounces each) flat anchovy fillets, drained and rinsed

8 ounces Roquefort cheese

1 teaspoon coarse salt

1 teaspoon coarsely cracked black pepper

½ cup fresh lemon juice

1 teaspoon Worcestershire sauce

½ teaspoon hot pepper sauce

⅔ cup freshly grated imported Parmesan cheese

1. Cut off the tough bottom inch or two from each head of romaine. Separate the leaves, rinse well, and soak in a large bowl of ice water for at least 30 minutes. Tear the leaves into large bite-size pieces and dry in a salad spinner. (The lettuce can be prepared up to 2 days ahead. Wrap loosely in a kitchen towel and store in the refrigerator in plastic bags.)

2. Meanwhile, heat the oven to 375°F. Brush the bread slices lightly on both sides with ½ cup of the olive oil. Arrange in a single layer on a couple of baking sheets and bake, turning once, until golden brown, 8 to 10 minutes per side. Let cool, then rub with the cut garlic. Cut the bread into ½- to ¾-inch cubes. (The garlic croutons can be made up to a day ahead. Store in a sealed plastic bag or airtight container at room temperature.)

3. In a large salad bowl, mash the crushed garlic with half the anchovies, half the Roquefort cheese, the salt, and black pepper. Stir in the lemon juice, Worcestershire, and hot sauce. Blend in the remaining 1 cup olive oil. Add the lettuce and toss to coat.

4. Coarsely chop the remaining anchovies. Add them to the salad along with the Parmesan cheese and garlic croutons. Toss again and crumble the remaining Roquefort cheese on top. Serve at once.

HERBED ROAST PORK LOIN

12 TO 14 SERVINGS

The last time I served this roast, I was greeted with the compliment, "I forgot how good a piece of meat can be." Juicy and tender and full of flavor, this simple roast can serve as a basis for the most elegant of meals. Best of all, it's one of the easiest ways I know to feed a crowd. If you don't have time for the succulent, slow-roasted method given below, you can start the roast in a 425°F oven for 15 minutes and then finish it at 325°F for 1½ hours longer, or until the pork registers 160°F.

2 pork loins, 6 pounds each, bones in but cracked by the butcher for easy carving, fat trimmed to a thin layer and scored in a diamond pattern

2 tablespoons coarse salt

1 tablespoon plus 1 teaspoon chopped fresh rosemary or 2 teaspoons dried

1 tablespoon plus 1 teaspoon black peppercorns

2 teaspoons fresh thyme leaves or 1 teaspoon dried

6 garlic cloves, crushed through a press

¼ cup fresh lemon juice

¼ cup extra-virgin olive oil

1. If the butcher has left any thick pieces of fat, trim them to a thin layer and score to match the rest of the roast. Wipe the roasts dry and place, bones down, in 1 or 2 roasting pans.

2. In a spice grinder or food processor, combine the salt, rosemary, peppercorns, and thyme. Process until the peppercorns are coarsely ground. In a small bowl, mix together the seasoned salt with the garlic, lemon juice, and olive oil. Smear this paste all over the pork loins. Set aside at room temperature for 3 to 4 hours or refrigerate overnight until 1 to 2 hours before roasting.

3. Heat the oven to 275°F. Roast the pork for 3 hours. Raise the oven temperature to 400°F and continue to roast 30 to 45 minutes longer, until the outside of the roast is nicely browned and the internal temperature registers 160° to 162°F. Let stand for about 10 minutes before carving.

CREAMY BUTTERMILK DO-AHEAD GRITS

12 TO 14 SERVINGS

Ask any Southerners and they'll tell you grits have to be made at the very last minute, just like risotto. Well, I've seen the top chef in America make risotto ahead, so I knew it could be done with grits. Just as with risotto, stopping the cooking before they are fully cooked is the secret. Extra liquid helps, too. Then the grits are finished off quickly just before serving. While you can use regular yellow cornmeal here, fresh stone-ground grits are worth the effort, whether you find them in a specialty store or from an online distributor of Southern ingredients.

2½ cups stone-ground grits, preferably coarsely ground

4 cups chicken stock

2 cups half-and-half

Salt and freshly ground pepper

6 tablespoons unsalted butter

2 cups cold buttermilk

1. In a large heavy pot, stir the grits into the cold chicken stock to make a thick slurry. Stir in the half-and-half, 1 teaspoon salt, and ¼ teaspoon pepper. Slowly bring to a boil, stirring. Reduce the heat to a simmer and cook, stirring often, until the grits are thickened and almost tender, 20 to 25 minutes.

2. Remove from the heat and stir in the butter, 2 tablespoons at a time, and then 1 cup of the buttermilk. Let stand at room temperature for up to 3 hours.

3. Stir in the remaining 1 cup buttermilk, return the grits to moderately low heat, and cook, stirring, until the mixture is thickened but still creamy and the grits are tender. Season with salt and pepper to taste.

OVEN-ROASTED GARLIC POTATOES

12 TO 14 SERVINGS

These crisp flavorful potatoes are great for any large dinner or buffet because they don't require peeling and all the messy preparation can be done a day ahead. Whenever I serve potatoes with the peel on, I try to use organic.

6 pounds baking potatoes, preferably organic

6 garlic cloves, peeled and cut in half

⅔ cup olive oil, preferably extra virgin, or other vegetable oil

2 teaspoons coarse salt

¾ teaspoon freshly ground pepper

1. Scrub the potatoes well and rub dry; do not peel. Cut lengthwise into long, ½-inch wedges. Dump the potatoes into a large pot of boiling salted water. Cover and return to a boil over high heat, about 2 minutes. Uncover and cook for 5 minutes. Drain and rinse under cold running water. Drain well. Spread the potatoes out on kitchen towels and let dry. (The recipe can be prepared to this point up to a day ahead. Refrigerate the potatoes in a covered container.)

2. Heat the oven to 325°F. In a small, heavy saucepan, steep the garlic in the oil over low heat until the garlic just begins to color, 10 to 15 minutes.

3. Spread out the potatoes on large baking sheets. Season with the salt and pepper. Drizzle the oil over the potatoes and toss gently to coat. (I cook the garlic cloves along with the potatoes and discard them before serving.) Bake, tossing with a spatula every 10 to 15 minutes, for 1 hour. Increase the oven temperature to 425°F and bake, tossing once or twice, until the potatoes are browned and crisp, 15 to 20 minutes longer.

Oven-Roasting Vegetables

When we think of cooking vegetables, blanching them in a large pot of boiling water or steaming them usually comes to mind first. But especially for large quantities, oven-roasting is an excellent, easy way to cook root vegetables such as potatoes, carrots, turnips, and onions. Whole garlic cloves, roasted in their skins, are delicious when prepared this way, and asparagus becomes a completely new treat.

To oven-roast a vegetable, peel off the outer skin and, if large, cut in half or quarters. Toss with enough good olive oil, preferably extra virgin, to coat lightly and season sparingly with coarse salt and freshly ground pepper. That's all there is to it. For a tender vegetable like asparagus, roast at a high temperature (450° to 500°F) for about 10 minutes, tossing once or twice. Squeeze a little lemon juice over them before serving. Roast root vegetables for a longer time at a lower temperature in the same roasting pan as the meat or fowl for extra flavor. Turn once or twice for even browning.

I frequently use a disposable aluminum roasting pan for easy cleanup. In a pinch, the vegetables can be roasted ahead, set aside at room temperature, and reheated in a hot oven for about 5 minutes just before serving.

GREEN BEANS WITH LEMON BUTTER

12 TO 14 SERVINGS

2½ pounds green beans, trimmed and broken in half

4 tablespoons unsalted butter, cut into pieces, or olive oil

1½ teaspoons grated lemon zest

¼ cup fresh lemon juice

Salt and freshly ground pepper

1. In a large pot of boiling salted water, cook the green beans over high heat until tender, 5 to 7 minutes. Drain in a colander and rinse under cold running water, tossing, for 20 seconds; drain. (The green beans can be blanched and refreshed up to 6 hours before serving. Set aside at room temperature or cover and refrigerate for longer keeping.)

2. Either return the beans to the hot pot or, if you have done them ahead, add them to a large saucepan set over high heat. Toss over the heat until excess moisture is evaporated, about 1 minute. Add the butter and toss over the heat until the butter is melted and the beans are hot and coated with butter, about 2 minutes. Add the lemon zest and lemon juice and toss. Remove from the heat and season with salt and pepper to taste; toss again and serve.

HAZELNUT ROULADE WITH BANANA CREAM AND RICH CHOCOLATE SAUCE

12 TO 14 SERVINGS

The recipe for the flourless cake used in this dessert was given to me many, many years ago by Lenore Gordon, the mother of my good friend Linda. She bakes it in a 10-inch springform pan for about 45 minutes to produce a stunning nut torte. I kept it a secret all this time, as she requested, but she's agreed to let me share it now. The only trick to this easy cake, which is really a fallen soufflé, is to grind the hazelnuts with a nut grinder to produce a light, fluffy nut flour—and there's no substitute for that tool. The roulade can be assembled up to a day ahead. It will yield 16 slices, so be forewarned—there really will be no seconds here, unless you want to have a second dessert standing by.

½ pound hazelnuts

9 eggs, separated

1 cup granulated sugar

½ teaspoon orange extract

½ teaspoon almond extract

1½ cups heavy cream

3 tablespoons confectioners' sugar

¾ teaspoon vanilla extract

4 to 5 medium bananas

Rich Chocolate Sauce (page 31)

1. Heat the oven to 375°F with a rack set in the upper third of the oven. Butter a 13 × 18-inch half-sheet or jellyroll pan. Line the pan with waxed paper, allowing the long ends to extend over the side a little, and butter the paper. Flour the entire pan; tap out any excess. Grind the hazelnuts in a nut grinder; no need to skin them first.

2. In a large bowl, beat the egg yolks lightly. Gradually beat in the granulated sugar and continue beating until the mixture is light in color and falls from the beater in a slowly dissolving ribbon, about 5 minutes. Beat in the orange and almond extracts.

3. In another large bowl, beat the egg whites until stiff but not dry. Sprinkle about one-third of the nuts over the egg yolk mixture. Scoop about one-third of the egg whites on top. Fold until partially blended. Repeat with half the remaining nuts and egg whites. Then add the remaining nuts and egg whites and fold just until the mixture is blended and no streaks are visible.

4. Turn the batter into the pan and bake in the upper third of the oven for 12 to 14 minutes, or until the cake is puffed and browned and slightly springy to the touch. Let cool in the pan on a large rack for 5 minutes.

5. Set a slightly dampened clean kitchen towel on top of the rack. Invert the pan to unmold the cake onto the towel. Carefully peel off the waxed paper. Cover with another dampened towel. Starting at one of the long sides, loosely roll up the cake in the towels. Let cool for 1 hour.

6. Meanwhile, beat the cream until it mounds softly. Gradually, add the confectioners' sugar and vanilla and beat until stiff.

7. After an hour, unroll the cake (if you wait longer, it will stiffen and may crack when you roll it). Remove the top towel and spread the whipped cream over the cake. Cut the bananas crosswise on the diagonal into ¾-inch-thick slices and arrange them on top of the cream. Roll up again, using the edge of the towel to help, and set the cake, seam side down, on a large serving platter. Cover with plastic wrap and refrigerate for up to 24 hours before serving. (If you don't have a large enough platter, refrigerate the cake on the half-sheet pan and cut the slices in the kitchen.)

8. To serve, reheat the chocolate sauce, if necessary. Drizzle a little of the warm sauce decoratively over the top of the roulade. Cut the roulade into 1-inch slices and spoon some sauce on top of each serving.

A Simple Buffet for All Seasons

FOR 12 TO 16

ASSORTED CHEESES AND CRACKERS

SOUR CREAM AND TWO-CAVIAR DIP (PAGE 191)
WITH BELGIAN ENDIVE AND POTATO CHIPS FOR DIPPING

THIN SLICES OF PEPPERONI OR SOPPRESSATA

OLIVES AND NUTS

TURKEY TONNATO

ROASTED BEET AND RICE SALAD WITH HAM, CHEESE, AND PEAS

YELLOW SQUASH WITH GREEN BEANS AND SWEET ONIONS

OR

LENTIL SALAD WITH GOAT CHEESE AND TOMATOES

FIELD MIX AND BABY SPINACH SALAD

CARAMEL PEACH COBBLER

OR

APRICOT-APPLE CRISP WITH VANILLA ICE CREAM OR CRÈME FRAÎCHE

ASSORTED COOKIES AND BROWNIES

No matter which season you find yourself in, serving food that is chilled or at room temperature is absolutely the easiest way to go. Not only is everything made in advance, nothing needs reheating. All you have to do is remember to take the food out of the refrigerator in time for it to return to room temperature, or to be sure it is not ice cold, when your company is ready to eat.

With a nod to the fruits and vegetables that are best at different times of the year, I've given you a choice of vegetables—yellow squash and green beans or lentils—and of desserts—peach cobbler or apricot-apple crisp—depending upon what's in the market. All the other dishes are true "evergreens."

For starters, most of the appetizers are purchased: cheeses, nuts, olives, salamis. If you have a favorite purchased nibble or an easy dip of your own, by all means put that out. If you want a longer cocktail hour and feel you need more food, pick any of the do-ahead hot appetizers—such as Mushroom-Leek Turnovers (page 249), Coriander Chicken Rolls (page 165), or Sweet and Tangy Shrimp Kebabs (page 96)—or dips you'll find elsewhere in this book.

The main course here—braised turkey breast sliced thin and coated with a piquant tuna fish sauce subtly flavored with capers and anchovies—is both easy and affordable. What's more, with a few appropriate garnishes, the platter will look elegant. I like to present the sauced turkey slices on one very large platter. You could create a bold rim made of bunches of fresh herbs, with lemon wedges, cut radishes, and cherry tomatoes or olives nestled in the sprigs or garnish simply, as suggested.

Adding to the color on the plate is the gorgeous, shocking-pink rice salad, studded with roasted beets, ham, cheese, capers, and pickles. Good thing it tastes as good as it looks! Summer squash and green beans flavored with browned onions is a lovely dish for the warmer months; the lentil salad with goat cheese works well in the winter. As a green salad to round out the plate, I suggest field greens, otherwise known as mesclun, and baby spinach, because both can be purchased prewashed in plastic bags. Salad is one of the most labor-intensive dishes you can prepare for a crowd, and having the greens all ready makes it easy. The best dressing to use is a simple vinaigrette, made with excellent extra-virgin olive oil and sherry vinegar, Champagne vinegar, or Banyuls vinegar, or balsamic vinegar and lemon juice, if you are so inclined.

Dessert also offers a seasonal choice of peach cobbler or apricot-apple crisp, both easy fruit desserts, which can be made completely in advance. Alternatively, you could choose from any of the frozen or refrigerated desserts in the book.

DO-AHEAD PLANNING

UP TO 3 DAYS IN ADVANCE: Roast the beets. Marinate them in the refrigerator.

UP TO 2 DAYS IN ADVANCE: Braise the turkey. Keep it refrigerated in its cooking liquid.

UP TO A DAY AHEAD: Prepare the caviar dip. Make the Tonnato Sauce. Cut up the ham and cheese; refrigerate them together in a sealed plastic bag or covered container. Boil the rice, if you like. Blanch the green beans. Make the caramel sauce for the cobbler. Peel the peaches, slice them, and toss with the caramel sauce. Mix all the dry ingredients for the cobbler topping and set them aside at room temperature; remove from the refrigerator about 1 hour before serving.

THE DAY OF THE PARTY: Slice the turkey and arrange it on a platter. Coat the turkey with the tuna sauce. Cover with plastic wrap and refrigerate. Finish the Roasted Beet and Rice Salad. Cover and refrigerate; remove from the refrigerator about 2 hours before serving. Finish the Yellow Squash with Green Beans and Sweet Onions or make the Lentil Salad with Goat Cheese and Tomatoes; set aside at room temperature. Bake the cobbler or make the Apricot-Apple Crisp.

SHORTLY BEFORE SERVING: Reheat the squash and beans, if desired; otherwise, the dish is also good at room temperature. Reheat the cobbler.

TURKEY TONNATO

12 TO 16 SERVINGS

Classic veal tonnato is reappearing everywhere on tony restaurant menus, often as a cold appetizer. Braised turkey breast, very thinly sliced, offers a fine alternative to the meat. In fact, when turkey is cloaked with the traditional sauce, made with canned tuna, mayonnaise, and capers, you'd be hard put to tell the two apart. Purchase fresh turkey if at all possible.

Tonnato is a traditional Italian sauce, but if tuna is just not to your taste, the technique for poaching turkey breast below is an excellent one, and you could just as well serve the meat sliced with the Romesco Sauce on page 39 or the Basil-Walnut Dressing on page 192.

1 young turkey breast, 6 to 7 pounds

1 tablespoon coarse salt

2 medium onions, halved

5 garlic cloves, smashed

2 medium carrots, quartered

2 celery ribs with leaves, cut in thirds

8 large parsley stems

2 imported bay leaves

1 teaspoon black peppercorns

1 whole clove

⅔ cup dry white wine

Tonnato Sauce (page 68)

Lemon slices, capers, chopped parsley, and chives, for garnish

1. Put the turkey breast in a stockpot. Add enough water to cover by 1 inch and the salt. Slowly bring to a boil, skimming to remove the foam as it rises to the top; it can take up to half an hour for the water to reach a boil. Reduce the heat to low. Add the onions, garlic, carrots, celery, parsley stems, bay leaves, peppercorns, whole clove, and white wine. Simmer very slowly until the internal temperature of the turkey registers 160°F, about 1 hour longer. The slower you cook the meat, the more tender it will be; adjust the heat as best you can so that the liquid bubbles very gently. If too much liquid evaporates, add a little more water.

2. When the turkey reaches 160°F, remove the pot from the heat and let the breast cool in the cooking liquid. As it sits, the internal temperature of the meat will increase to about 170°F. Refrigerate the turkey in its cooking liquid overnight or for at least 6 hours.

3. Remove the turkey to a cutting board. Strain the cooking liquid to remove the solids. Set aside about ⅔ cup for the tonnato sauce, which follows. Save the rest for soup or stock; it freezes perfectly and is an excellent alternative to chicken stock. Carve the turkey by first cutting both "fillets" off either side of the breast bone. Then cut the meat crosswise on an angle into thin slices; a very sharp carving knife or even an electric knife is the best tool for this.

4. Arrange the slices, overlapping just slightly, on 1 or 2 large platters; don't stack the slices, because you want to make sure each piece gets plenty of sauce. Coat the turkey slices with the tonnato sauce; if you have any extra, put it out in a sauceboat with a ladle. Garnish the platter(s) with lemon slices. Sprinkle the capers, chopped parsley, and chives over the sauce. Serve slightly chilled but not ice cold.

TONNATO SAUCE

MAKES ABOUT 3 CUPS

Although traditionally served over cold sliced veal, this thick savory cold sauce is equally compatible with turkey or even pork. It will keep well in a covered container in the refrigerator for up to 5 days, though I prefer to prepare it just a day ahead, when I poach the turkey, so it has a fresher taste.

1 cup mayonnaise

1 can (6 ounces) tuna packed in olive oil (do not use water-packed tuna for this dish), drained

1 can (2 ounces) anchovy fillets, drained

⅓ cup fresh lemon juice

¼ cup fruity extra-virgin olive oil

2½ tablespoons capers, either salted capers, well rinsed, or nonpareil brined capers

⅔ cup poaching liquid, reserved from the turkey recipe above

Salt and freshly ground pepper

1. In a food processor, combine the mayonnaise with the tuna, anchovies, lemon juice, olive oil, and capers. Puree until smooth.

2. With the machine on, drizzle the oil through the feed tube. Add ⅓ cup of the poaching liquid. If the sauce is too thick, add more liquid, 1 or 2 tablespoons at a time. Season lightly with salt, generously with pepper. Cover and refrigerate until serving time.

ROASTED BEET AND RICE SALAD WITH HAM, CHEESE, AND PEAS

12 TO 16 SERVINGS

Perhaps because she is married to one of Italy's premier wine makers, Giovanna Folinari Ruffino prides herself on her food and enjoys entertaining with elegance. This tasty, shocking-pink salad has enough ham, cheese, and vegetables to serve as a lovely first course, especially in summer when something cool is welcome, but because of its striking color, I like to present it as part of a buffet. Giovanna garnishes the top with a pink rose from her garden.

1 bunch of fresh beets

¼ cup plus 3 tablespoons red or white wine vinegar

⅓ cup plus 2 tablespoons extra-virgin olive oil

1 teaspoon sugar

3 cups long-grain white rice

Salt and freshly ground pepper

8 ounces flavorful ham, such as baked Virginia or Black Forest, sliced ⅜ inch thick

8 ounces Emmentaler Swiss cheese

1 cup peas, cooked fresh or thawed frozen

⅔ cup pitted green and/or Kalamata olives, sliced or coarsely chopped

½ cup minced fresh chives or thinly sliced scallions

½ cup sliced cornichons or kosher dill pickles

2 tablespoons capers, preferably salted, rinsed and drained

1. Heat the oven to 375°F. Cut off the tops of the beets, leaving just a couple of inches of stem. Wrap each beet

Setting the Scene

For a large party, the presentation of the food means a lot. It sets the tone of the party as much as the decor of the room, flowers, or music. In essence, the food is the theme of the party, and how you set it out reflects your expectations of what the event will be like. If you've pulled out your best china, silver, and linen and set places formally around a table, guests will behave differently from those occasions when you've piled up the food informally in colorful bowls on a picnic table with stacks of paper plates.

I like party food to be plentiful, colorful, and tasty. If the food looks wonderful to begin with, garnishes can be held to a minimum. However, a little color contrast always helps, especially with some foods that are not that great to look at. When a dish does need garnish, try to pick something appropriate. If you've used fresh tarragon or dill in a recipe, use that as your embellishment. Lemons, limes, and radishes—sliced, carved, or cut into wedges—as well as cherry tomatoes and olives, are common but indispensable adornments. Whenever possible, arrange the garnish so that it won't be destroyed as soon as the first person digs in. For large crowds, I design my decorations around the rim of the platter rather than in the center.

Professionals offer other tricks. Simple geometric arrangements on dark platters create a stylish, dramatic effect. Clear plastic blocks can be employed to establish different heights on a buffet table, adding another dimension to the visual interest. Simply lining a bowl or platter with a contrasting colored leaf—green kale or red cabbage—can dress up a salad.

Try to keep dishes refilled and fresh looking throughout the party. One way to do this is to put out only half of what you have to serve. When the food has diminished less than halfway, or whenever it looks tired, whisk the bowl or platter into the kitchen and refill; at the same time, refresh it with a new garnish.

And if your party has a theme, play it to the hilt. Carry out the idea not only in the food itself and the way it's garnished and presented but in the decorations and accessories you set around the room. And don't forget the music!

or 2 together in heavy-duty foil and place directly on the rack of the oven. Roast for 45 to 60 minutes, until the tip of a small knife pierces the beets easily. Remove and let cool, then rub off the skin and cut the beets into ½-inch dice.

2. Put the diced beets in a bowl and marinate in 3 tablespoons of the vinegar, 2 tablespoons of the olive oil, and the sugar.

3. In a large pot of boiling salted water, cook the rice until tender but still firm, 12 to 15 minutes. Drain and rinse with cold running water until cooled; drain well.

4. In a large bowl, whisk the remaining ⅓ cup olive oil and the ¼ cup vinegar with 1 teaspoon salt and ¼ teaspoon pepper. Toss to thoroughly coat the rice with the vinaigrette.

5. Dice the ham and finely dice the cheese. Add both to the rice along with the beets and their marinade. Toss to mix well. Add the peas, olives, chives, cornichons, and capers to the rice and toss again gently. Season with additional salt and pepper to taste. Let stand for at least 30 minutes, stirring several times, before serving.

YELLOW SQUASH WITH GREEN BEANS AND SWEET ONIONS

12 SERVINGS

If you're making this dish shortly before serving it, you can use red onions, which look pretty with the other vegetables. But if you do it a day ahead and reheat it, which is fine, the red onions will turn gray. If that's the case, better opt for Vidalias or other sweet onions—or even regular yellow onions. If you have fresh basil in your garden, a couple of tablespoons shredded makes a nice alternative to the marjoram, but do not use dried basil. Keep an eye on the squash so that it cooks only until softened but still holds its shape; this variety can turn mushy very quickly.

2½ pounds small yellow (summer) squash

1¼ pounds green beans, the thinner the better

2 medium red, Vidalia, or yellow onions

½ cup extra-virgin olive oil

Salt and freshly ground pepper

1 tablespoon chopped fresh marjoram or oregano or ¾ teaspoon dried

1. Trim the squash and beans. Cut the squash crosswise into thick slices; if parts of the squash are very wide, halve them lengthwise first. Break the beans in half. Slice the onions.

2. Bring a large saucepan of salted water to a boil. Add the green beans and cook until they are barely tender and bright green, 3 to 4 minutes (they will finish cooking with the squash). Drain in a colander and rinse under cold running water; drain well.

3. In a large flameproof casserole or wide heavy saucepan, heat the olive oil over moderate heat. Add the onions and cook, stirring occasionally, until they are golden, about 10 minutes.

4. Add the squash slices, season with salt and pepper, and raise the heat to moderately high. Cook, stirring gently, until you can see a slight change in the squash and the slices are coated with oil, about 5 minutes.

5. Add the marjoram and the beans. Cover and cook until both the squash and beans are just tender, 5 to 7 minutes longer. Check the seasoning and serve hot or at room temperature.

LENTIL SALAD WITH GOAT CHEESE AND TOMATOES

12 SERVINGS

Two kinds of tomatoes here—sun-dried and fresh—lighten up the lentils and add a lovely sweet note. In winter, when good tomatoes are harder to come by, you might opt for "tomatoes on the vine" or plum tomatoes, which tend to have more flavor year round. Another tip is to let them stand at room temperature for a couple of days before using them so that they ripen fully.

1 pound lentils

⅓ cup plus 3 tablespoons extra-virgin olive oil

2 medium yellow onions, finely diced

2 medium carrots, peeled and finely diced

2 celery ribs, finely diced

1 dried chipotle chile or ¼ to ½ teaspoon crushed hot red pepper

1 teaspoon coarse salt

⅓ cup sherry vinegar or red wine vinegar

8 large sun-dried tomato halves (about 3 ounces), finely diced

½ large red onion, diced

1 teaspoon coarsely cracked black pepper

4½ ounces mild white goat cheese, such as Coach Farm or French chèvre

⅓ cup plus 2 tablespoons chopped parsley

4 or 5 ripe tomatoes, cut into wedges

1. Rinse the lentils and pick over to remove any grit.

2. In a large flameproof casserole, heat 3 tablespoons of the olive oil. Add the yellow onions, carrots, and celery and sauté over moderately high heat until the onions are just beginning to turn golden brown, 7 to 10 minutes.

3. Add the lentils, chipotle chile, and 6 cups of water. Bring to a simmer and cook, partially covered, stirring occasionally, for 15 minutes. Season with the salt and cook until the lentils are just tender but not falling apart and almost all the liquid is evaporated, 5 to 10 minutes, or longer if the lentils are old. Boil for a few minutes, if necessary, to evaporate excess liquid.

4. Turn the lentils into a large bowl and drizzle on the remaining ⅓ cup olive oil and the vinegar; toss lightly. Add the sun-dried tomatoes, red onion, and black pepper. Crumble half the cheese into the salad, add ⅓ cup of the parsley, and toss again. Season with additional salt to taste. Let stand, tossing occasionally, until cooled to room temperature.

5. Turn into a serving bowl or deep platter. Crumble the remaining goat cheese over the top and dust with the 2 tablespoons parsley. Surround with the tomato wedges. Serve at room temperature or slightly chilled.

CARAMEL PEACH COBBLER

12 TO 16 SERVINGS

Buttermilk adds a rich, nutty flavor that I adore to any batter, especially one that contains butter (the buttermilk itself is low in fat). If you don't have it on hand, though, you can adjust the recipe to use regular milk or half-and-half by omitting the baking soda and increasing the baking powder to 4 teaspoons.

3½ to 4 pounds ripe but firm peaches

10 tablespoons unsalted butter

½ cup packed dark brown sugar

½ cup heavy cream

1 teaspoon fresh lemon juice

1⅓ cups granulated sugar

¾ teaspoon vanilla extract

2 cups all-purpose flour

½ cup yellow cornmeal, preferably stone ground

1 tablespoon baking powder

¾ teaspoon baking soda

¼ teaspoon salt

1 cup buttermilk

1. Heat the oven to 375°F. Bring a large saucepan of water to a boil. Gently add the peaches to the water in 2 batches and cook for about 10 seconds. Remove with a skimmer or slotted spoon to a colander and rinse under cold running water. The peels will slip right off. Cut the peaches into ½- to ¾-inch slices and discard the pits. Put the peaches in a shallow 16-inch oval casserole or other 4-quart baking dish.

2. In a deep medium saucepan, melt 4 tablespoons of the butter. Add the brown sugar, heavy cream, and lemon juice. Boil, stirring occasionally, for 5 minutes. Add 1 cup of the granulated sugar and boil for 10 minutes longer, or until the caramel is thick. Remove from the heat and let cool slightly, then stir in the vanilla. Drizzle the caramel over the peaches and toss to mix.

3. In a mixing bowl, combine the flour and cornmeal with the remaining ⅓ cup sugar, the baking powder, baking soda, and salt. Whisk to blend. Cut the remaining 6 tablespoons butter into small cubes and pinch with your fingers to blend into the dry ingredients. When the butter is the consistency of oats, add the buttermilk and stir until just blended. Dollop the batter over the peaches. Don't worry about gaps; they will fill in as the cobbler bakes.

4. Bake the cobbler in the center of the oven for 30 to 35 minutes, or until the fruit is bubbling and the topping is cooked through and nicely browned. Serve warm or at room temperature, with a scoop of vanilla ice cream.

APRICOT-APPLE CRISP

12 SERVINGS

In some circles, creamy vanilla ice cream is considered a must with a warm fruit dessert like this. I prefer a minimum of sugar in my sweets; if your apples are very tart, you may wish to toss them with an extra tablespoon. Nothing goes better with a fruit crisp than a scoop of vanilla cream.

½ pound dried apricots

2 tablespoons dark rum, such as Myers's, optional

10 tablespoons unsalted butter

½ teaspoon almond extract

8 large cooking apples, such as Granny Smith or Cortland (I like to use a mix for more complex flavor)

⅔ cup chopped toasted almonds

⅓ cup plus 3 tablespoons sugar

¾ cup plus 2 tablespoons all-purpose flour

¼ teaspoon salt

1. Cut the apricots into halves or quarters, depending on their size. Put them in a small heatproof bowl and add just enough boiling water to barely cover them. Add the rum if you're using it and let stand for at least 20 minutes, or until softened.

2. Heat the oven to 375°F. Use 1 tablespoon of the butter to grease a shallow 9 × 14-inch baking dish. Melt 3 tablespoons of the butter and set aside to cool. Stir in the almond extract.

3. Peel and core the apples and cut them into short slices, about 1 inch long and ½ inch thick. Put them in the baking dish. Drain the apricots and add them, along with the almonds, to the apples. Drizzle the melted almond butter over the fruit. Sprinkle on 3 tablespoons of the sugar and toss to mix. Spread the fruit and nuts evenly in the dish.

4. In a medium bowl, combine the flour, salt, and the remaining ⅓ cup sugar. Cut the remaining 6 tablespoons butter into small dice, add it to the flour mixture, and pinch with your fingertips until it is blended into coarse crumbs. Squeeze the nut-crumb mixture into nuggets and sprinkle evenly over the top of the fruit.

5. Bake the crisp for 40 to 45 minutes, or until the apples are tender and the crust is browned. Serve warm or at room temperature.

Tuscan Lunch

For 12 to 16

PROSCIUTTO WITH FRESH FIGS OR MELON AND ARUGULA

RIBOLITTA

TIRAMISÙ

ESPRESSO

Everyone in the know told me I had to have *ribolitta* in Florence. What the dish was exactly no one could tell me. I had no idea until the first piping hot bowl was plunked before me in a crowded trattoria, and even then it wasn't clear. I had just finished polishing off a gargantuan helping of silky pink prosciutto the owner's aged father was slicing by hand in the corner—with expert precision, I might add—and knew that half a side of beef or a whole roasted rabbit was yet to come.

It was clear from the commotion on either side of the customary communal table that ribolitta was the favored choice of food-loving Florentines for their *prima piatta,* or first course. On a cold rainy day in that magical medieval stone city, it was chosen even over polenta or pasta, and my curiosity was heightened even further. But I was unprepared for the dark, fragrant mélange of I knew not what that appeared before me: purplish brown, of an indescribable texture similar to porridge, clearly from some sort of vegetable origin, with a flavor and aroma that was immediately addictive. I became determined on the spot to reproduce ribolitta in my own home, and I did so only a few weeks later, as soon as I returned, having sampled the concoction at several other restaurants, including Cibreo, which had the best and courteously gave me a list of the main ingredients. As with most great soups, there must be as many recipes for this dish as there are cooks. This is mine.

With a nod to that favorite Tuscan lunch that I enjoyed, I suggest beginning with a colorful plate of rosy prosciutto, sliced paper thin, draped over a fresh fig, quartered lengthwise. A small bouquet of baby arugula, a grinding of fresh pepper, and a lime wedge complete the delightful starter. Just pass a cruet of your best extra-virgin olive oil and a basket of sesame-crusted semolina bread on the side. For dessert, another crowd-pleaser—tiramisù, made an easy way and waiting leisurely in your fridge until it's time to serve.

DO-AHEAD PLANNING

UP TO 3 DAYS BEFORE YOU BEGIN THE SOUP: Make the Simple Meat Stock on page 77. If you have a lot of room in your freezer, it can be made up to 2 months in advance.

UP TO A DAY BEFORE YOU COOK THE SOUP: Cut the Italian bread into chunks and allow it to become stale.

UP TO 2 DAYS BEFORE YOU PLAN TO SERVE THE SOUP: Chop the vegetables and prepare the Ribolitta through Step 3. This will take about 30 minutes of preparation time and 2½ hours cooking, all but about 10 minutes of it unattended.

UP TO A DAY IN ADVANCE: Make the Tiramisù.

ABOUT 3 HOURS BEFORE SERVING: Remove the Ribolitta from the refrigerator.

UP TO 2 HOURS BEFORE SERVING: Assemble the plates of prosciutto, fig or melon, and arugula. Garnish each plate with a wedge of lime. Cover loosely with plastic wrap.

ABOUT HALF AN HOUR BEFORE SERVING: Reheat the soup very slowly so the bottom doesn't burn. Thicken it with the stale bread as directed in Step 4.

RIBOLITTA

MAKES ABOUT 6 QUARTS; 12 TO 16 SERVINGS AS A MAIN COURSE

By the way, you should know that the same thickened soup is also called *minestrone di pane,* minestrone thickened with bread, which demystifies its unique character. Its pet name, *ribolitta,* which means "reboiled," is clearly explanatory. And *minestrone* means "big soup." It is silly to make a small amount of minestrone and impossible to make a small pot of ribolitta.

A simple meat stock recipe follows the ribolitta; it contains just three ingredients. This stock base is important here, and I urge you to make your own. The small extra effort is well worth the quantum improvement in flavor over canned broth in this soup.

3 medium red onions, chopped

6 tablespoons extra-virgin olive oil

2 cups chopped carrots

2 cups chopped celery

6 garlic cloves, finely chopped

2 cups dry red wine, preferably a Montepulciano

1 can (28 ounces) Italian peeled tomatoes in juice

3 quarts Simple Meat Stock (opposite page)

1 pound red cabbage, cut into ½-inch pieces

1 pound green cabbage, cut into ½-inch pieces

1½ pounds russet (baking) potatoes, peeled and cut into ½-inch dice

2 imported bay leaves

1 teaspoon dried oregano

½ teaspoon crushed hot red pepper

1¼ pounds zucchini, cut into ½-inch dice

1 pound cauliflower, coarsely chopped

1 large bunch of Swiss chard, preferably the red variety, well rinsed, leaves and stems cut into 1-inch pieces

1 large bunch of lacinato, or dinosaur kale, well rinsed, leaves coarsely shredded, stems cut into 1-inch pieces

2 cups cooked or drained canned cannellini or other white beans

Coarse salt and freshly ground black pepper

8 ounces Italian bread, day old or left to dry out for at least several hours

Freshly grated imported Parmesan cheese and/or your best olive oil, as accompaniment

1. In a very large soup pot, cook the red onions in the olive oil, covered, over moderate heat for 3 minutes. Add the carrots, celery, and garlic and continue to cook covered, stirring occasionally, until all the vegetables are softened and the onions are lightly colored, 7 to 10 minutes longer.

2. Add the wine and the tomatoes with their juices. With a large spoon, break up the tomatoes by pressing them against the side of the pot. Add the meat stock and bring to a boil. Add the red and green cabbage, potatoes, bay leaves, oregano, and hot pepper. Reduce the heat to moderately low and simmer, partially covered, for 30 minutes.

3. Add the zucchini, cauliflower, Swiss chard, kale, and beans. Season with salt and pepper. Simmer, partially covered, 1½ to 1¾ hours, adding 1 or 2 cups of water if needed. The soup should be thick but have plenty of liquid to cook in. At this point, the vegetables should be broken down into a very coarse puree, with some larger pieces probably still intact. (The recipe can be made ahead to this point up to 3 days in advance; it is best made a day in advance, cooled completely, and then refrigerated, or it can be frozen for up to 2 months.)

4. Before serving, reheat the soup and tear or crumble the bread into the pot. Season with additional salt and pepper to taste. Simmer, uncovered, for about 30 minutes, or until the bread has blended into the soup and the vegetables are so broken down they are almost unrecognizable; the mixture will be as thick as porridge. In Italy, they say a spoon should be able to stand up in the bowl, but we don't want to build Roman roads here.

5. Ladle the ribolitta into big soup plates and pass the Parmesan cheese and/or olive oil.

SIMPLE MEAT STOCK

MAKES ABOUT 3½ QUARTS

I make this stock as simple as possible, so it can be seasoned to suit almost any soup. When it's done, the meat can be used for pot pies or another dish.

3 to 3½ pounds beef shank center-cut

3 medium onions, quartered

2 imported bay leaves

1. Heat the oven to 425°F. Place the beef shank and onions in a shallow roasting pan and roast, turning once, 45 to 55 minutes, or until the meat and onions are nicely browned. Transfer to a large stockpot.

2. Pour off any fat from the roasting pan. Pour 2 cups of water into the pan, set over moderately high heat, and bring to a boil, scraping up all the brown bits from the bottom of the pan. Pour into the stockpot.

3. Add 4½ more quarts of water to the stockpot and bring to a boil, skimming off any foam that rises to the top. Add the bay leaves, reduce the heat to moderately low, and simmer, partially covered, 3½ to 4 hours.

4. Strain the stock. If it is not reduced enough, boil it down until it is reduced to 3½ to 4 quarts. Let cool, then cover and refrigerate overnight. The next day, scrape the fat off the top.

TIRAMISÙ

12 TO 16 SERVINGS

While it sometimes seems as if this creamy Italian dessert is everywhere, there is a reason for that: It is immensely popular. It's also a dessert that improves upon resting in the refrigerator and is best made at least 6 hours or even a day ahead. The ladyfingers would be difficult to bake from scratch, but they're purchased, so making the dish is relatively effortless. And since the portions are scooped out to serve, everyone can have the size he or she wishes.

By the way, I make no claims for authenticity here, which is not so terrible, because tiramisù is a relatively modern recipe, and there are many variations. Mascarpone, a thick Italian version of crème fraîche, is a key ingredient in the original, but because of the expense and difficulty of finding it everywhere, I've opted for ordinary heavy cream mixed with a little sour cream to enrich a quick-stirred pudding. This is a little heavier than the more usual zabaglione mixture but much easier. If you're in a real pinch for time and you don't tell anyone, you can even substitute instant vanilla pudding.

Vanilla Pudding (opposite page)

¼ cup Kahlúa

1 cup heavy cream

½ cup sour cream

3 tablespoons confectioners' sugar

2 packages (7 ounces each) ladyfingers or *savoiardi*

2 cups espresso or very strongly brewed coffee

1½ tablespoons unsweetened cocoa powder

Curls of bittersweet or semisweet chocolate, for garnish

1. Make the vanilla pudding. Beat in the Kahlúa. Chill, whisking once or twice as it cools, until the pudding begins to set, 30 to 45 minutes.

2. Whisk together the heavy cream, sour cream, and confectioners' sugar. Beat until the cream just peaks. Fold this cream into the cool vanilla pudding.

3. Pour half the espresso into a wide shallow bowl. One by one, slowly turn half the ladyfingers in the espresso to soften and use them to line the bottom of a large shallow casserole or baking dish—a 16-inch oval works well. Drizzle the espresso remaining in the bowl over the ladyfingers. Spoon about 3 cups of the Kahlúa cream over the ladyfingers to cover them.

4. Turn the remaining ladyfingers in the remaining espresso and use them to cover the cream in the dish, breaking them in half where necessary to fit. Drizzle any espresso remaining in the bowl over the second layer of ladyfingers. Top with the remaining Kahlúa cream. Cover and refrigerate for at least 6 hours or overnight. Just before serving, sprinkle the cocoa through a sieve to dust the top of the dessert. Garnish with chocolate curls just before serving.

VANILLA PUDDING

MAKES ABOUT 4 CUPS

Although in a pinch you could substitute a packaged pudding, this recipe is so simple, there really is no need. Because of the cornstarch, curdling of the eggs is not a problem, and the taste of "made-from-scratch" is always better.

¾ cup sugar

⅓ cup cornstarch

4 cups milk

2 whole eggs

4 egg yolks

4 tablespoons unsalted butter

1 tablespoon vanilla extract

1. In a large heavy saucepan, combine the sugar and cornstarch. Gradually whisk in the milk so there are no lumps. Slowly bring to a boil over moderate heat, stirring and scraping the bottom often with a wooden spoon to avoid scorching. Reduce the heat to low.

2. Lightly beat the whole eggs and egg yolks in a medium bowl. Slowly whisk in about 1 cup of the thickened milk to warm the eggs. Gradually whisk the egg mixture back into the hot milk in the pan. Boil, stirring, for about 30 seconds. (Don't worry, the cornstarch will prevent the eggs from curdling.)

3. Remove from the heat and beat in the butter, 1 tablespoon at a time. Let cool slightly, then whisk in the vanilla. To speed cooling, stir over a bowl of ice and water. Cover and refrigerate until set.

Indian Buffet

FOR 12 TO 16

SLOW-COOKED AROMATIC LEG OF LAMB

CREAMY CHICKEN CURRY WITH CASHEWS AND COCONUT MILK

MIXED VEGETABLE CURRY WITH TURMERIC AND MUSTARD SEEDS

MINTED CHERRY CHUTNEY

CUCUMBER-TOMATO RAITA WITH CILANTRO AND TOASTED CUMIN

JASMINE RICE

CUT-UP TROPICAL FRUIT

INDIAN RICE PUDDING WITH CARDAMOM AND PISTACHIO NUTS

Because so much of Indian food can be prepared ahead of time and because many dishes are best served warm or at room temperature—as opposed to piping hot—this savory cuisine is ideal for entertaining large numbers of people. While all the food is richly spiced, when you cook it at home, you can tailor the level of heat to your own preference—or to that of children, who usually prefer much milder food. The seasoning suggested in the recipes is geared to a relatively sophisticated palate, one that enjoys a little heat. Note, however, that not all the dishes are spicy.

Most of these recipes are from the north of India, where people do eat meat. Vegetables, legumes, cool yogurt-based saucy salads called raitas, and breads are such an important part of the national cuisine, though, that vegetarians can fare extremely well at this banquet. And with few exceptions, such as the lamb curry and the rice pudding for dessert, all these dishes are quite low in fat.

If you have not practiced Indian cooking before, you can relax, because there is very little technique to learn. You may have to enlarge your spice rack with a single trip to the market. Ground coriander, cumin, turmeric, and cardamom lead the list, with black mustard seeds and saffron completing it. Since these spices last well for 6 months on the shelf and since many are used in Mexican cooking and other recipes, it's a worthwhile investment. Fresh ginger, unsweetened grated coconut, and cilantro are the only other ethnic items you'll need to purchase, and most supermarkets now stock these. For convenience, I've cheated in these recipes and used a mix of butter and vegetable oil, rather than the traditional Indian *ghee,* which is a type of clarified butter. You may use all oil for health purposes, with only a slight loss of richness and flavor, or substitute all clarified butter for best results.

While the menu list may appear a bit daunting, if you follow the timetable, you'll be surprised how far ahead most of these recipes can be prepared. Also, you can cut down on time and effort by picking and tailoring what you want to serve. For example, you can easily prepare just the chicken or lamb rather than both; simply double the recipe. This menu can be enhanced and elaborated upon by buying any assortment of prepared Indian pickles and chutneys. In my opinion, the only real hard part is in cooking rice for so many people. If you have an electric rice cooker, this is the time to pull it out.

DO-AHEAD PLANNING

UP TO 2 WEEKS IN ADVANCE: Make the Minted Cherry Chutney. Refrigerate in a covered container.

UP TO 2 DAYS IN ADVANCE: Prepare the Slow-Cooked Aromatic Leg of Lamb through Step 2.

UP TO A DAY AHEAD: Prepare the Creamy Chicken Curry, cooking it the minimum amount of time. Finish the lamb, if you like. Blanch the green beans and cut up the cauliflower and carrots for the vegetable dish. Make the rice pudding; refrigerate in a covered container.

UP TO 4 HOURS IN ADVANCE: Make the raita. Prepare the Mixed Vegetable Curry but do not add the lemon juice.

SHORTLY BEFORE SERVING: Make the rice. Gently reheat the lamb, chicken, and vegetables. Add the lemon juice to the vegetable curry.

SLOW-COOKED AROMATIC LEG OF LAMB

12 TO 16 SERVINGS

Rich and mellow, this unusual north Indian lamb, called *raan*, is cooked at a very low temperature until it is way past rosy. Every bit of fat is leached out; the meat ends up butter soft and saturated with flavor. Be sure to allow enough time for the leg to marinate for 2 days before cooking. After it is done, you can slice the lamb, cover it with sauce, and reheat it later in the day or even the next day. I like to garnish the platter with a large sprig of mint or cilantro.

1 semi-boneless whole leg of lamb, 6 to 7 pounds

3 tablespoons garam masala

2 tablespoons demerara sugar or light brown sugar

1 tablespoon coarse salt

½ teaspoon cayenne pepper

2 inches of fresh ginger, peeled and shredded on the large holes of a box grater (about ⅓ cup)

6 garlic cloves, crushed through a press

¼ cup fresh lime juice

1½ cups plain yogurt

½ teaspoon saffron threads

1. Trim as much fat as you can from the lamb. Make a number of slits all over the leg, cutting about 2 inches long and 1 inch deep. (Since the meat is slow-cooked until well done, you don't need to worry about losing juices when you pierce it.) Put the leg in a heavy non-reactive lidded casserole that holds it snugly; I prefer enameled cast iron.

2. In a small bowl, mix together the garam masala, sugar, salt, cayenne, ginger, garlic, lime juice, and 1 cup of the yogurt. Smear the spiced yogurt all over the leg of lamb, pressing it down into the slits. Cover the casserole and refrigerate the lamb for at least 24 and preferably 48 hours.

3. Heat the oven to 275°F. Soften the saffron in ¼ cup cold water. Bring 1 cup of water to a boil. Stir in the softened saffron with its water and pour it all over the lamb. Set in the oven, covered, and braise for 3½ hours.

4. Remove the lamb to a carving board. Skim as much fat as possible off the liquid in the casserole; there will be quite a bit. Boil the remaining liquid for 3 to 5 minutes, until concentrated and delicious. Whisk in the remaining ½ cup yogurt.

5. Carve the lamb into thin slices. Arrange on a large platter with a lip. Pour the juices from the casserole over the lamb. Serve at once or cover and refrigerate. Reheat gently before serving.

CREAMY CHICKEN CURRY WITH CASHEWS AND COCONUT MILK

12 TO 16 SERVINGS

For a crowd, this easy recipe cannot be beat for simplicity and flavor. Chunks of boneless chicken are marinated in yogurt and spices for 1 to 3 hours, then cooked slowly in the marinade with browned onions, coconut milk, and diced tomatoes until succulent and tender.

5 to 6 pounds skinless, boneless chicken breasts

MARINADE

⅔ cup roasted cashew nuts

¼ cup chopped fresh ginger

1½ tablespoons chopped garlic

¼ cup fresh lemon juice

3 tablespoons ground coriander

1½ tablespoons ground cumin

1 teaspoon ground cardamom

2 tablespoons sugar

1 tablespoon coarse salt

½ teaspoon cayenne pepper

2 cups plain yogurt, low-fat if you like

FINISHING SAUCE

⅓ cup clarified butter or 2 tablespoons vegetable oil and 4 tablespoons unsalted butter

2 medium onions, thinly sliced

1 can (14 ounces) unsweetened coconut milk

1 can (14½ ounces) diced peeled tomatoes, drained

Coarsely chopped cashews and cilantro or mint, for garnish

1. Trim any fat and bits of cartilage from the chicken breasts. Cut the chicken into 1- to 1½-inch chunks.

2. In a food processor, combine the cashews, ginger, garlic, lemon juice, coriander, cumin, cardamom, sugar, salt, cayenne, and 1 cup of the yogurt. Process until as smooth as possible. Transfer to a large bowl and stir in the remaining 1 cup yogurt. Add the chicken and stir to coat. Cover and refrigerate for 1 to 3 hours. (Do not overmarinate or the chicken will soften too much.)

3. Heat the oven to 325°F. In a large skillet, set the clarified butter over moderately high heat. Add the onions and cook, stirring from time to time and reducing the heat slightly if necessary to prevent burning, until the onions are golden brown, 10 to 15 minutes. Add the coconut milk and heat, stirring, until melted and warm. Stir in the diced tomatoes.

4. Scrape the onions and sauce into a large casserole or baking dish at least 3 inches deep or divide everything between 2 dishes. Add the chicken and its marinade and stir to mix. Cover tightly with foil and bake for 1¼ to 1½ hours, or until the chicken is just barely opaque in the center. (It will continue to cook as it stands and will, of course, cook even more if you reheat it.)

5. If made ahead, cover and refrigerate. Reheat very gently. Serve garnished with a heavy sprinkling of chopped cashews and cilantro or mint.

MIXED VEGETABLE CURRY WITH TURMERIC AND MUSTARD SEEDS

12 TO 16 SERVINGS

Deceptively simple, this dry curry is pretty, with green beans, orange carrots, and cauliflower colored bright yellow from the turmeric. Black mustard seeds, which have a pleasant, nutty taste when toasted, are worth looking for in an Asian market if you can't find them in your supermarket. A hit of hot pepper and the refreshing zing of lemon juice make this the perfect accompaniment to almost any other Indian dish.

1½ pounds green beans

1 large head of cauliflower (2½ pounds)

1 pound carrots

¼ cup peanut oil

2 medium onions, chopped

2 tablespoons black mustard seeds

2 teaspoons turmeric

½ teaspoon cayenne pepper

1 teaspoon salt

⅓ cup fresh lemon juice

1. Trim the ends of the green beans and cut them into 1½-inch pieces. Cook in a large pot of boiling salted water until tender, 4 to 5 minutes. Drain and rinse under cold running water until cool; drain well.

2. Trim the cauliflower and separate the head into small florets. Peel the carrots and cut them on a slight angle into fairly thin slices. (The recipe can be prepared to this point up to a day in advance.)

3. In a wok or large flameproof casserole, heat the oil over moderately high heat. Add the onions and cook, stirring often, until golden, 4 to 6 minutes. Add the mustard seeds, turmeric, and cayenne. Cook, stirring, for 2 minutes, or until the mustard seeds begin to pop.

4. Add the cauliflower and carrots, season with the salt, and stir to mix with the turmeric oil. Pour in 1 cup water, cover, and cook, stirring to move the vegetables from the bottom to the top several times, until they are almost tender, 5 to 7 minutes.

5. Uncover, raise the heat to high, and cook, stirring often, until the vegetables are tender and most of the liquid is evaporated. Sprinkle on the lemon juice, stir, and serve.

MINTED CHERRY CHUTNEY

MAKES ABOUT 3½ CUPS

If you're pressed for time, there's nothing wrong with buying a jar or two of mango chutney, but it is a pricey alternative. This unbelievably easy homemade version is not even cooked. While dried cherries make a more unusual offering, plain ordinary raisins make a fine substitute.

2 cups dried cherries

1½ inches of fresh ginger

4 garlic cloves

1 cup fresh mint leaves

¼ cup rice vinegar

½ teaspoon salt

½ teaspoon coarsely ground pepper

1. Put the cherries in a glass measuring cup or other heatproof glass container. Add 1 cup very hot water and let soak for 20 minutes, or until softened.

2. Coarsely chop the ginger and garlic. Place in a food processor with half the mint, the vinegar, salt, and pepper. Drain the cherries, reserving the water. Add the water to the food processor. Puree until the ginger, garlic, and mint are finely chopped.

3. Add about one-fourth of the cherries and chop finely. Add the remaining cherries and mint and pulse until coarsely chopped. If you have time, transfer to a covered container and refrigerate for a day or two to mellow.

CUCUMBER-TOMATO RAITA WITH CILANTRO AND TOASTED CUMIN

MAKES ABOUT 7 CUPS

Cool and refreshing, Indian-style yogurt salad goes well with almost any spicy grilled meat or stew. The small amount of sugar balances the acidity of the yogurt and lemon juice and provides balance to the hot pepper.

2 cups diced seeded cucumber

1½ cups diced seeded tomatoes

1 cup coarsely chopped cilantro

½ cup finely diced white onion

2 tablespoons fresh lemon juice

2 teaspoons sugar

½ teaspoon salt

¼ teaspoon cayenne pepper

3 cups plain yogurt

2 tablespoons unsalted butter

1 tablespoon cumin seeds

1. In a large bowl, mix together the cucumber, tomatoes, cilantro, onion, lemon juice, sugar, salt, cayenne, and yogurt. Set the raita aside.

2. Melt the butter in a small skillet over moderate heat. Add the cumin seeds and cook, shaking the pan once or twice, until toasted and fragrant, 2 to 3 minutes.

3. Drizzle the cumin butter with seeds over the raita. Stir to blend. Serve at once or cover and refrigerate for up to 4 hours.

INDIAN RICE PUDDING WITH CARDAMOM AND PISTACHIO NUTS

12 TO 16 SERVINGS

Cardamom adds an irresistible taste to what is already the ultimate comfort dessert.

1 tablespoon ground cardamom

1 teaspoon ground cinnamon

6 tablespoons unsalted butter

3 cups basmati or jasmine rice

3 cups milk

3 cups half-and-half

1¼ cups sugar

1 cup chopped pistachio nuts

1. In a wide heavy saucepan or flameproof casserole, cook the cardamom and cinnamon in the butter over moderately low heat for 30 seconds. Add the rice and stir to coat with the butter. Stir in 4 cups water, cover, and cook for 7 minutes, or until most of the water has been absorbed and the rice is about half-cooked.

2. Pour in the milk and half-and-half. Stir in the sugar. Bring to a simmer, reduce the heat to low, and continue to cook, partially covered, until the rice is soft and the liquid forms a thick sauce, about 25 minutes.

3. Remove from the heat and stir in ¾ cup of the pistachio nuts. Let cool, then cover and refrigerate until serving time. Garnish with the remaining chopped pistachios.

Italian Abbondanza

FOR 12 TO 16

ANTIPASTO SALAD

HERBED GARLIC BREAD

ITALIAN MEAT SAUCE WITH PASTA

BRAISED BEEF AND PORK FROM THE MEAT SAUCE,
ALONG WITH SAVORY MEATBALLS OR SAUSAGES

STEAMED BROCCOLI OR ESCAROLE, OR
BROCCOLI RABE SAUTÉED IN OLIVE OIL WITH GARLIC

TIRAMISÙ (PAGE 78)

ESPRESSO WITH SAMBUCA OR ANISETTE

There's a reason Italian cookbooks have remained the leading ethnic category for at least a decade. Everyone loves the food! This menu is a tad retro but authentic nonetheless. Part of the fun of this meal is the number of courses—four in all, which allows a full evening around the table.

We begin with a generous antipasto salad platter, more assembled than prepared. This is where you get to buy lots of goodies and save your energy for another course. Crisp romaine lettuce is laden with prosciutto, provolone cheese, soppressata, fresh mozzarella, pickled Italian peppers (pepperoncini), olives, tomatoes, onions, and just about any other taste treat you'd like to add.

Buttery herbed garlic bread accompanies both the antipasto salad and the pasta that follows. The sauce is Italian "gravy," an amazingly intense tomato sauce flavored with the beef and pork that are cooked in it in large pieces and removed. The sauce is easy to make, but it is time consuming. The plus is that you can make it a week or two ahead and freeze it, or days ahead and refrigerate it. Plenty of excellent freshly grated imported Parmesan cheese is, of course, mandatory with the pasta.

The third course is a heaping platter of the meats cooked in the tomato sauce—namely beef chuck or top round and pork loin or boneless country ribs—sliced and served with a drizzle of the same sauce that went on the pasta. A steamed or sautéed green vegetable is a must to accompany the meat, and I suggest a simple but interesting broccoli partly because it is such an easy vegetable to find fresh. Alternatively, you could serve braised escarole or chard or broccoli rabe. Use your favorite recipe.

Dessert is an easy tiramisù, which should be made a day ahead. If that last course feels like too much to do, you can offer purchased *cannoli* or other Italian pastries, or you could serve fruit and cheese, as they do in Italy. Either way, no one will go away hungry from this meal, and you'll get as many compliments from the children as you will from the adults.

DO-AHEAD PLANNING

UP TO 2 WEEKS IN ADVANCE: Make the Italian Meat Sauce. Freeze the meats whole right in the sauce in a large covered container. Or make the dish up to 3 days in advance and store it in the refrigerator.

UP TO 2 DAYS IN ADVANCE: Separate the romaine leaves. Rinse them well and spin dry. Wrap the lettuce in a clean kitchen towel, roll it up loosely, and store in a plastic bag.

THE DAY BEFORE: Make the meatball mixture, if you are making meatballs. Prepare whatever green vegetable you are cooking so it is all ready to go into the pot. Make the Tiramisù.

THE MORNING OF THE DINNER: Grate all the Parmesan cheese you'll need for the meal. Prepare the Herbed Garlic Bread through Step 2. If you are making meatballs, brown them and braise them in the tomato sauce; remove and refrigerate separately. If you are serving sausages, cook them until browned outside and no longer pink inside; drain off the fat and refrigerate the sausages.

ABOUT 2 HOURS BEFORE DINNER: Assemble the Antipasto Salad but do not dress. Cover the platter with a loose sheet of plastic wrap; set aside at room temperature. Prepare the vegetable you will be serving with the meats; undercook slightly and set aside at room temperature. Slice the cold meats. Arrange them on a heatproof platter; if serving sausages, add them to the platter. Drizzle 1 to 1½ cups of the tomato sauce over the meats. Cover with foil and set aside. Slowly reheat the tomato sauce. Set aside, covered, off the heat.

JUST BEFORE SERVING: Dress the Antipasto Salad. Bake the Herbed Garlic Bread. Reheat the sauce again while warming the meatballs or sausages in the sauce. Cook the pasta. Reheat the vegetable.

ANTIPASTO SALAD

12 TO 16 SERVINGS

Who says you have to make everything yourself? With the exceptions of the lettuce and tomatoes, all the ingredients for this immensely appealing salad can be purchased in one place: the deli counter of your local supermarket. If for some reason they don't carry pickled artichokes or roasted red peppers, go an aisle or two over and buy them in jars. Either pass cruets of olive oil and red wine vinegar at the table or whisk them together in a 3 to 1 ratio with a tiny pinch of salt, a large pinch of sugar, a generous grinding of pepper, and about ½ teaspoon dried oregano to make an Italian vinaigrette.

Balsamic vinegar is immensely popular these days, and if it's your preference, by all means use it, but I find the sweetness cloying in a salad like this. The greater acidity of the wine vinegar cuts through the fat of the meats and cheeses.

2 large heads of romaine lettuce (about 2½ pounds)

1 pound sharp provolone, in one chunk

1 pound fresh mozzarella cheese

1 pound roasted red bell peppers

2 medium fennel bulbs or 4 celery ribs

1 medium white onion

8 large or 16 small pickled artichoke hearts, optional

¾ pound prosciutto, sliced paper thin

¾ pound thinly sliced soppressata, Genoa salami, or your favorite

15 to 16 ounces pepperoncini, jarred or from the deli

½ pound good olives, your choice of green and/or black

1½ cups grape tomatoes or 3 medium tomatoes, cut into wedges

1. Separate the lettuce leaves, rinse well, and spin dry. If not using at once, loosely wrap in a clean kitchen towel in a plastic bag or container and refrigerate.

2. Cut the provolone and mozzarella into 16 or more rectangles or strips each. Cut the roasted peppers into thick wedges or slices. Trim the tops off the fennel bulbs and cut the fennel down the middle; then cut each half into slices. Thinly slice the onion.

3. Up to 2 hours in advance, line 1 or 2 large platters with the whole romaine leaves or cut the lettuce into thick strips and use those to make a bed. Arrange all the "goodies" on top. Dress just before serving or pass cruets of good olive oil and vinegar at the table.

HERBED GARLIC BREAD

MAKES 2 LOAVES; 12 TO 16 SERVINGS

Sure, you can buy garlic bread at the store, but it won't taste the same as homemade, prepared with sweet butter and fresh garlic, not the harsh dehydrated powder.

2 long loaves of Italian bread

2 sticks (½ pound) unsalted butter, at room temperature

3 garlic cloves, crushed through a press

1 teaspoon dried oregano

½ teaspoon dried thyme

Coarse salt and freshly ground pepper

1. Cut each loaf of bread in half horizontally, leaving one side just slightly attached so you can open it up like a book.

2. Blend the butter with the garlic, oregano, and thyme. Season with salt and pepper to taste. Spread the garlic-herb butter evenly over the bread to cover all 4 halves.

3. Heat the broiler. Set the bread on a baking sheet or a sheet of foil and broil 4 to 6 inches from the heat until the bread is golden brown. Separate the halves and cut each into 1-inch-thick slices. Serve hot.

ITALIAN MEAT SAUCE WITH PASTA

MAKES 3½ TO 4 QUARTS SAUCE, PLUS ENOUGH MEAT FOR 12 TO 16 SERVINGS

Ask Italians about this dish and they'll call it "gravy." Unlike the ground meat sauce most of us are familiar with, whole pieces of meat are used as the base in this authentic, intense tomato sauce. I like beef chuck or top round and, of course, the traditional pork roast, which yields the distinctive rich taste. If I have time, I make my own meatballs for a third offering; if not, I buy a good sausage.

This is an easy recipe, but the sauce must simmer slowly for several hours. On the other hand, it is better if made a day or two in advance, and it freezes beautifully, with the meats right in the sauce.

The dish is served in two courses: first the sauce by itself over pasta; then the meats are sliced and offered as a separate course, with a little extra sauce spooned on top. A green vegetable usually accompanies the meat. Serve the sauce over penne, shells, or *strozzapreti.*

⅓ cup plus 2 tablespoons extra-virgin olive oil

1 large onion, finely chopped

3 garlic cloves, chopped

1½ teaspoons sugar

1 large can (6 ounces) tomato paste

2 cups dry red wine

3 cans (28 ounces each) Italian peeled tomatoes

1 tablespoon dried oregano

1 tablespoon salt

1 teaspoon freshly ground black pepper

½ teaspoon crushed hot red pepper

3½ to 4 pounds beef chuck, in one piece

3 to 3½ pounds boneless pork loin roast, excess fat trimmed off

Savory Meatballs (recipe follows) or 2 pounds Italian sausages, sweet and/or hot

2 to 3 pounds imported pasta

Freshly grated imported Parmesan cheese

1. In a very large stockpot, heat ⅓ cup of the olive oil over moderately high heat. Add the onion and cook, stirring occasionally and reducing the heat to moderate if the onion starts to burn, until it is very soft and golden in color, 7 to 10 minutes. Add the garlic and cook 2 minutes longer. Sprinkle on the sugar. Add the tomato paste and cook, stirring with a wooden spoon, until the tomato paste starts to cook with the oil and looks a little like chopped meat, 3 to 5 minutes.

2. Pour in the wine, stirring to blend it with the tomato paste. Bring to a boil, scraping up any browned bits from the bottom of the pot. Let the wine cook for 5 minutes, then add all the tomatoes with their liquid, squeezing them through your hands as you add them to break up the pieces. Add the oregano, salt, black pepper, hot pepper, and 2 cups water. Bring the sauce slowly to a boil, then reduce the heat to a simmer.

3. While the sauce is coming to a boil, pat the chuck dry. Season generously with salt and pepper. In a large heavy skillet, preferably cast iron, heat the remaining 2 tablespoons olive oil over high heat. Add the meat to the hot oil and sear it well, turning only after each side has browned, until the meat is crusty and nicely browned all over, about 10 minutes. Transfer the beef to the tomato sauce.

4. Cut the pork roast in half, if necessary, to fit the skillet. Season with salt and pepper. Add to the hot oil and cook, turning, until nicely browned, 10 to 12 minutes. Turn and cook the second side for 5 minutes. Add the pork to the sauce. Pour off any excess fat from the skillet. Add 2 cups water and bring to a boil, scraping up any brown bits with a wooden spoon. Pour this liquid into the sauce.

5. Loosely cover the sauce and simmer for a minimum of 3 hours, and preferably 4 to 5 hours. The sauce will develop a rich, dark flavor. Stir occasionally, scraping the bottom so it doesn't scorch. If the sauce becomes too thick, add a little water. When you're through, remove from the heat and let the meats cool in the sauce. (The recipe can be made to this point in advance and refrigerated for up to 3 days or frozen for up to 3 months.)

6. When you're ready to serve, gently reheat the meats in the sauce. If you've made the meatballs, finish them off in the sauce. If you're serving sausages, prick them and brown in a skillet or in the oven before adding to the sauce. Slice the beef and pork roast against the grain. Cut the sausages into 2-inch chunks. Transfer the meats to a flameproof casserole. Ladle 2 cups of sauce over the meats. Cover with foil and keep warm in a low oven until you're ready for the meat course.

7. In a large pot of boiling salted water, cook the pasta until al dente, 10 to 11 minutes. Drain and return to the pot. Toss with enough sauce to coat lightly. Transfer to a pasta bowl and ladle more sauce on top. Pass the Parmesan cheese on the side.

SAVORY MEATBALLS

MAKES ABOUT 24

Light and subtly seasoned, these delicious meatballs turn ordinary spaghetti into a gourmet dish. Leftovers, if you have any, make a great sandwich.

1½ pounds meat loaf mix or ½ pound *each* ground beef, ground pork, and ground veal

2 eggs

½ cup freshly grated imported Parmesan cheese

½ cup chopped parsley

2 garlic cloves, crushed through a press

1 teaspoon dried marjoram

¼ teaspoon freshly grated nutmeg

1 teaspoon salt

½ teaspoon freshly ground pepper

2 slices of firm-textured white bread, left out to dry

⅓ cup heavy cream

Olive oil

1. Put the ground meat in a moderately large bowl. Beat the eggs lightly with a fork and add to the meat along with the cheese, parsley, garlic, marjoram, nutmeg, salt, and pepper.

2. Tear the bread into pieces and soak in the cream in a small bowl for 10 minutes, or until softened. Add to the meat mixture and blend lightly, preferably with your hands, until evenly combined. Form into 1½- to 2-inch meatballs.

3. Heat a thin film of olive oil in a large nonstick skillet over moderately high heat. Add the meatballs, in batches if necessary, and sauté, turning several times so that they hold their shape, until browned. Drain on paper towels.

4. Finish cooking the meatballs by braising them slowly in the Italian Meat Sauce (Step 6, above) for 15 to 20 minutes.

Backyard Barbecue

FOR 16

GRILLED STUFFED GRAPE LEAVES

SWEET AND TANGY SHRIMP KEBABS

GRILLED CLAMS

GRILLED PEPPER-LIME CHICKEN

GRILLED CORN, SAN MIGUEL STYLE

GRILLED SWEET ONION SALAD

BLACK BEAN SALAD WITH TOASTED CUMIN
AND JALAPEÑO PEPPERS

GARDEN TOMATOES, CUCUMBERS, AND RADISHES

CHOCOLATE COOKIE ICE CREAM CAKE

Outdoor grilling is the favorite form of entertaining for many Americans. Count me in! I love those glowing coals and the rich, smoky flavor they impart to food. I'm especially comfortable with the casual, more informal style of entertaining grilling allows.

Most of the dishes in this menu are prepared over a charcoal (or gas) fire, and for a crowd, you'll need one or two very large grills. I recommend cooking the chicken and the onions for the salad before everyone arrives. The chicken can be reheated in the oven or on the grill just before serving, or it can be put out at room temperature, as the other food is.

All three appetizers are done on the barbecue, but they cook very quickly. Since the grape leaves are stuffed in advance, you need only brush them with oil before setting them on the grill. The shrimp are marinated and skewered—ready to cook when you are. The clams need only a light scrubbing beforehand. Then store them in the refrigerator in a loosely covered bowl; don't leave them in a bowl of water or wrap them airtight or they will suffocate. They cook in just a minute or two, and they're delicious.

While the hors d'oeuvre are eclectic, the flavors of Mexico are apparent in the tart lime of the chicken, in the toasted cumin seeds that are the secret of this fabulous black bean salad, and in the grilled corn. Since the corn works well with the new sweet hybrids we see in the supermarket almost year round, you don't have to wait until August to enjoy it, and it's guaranteed to be a big hit. With so much grilling, I prefer a completely done-in-advance ending to this fabulous barbecue, so I can relax. Nothing is more popular with adults and children alike than an ice cream cake, and no flavors are more popular than chocolate and vanilla. This is an almost-instant dessert, requiring little more than assembly, but you can be sure its popularity will be in inverse proportion to the amount of effort it takes. Chocolate wafer crumbs, mini chocolate chips, and toasted almonds add irresistible crunch in contrast to the silky cold ice cream.

DO-AHEAD PLANNING

UP TO 3 WEEKS IN ADVANCE: Make the ice cream cake. Double wrap tightly and freeze.

UP TO 2 DAYS IN ADVANCE: Soak the black beans.

THE DAY BEFORE THE BARBECUE: Stuff the grape leaves. Scrub the clams. Marinate the chicken. Blanch the corn on the cob. Cook the black beans and make the Black Bean Salad.

THE MORNING OF THE PARTY: Marinate the shrimp. Up to 3 hours ahead, skewer the shrimp but leave them in their marinade.

ABOUT 2 HOURS BEFORE GUESTS ARRIVE: Grill the chicken. Grill the onions and finish the Sweet Onion Salad. Remove the bean salad from the refrigerator. Prepare platters of sliced tomatoes, cucumbers, and radishes; cover with a damp cloth and set aside.

SHORTLY BEFORE SERVING: Brush the grape leaves with oil and grill them. Grill the shrimp. Grill the clams. Reheat the chicken. Grill the corn.

GRILLED STUFFED GRAPE LEAVES

MAKES 64

These irresistible appetizers were first served to me by noted cookbook author Rose Levy Beranbaum at her country home. I made them for a video demonstration and couldn't keep the crew from eating every last one. I originally wrote the recipe for a smaller amount but found we never managed to eat less than four per person, so halve this only if you dare.

64 grape leaves in brine (about two-thirds of an 8-ounce jar)

2 logs (9 ounces each) mild goat cheese, such as Coach Farm or Montrachet

32 sun-dried tomato halves packed in olive oil, drained and cut lengthwise in half

Extra-virgin olive oil

1. Rinse the grape leaves and soak them in cold water for at least 1 hour to remove some of the brine. Drain and pat dry. If they have stems, remove them.

2. For each hors d'oeuvre, cut a thin slice of goat cheese and squeeze into a small cylinder. Set in the middle of the bottom edge of a grape leaf. Top with a piece of sun-dried tomato. Fold in the edges and roll up. Set aside, seam side down. (The grape leaves can be stuffed up to a day ahead. Wrap and refrigerate.)

3. Light a charcoal or gas grill to produce a hot fire. Brush the stuffed grape leaves with olive oil and grill over hot coals, turning once, until the leaves are lightly toasted and the cheese is heated through, 3 to 4 minutes. Serve hot.

SWEET AND TANGY SHRIMP KEBABS

12 TO 16 SERVINGS

Because these shrimp are so tasty, they don't need any dipping sauce. For best flavor, serve them hot off the grill.

2 pounds medium or large shrimp, shelled and deveined

½ cup orange juice, preferably fresh

3 tablespoons fresh lemon juice

½ cup ketchup

¼ cup soy sauce

2 tablespoons Asian sesame oil

1½ tablespoons brown sugar

2 garlic cloves, smashed

1. Rinse the shrimp and drain well. In a mixing bowl, combine the orange juice, lemon juice, ketchup, soy sauce, sesame oil, and brown sugar. Whisk to blend well. Add the garlic and shrimp and stir to coat. Marinate at cool room temperature for 1½ to 2 hours or up to 6 hours in the refrigerator.

2. Light a hot fire in a barbecue grill or preheat your broiler. Thread the shrimp onto long bamboo skewers that have been soaked in cold water for at least 30 minutes. Skewer them tip to tail so that they don't fall around and allow 3 per skewer.

3. Grill or broil the shrimp as close to the heat as possible for 1½ to 2 minutes on each side, or until they are nicely browned.

GRILLED CLAMS

MAKES 48

Clams on the grill are absolutely no work, and they're something of a conversation piece. They cook in just a minute or two over hot coals, and guests can watch as they pop open, their juices bubbling and sputtering over the fire. I like these absolutely pure, with maybe a squeeze of lemon, but you can offer seafood cocktail sauce, if you wish.

4 dozen littleneck or cherrystone (hard-shell) clams

Lemon wedges

1. Choose tightly closed clams with unbroken shells. Scrub the clam shells to remove any loose grit. Refrigerate the clams, loosely wrapped, for up to 24 hours before cooking.

2. Light a charcoal or gas grill and get a hot fire going. Set the clams, right side up, on the grill rack. The long, black hinges should be on the left; otherwise the clams will open upside-down and the juices will spill out. Not a tragedy if it happens—you can still eat them, and they'll still be delicious. Grill the clams over hot coals until they just open and the juices come bubbling up, 1 to 2 minutes. Serve with lemon wedges.

GRILLED PEPPER-LIME CHICKEN

16 SERVINGS

Simplicity stars in this savory chicken that can't go wrong. Your only challenge is grilling without having the coals catch fire. For this reason—and to reduce fat and cholesterol—I often opt for removing the skin from the chicken. If you do so, the cooking time will be about 5 minutes less.

4 chickens, about 3 pounds each, quartered

1 cup fresh lime juice (from 7 or 8 limes)

¾ cup extra-virgin olive oil

1 tablespoon coarse salt

1½ tablespoons coarsely cracked black pepper

2 teaspoons hot pepper sauce

2 medium onions, sliced

Lime wedges

1. Trim off any excess fat from the chickens. Rinse and pat dry. With a small knife, stab the pieces of chicken in 2 or 3 of the meatiest spots.

2. In a large bowl, whisk together the lime juice, olive oil, salt, pepper, and hot sauce. Add the chicken and onions and toss to coat with the marinade. Let stand, turning occasionally, for at least 1 hour at room temperature or cover and refrigerate for up to 8 hours.

3. Heat the grill or broiler. Over medium-hot coals or about 6 inches from the broiler, cook the chicken, skin toward the heat, for 5 minutes. Baste, turn, and baste again. Cook for 10 minutes with the skin away from the heat. Baste, turn, and baste. Finish with the skin toward the heat for 5 to 10 minutes, until done and still juicy but no longer pink. Serve with wedges of lime to squeeze over the chicken.

GRILLED CORN, SAN MIGUEL STYLE

MAKES 16 EARS

San Miguel de Allende is a picturesque colonial village in the lush Guanajuato region of Mexico. Behind its cathedral, the colorful food market bustles with shoppers every day of the week. The smell of fresh tortillas mixes with sweet tropical fruit, pungent fresh herbs, and grilled meats. Snacks are sold along the street, including this savory grilled corn, sprinkled with lime juice and cheese.

Exact measurements don't make sense for this recipe. Make as many ears as you like—I usually allow 2 per person.

Fresh ears of corn

½ cup mayonnaise

1¼ teaspoons hot pepper sauce

1 cup grated aged Sonoma Jack or Pecorino Romano cheese

3 or 4 limes, cut into wedges

1. As soon as you get the corn home, shuck the ears and blanch the corn in a large pot of boiling salted water for 2 to 3 minutes, just to soften it slightly. Drain and rinse under cold water to stop the cooking. (The corn can be blanched up to a day ahead. Hold at room temperature for up to 4 hours or in the refrigerator for longer. Be sure it is returned to room temperature before grilling.)

2. Light the grill. Mix the mayonnaise with the hot sauce. Put the corn over hot coals and cook, basting with the mayonnaise and turning, until lightly browned all over, 5 to 10 minutes. Remove from the heat and immediately sprinkle the grated cheese over the hot corn. Serve at once with lime wedges.

Grilling

Grilling is a delightful, low-fat way to cook, whether you're barbecuing over charcoal or gas, whether you have a covered kettle grill or a small hibachi. To avoid a chemical taste on the food, I use an electric starter. When that's not possible, I use ordinary vegetable cooking oil instead of a petroleum starter. It works remarkably well.

Almost all foods derive extra flavor from grilling. If I'm going to the trouble of lighting the barbecue, I follow one of two strategies: Either I grill as much of the meal as possible, parboiling vegetables if necessary so they don't take forever, or I grill the main course and make sure that everything else is done ahead and served either chilled or at room temperature. I almost never run back and forth between the barbecue and the stove. For a crowd, I'll frequently grill ahead and reheat the food in the oven or on the grill for convenience.

All kinds of wood chips and chunks are making their appearance these days—mesquite, hickory, pinion/piñon, applewood, cherry. They provide extra flavor; some burn longer than charcoal, and some provide an extra-hot fire when you need it.

I prefer the chunks because they don't disappear as fast and can be used for smoking as well as grilling. All wood must be soaked for at least 30 minutes before putting it on the grill, or it will flare up and burn off. This is particularly important for smoking.

GRILLED SWEET ONION SALAD

16 SERVINGS

Though this dish can be made with either red or sweet yellow onions, the combination of the two is pretty.

4 large red onions (about ½ pound each)

4 large sweet yellow (Spanish) or Vidalia onions (about ¾ pound each)

About ½ cup extra-virgin olive oil

Coarse salt

1. Peel the onions and cut them into ⅜-inch-thick slices (do not separate the rings at this point). Light a charcoal or gas grill and adjust the fire or temperature setting so that the coals are hot.

2. Brush the onion slices on one side with oil. Set them on a grilling rack over the coals, oiled side down. Press down with a wide, flat spatula to help the heat penetrate the slices. Grill until the bottoms are lightly browned but not charred, 3 to 5 minutes. Brush the tops with oil, turn the slices, and cook, again pressing with the spatula, until the second side is browned and the onions are softened but still slightly crunchy, 3 to 5 minutes longer.

3. Transfer the grilled onion slices to a serving bowl and separate into rings. Season lightly with coarse salt and drizzle on the remaining olive oil. Toss to mix. Serve warm or at room temperature.

BLACK BEAN SALAD WITH TOASTED CUMIN AND JALAPEÑO PEPPERS

16 TO 20 SERVINGS

Although there is a quick method for softening dried beans, I suggest soaking them overnight for more uniform texture.

2 pounds black turtle beans (*frijoles negros*)

1 large imported bay leaf

1½ tablespoons cumin seeds

½ cup sherry vinegar

⅔ cup extra-virgin olive oil

1 large sweet onion, finely diced

2 medium green bell peppers, finely diced

2 medium red bell peppers, finely diced

1 large yellow bell pepper, diced

1 or 2 jalapeño peppers, seeded and minced

2 garlic cloves, crushed through a press

1½ teaspoons salt

Freshly ground pepper

1. Rinse the beans well and pick them over to remove any grit. Put them in a large, heavy pot with enough cold water to cover by at least 2 inches. Let stand overnight.

2. Drain the beans into a colander. Return them to the pot with the bay leaf and fresh water to cover by 2 inches. Bring to a boil, then reduce the heat and simmer until the beans are tender but still firm enough to hold their shape, 1½ to 2 hours. Drain the beans; discard the bay leaf.

3. Meanwhile, in a small dry skillet, toast the cumin seeds over moderately high heat, shaking the pan frequently to toss them, until they are toasted and fragrant, about 2 minutes. Pour into a small bowl and set aside.

4. In a large bowl, combine the warm beans with the vinegar and oil. Toss to coat. Add the onion, bell peppers, jalapeños, garlic, salt, and toasted cumin. Toss to mix. Let stand, tossing occasionally as the salad cools. Season with additional salt and black pepper to taste. Serve at room temperature. (The salad keeps well overnight. Cover and refrigerate; let return to room temperature before serving.)

CHOCOLATE COOKIE ICE CREAM CAKE

16 TO 20 SERVINGS

Not everyone has a Carvel's in the neighborhood, and just in case you don't, here is an easy and irresistible frozen dessert the entire family will love. It is also a fraction of the cost. The basic recipe is simple: Crumbled chocolate wafer cookies, mini chocolate chips, and chopped toasted almonds are layered with vanilla ice cream in a springform pan. As long as the finished dessert is tightly wrapped so it doesn't pick up any freezer odors, you can make this weeks, or even months, in advance and pull it out whenever you need a crowd-pleasing dessert.

The cake will be easier to cut if you let it stand at room temperature for about 5 minutes, assuming it's not too hot outside. To cut easily, have a tall glass of hot water next to your knife. Between cuts, dip the knife into the hot water and quickly wipe it dry before the next cut.

1 cup natural almonds (about 4 ounces)

1 box (9 ounces) chocolate wafer cookies

1½ cups mini chocolate chips

2 half-gallon packages French vanilla ice cream

1. Heat the oven to 375°F. Spread out the nuts on a small baking sheet and toast them in the oven until lightly browned and fragrant, about 12 minutes. Transfer to a plate and let cool.

2. Break up the cookies roughly into quarters. In 3 batches, combine the toasted almonds and chocolate cookies in a food processor and pulse to chop very coarsely. Transfer to a bowl and mix in the chocolate chips.

3. Line the bottom round of a 10-inch springform pan with waxed paper, parchment, or foil. Open one of the ice cream packages and use a large knife to cut the ice cream into ¾- to 1-inch slices. As you cut each one, fit it flat on the bottom of the springform pan. When most of the bottom is covered, smooth with a spatula or with your fingers (the easiest tool) to fill in any gaps. Sprinkle one-third of the chocolate-almond crumbs over the ice cream to make an even layer. Cover with another layer of ice cream, opening the second package when you need it. Add another layer of half the chocolate-almond crumbs. Cover with the remaining ice cream and top with the remaining chocolate-almond crumbs. Double wrap in plastic and freeze.

4. A couple of hours before serving, remove the cake from the freezer and unwrap. Using a blunt knife dipped in hot water, cut around the side of the pan to separate the ice cream from the metal. Remove the side ring of the pan. Smooth the sides with a rubber spatula and place in the freezer for 5 to 10 minutes to firm the cake up, then rewrap and return to the freezer until serving time.

Couscous Party

FOR 16

COUSCOUS WITH LAMB, CHICKEN, AND SWEET POTATOES

MARINATED BLACK OLIVES

PICKLED TURNIPS

ORANGE-RADISH SALAD

PITA BREAD

MINT TEA

LEMON ICE WITH COINTREAU AND STRAWBERRIES

There aren't a lot of restaurants where you can find a good couscous these days, and since it's festive one-dish party food, why not at your house? Couscous is a great Mediterranean dish that is a meal in itself. Only a few colorful accompaniments are needed to create a veritable feast. The hot sauce, olives, and tangy, refreshing salads that accompany it make a striking, tantalizing spread.

Paula Wolfert, author of, among others, *The Slow Mediterranean Kitchen* and *The Cooking of South-West France,* brought authentic couscous into the American kitchen in her delightful classic *Couscous and Other Good Food from Morocco.* I am indebted to her for the Orange-Radish Salad and for being so generous with her knowledge. Nonetheless, I confess at the outset that for ease of preparation I have opted for the precooked couscous sold in supermarkets across the country. So that you can be as relaxed as your guests, cook the meat and vegetables for the couscous a day in advance. The couscous grain itself is prepared in stages the day of the party.

If oranges and radishes sound like an odd couple to you, you're in for a pleasant surprise. The bite of the radish and the refreshing sweetness of the orange match beautifully, as do their colors. Marinated Black Olives and pink Pickled Turnips add additional fillips of flavor.

For a lovely, simple dessert, appropriately light after the couscous, buy a good-quality lemon ice. Pack it into a metal ring mold, freeze it solid, and unmold onto a platter (use a hot towel, if necessary, to unmold). Drizzle Cointreau over the sorbet, which will help soften it enough to serve, and fill the center with fresh strawberries and/or blueberries.

DO-AHEAD PLANNING

UP TO 1 MONTH IN ADVANCE: Marinate the olives.

UP TO 10 DAYS IN ADVANCE: Make the Pickled Turnips. Freeze purchased lemon ice in a ring mold.

THE DAY BEFORE THE PARTY: Prepare the Couscous with Lamb, Chicken, and Sweet Potatoes through Step 4.

UP TO 6 HOURS BEFORE SERVING: Give the couscous its first cooking and spread it out to dry.

UP TO 3 HOURS BEFORE SERVING: Make the Orange-Radish Salad through Step 2.

ABOUT 30 MINUTES BEFORE SERVING: Steam the couscous. Finish the Couscous with Lamb, Chicken, and Sweet Potatoes. Finish the Orange-Radish Salad. Unmold the lemon ice ring and return to the freezer until ready to serve.

COUSCOUS WITH LAMB, CHICKEN, AND SWEET POTATOES

16 TO 18 SERVINGS

For convenience, I use the precooked couscous that is sold in boxes in most supermarkets. If you own a *couscousière*, by all means use it, but the dish can be made in any large (at least 9-quart) pot, preferably an enameled cast-iron casserole or heavy stockpot. If you don't have a pot large enough, make the couscous in two smaller ones.

½ cup extra-virgin olive oil

4 pounds boneless lamb shoulder, trimmed of all excess fat and cut into 1½-inch pieces

4 medium onions, thickly sliced

1 teaspoon powdered ginger

1 teaspoon ground cinnamon

½ teaspoon freshly grated nutmeg

½ teaspoon ground coriander

½ teaspoon freshly ground black pepper

¼ teaspoon cayenne pepper

¼ teaspoon turmeric

2 large pinches of saffron threads

1 can (28 ounces) Italian peeled tomatoes, cut in half, with their juices reserved

2 tablespoons sugar

2 teaspoons salt

8 medium carrots, peeled and cut crosswise on the diagonal into 1½-inch lengths

1 cup raisins

4 sweet potatoes (about 2 pounds), peeled, cut lengthwise in half and then into ¾-inch slices

3 pounds skinless, boneless chicken breasts and/or thighs, cut into 1- to 1½-inch pieces

8 small zucchini (about 2 pounds), cut lengthwise in half and then into 1½-inch lengths

1 cup slivered blanched almonds (4 ounces)

2 tablespoons fresh lemon juice

2 teaspoons to 2 tablespoons harissa or sambal oelek, depending on how hot you like it, plus additional for the sauce

Couscous (opposite page)

1. In a large flameproof casserole, heat 3 tablespoons of the olive oil over moderately high heat. Add the lamb and sauté, stirring frequently, until the lamb is browned on the outside, about 10 minutes. Using a slotted spoon, remove the meat to a bowl. Pour the fat from the pan.

2. Add the remaining 5 tablespoons olive oil to the same casserole and reduce the heat to moderate. Add the onions, cover, and cook for 5 minutes. Uncover and continue to cook, stirring occasionally, until the onions just begin to brown, 10 to 15 minutes longer.

3. Add the ginger, cinnamon, nutmeg, coriander, black pepper, cayenne, turmeric, and saffron. Cook, stirring, for 1 minute to toast the spices. Return the lamb to the pan along with any juices that have collected in the bowl.

4. Add the tomatoes and their liquid along with enough water to barely cover the meat. Stir in the sugar and salt. Partially cover and simmer for 1 hour.

5. Add the carrots and raisins and simmer for 30 minutes longer, or until the lamb is tender. (The recipe can be prepared to this point up to a day in advance. Let cool, then cover and refrigerate. Scrape off any surface fat and reheat before proceeding.)

6. Add the sweet potatoes and simmer for 5 minutes. Add the chicken, zucchini, almonds, lemon juice, and harissa to taste. Simmer until the chicken is cooked through but still moist and the vegetables are tender, about 10 minutes longer.

7. To serve, mound the cooked couscous on a large platter or in a shallow serving bowl. With a perforated skimmer or slotted spoon, transfer the meat and vegetables to the platter, arranging them around the couscous. Serve most of the broth in a separate bowl with a ladle; use to moisten the couscous. In a small bowl, mix some of the broth with additional harissa to taste to pass as a hot sauce.

Couscous

Couscous is Moroccan pasta—tiny grains of semolina wheat flour. (The word also refers to the entire dish of the cooked grain with whatever vegetables, meats, and sauce are served with it.) Like any dried pasta, couscous expands when it is cooked. Traditionally, couscous is steamed three times. In between steaming, it is dried and raked with the hands, so that when it is finally served, each grain is separate, light, and fluffy. If you don't precook the couscous, it will expand in your stomach, giving you the uncomfortable feeling of having eaten too much.

These days, most couscous is precooked, which means it fluffs up much more with one cooking and can even be combined directly with liquid rather than being steamed. Even the couscous sold by the pound at health food stores and Middle Eastern groceries has most likely been precooked. For a crowd, I recommend this type of couscous. It needs only one or at most two steamings and is easy to handle.

I've experimented with cooking the couscous directly in the broth it will be served with and found it turned out leaden and heavy. For a big party, cook the pasta in boiling salted water as directed in the recipe the morning of the party. Spread it out on a baking sheet or in a roasting pan and let it dry, occasionally raking the couscous and breaking up any clumps with your fingers, until the grains are dry and not tacky to the touch. Cover with plastic wrap and a kitchen towel and set aside at room temperature. Shortly before serving, moisten the couscous, dump it into a colander, and steam, uncovered, over boiling water or over the stew with which you are going to serve it for 20 minutes, until heated through.

Then turn it out onto a platter or into a large bowl, top with a few tablespoons of butter and fluff up. Encourage guests to moisten the couscous with broth and/or hot sauce made from harissa, Middle Eastern chile paste, mixed with some of the broth.

COUSCOUS

16 TO 18 SERVINGS

If you've bought the couscous loose, be sure it is the precooked kind.

3 pounds couscous

3 tablespoons unsalted butter, cut into tablespoons

1. For every 1 cup of couscous, bring 1½ cups salted water to a boil. Add the couscous, stir, cover, and remove from the heat. Let stand for about 5 minutes, or until all the liquid is absorbed. Spread out the couscous in a roasting pan and let dry, occasionally raking the couscous with your fingers and breaking up any lumps. When the couscous is no longer sticky, cover with plastic wrap and a kitchen towel and set aside at room temperature. (The recipe can be prepared to this point up to 6 hours before serving.)

2. About half an hour before serving, moisten the couscous with 1½ cups water. Dump into a colander set over a pot of boiling water (depending on the size of your colander, this may be easier to do in 2 batches). Steam the couscous, uncovered, for 20 minutes, or until hot. Transfer to a bowl, toss with the butter, and serve.

MARINATED BLACK OLIVES

MAKES ABOUT 1½ QUARTS

You won't believe the difference a simple marinade makes for even an ordinary supermarket olive. Since these are so easy and only improve upon standing, I like to make a big batch.

2 pounds Moroccan or Mediterranean black olives (try at your deli counter or look for Peloponnese or Progresso brand on the shelf)

6 small dried hot red peppers

6 garlic cloves, smashed

2 tablespoons herbes de Provence

Extra-virgin olive oil

Put the olives in a stone crock or glass jar; use two if necessary. Add the hot peppers and garlic. Sprinkle on the herbes de Provence and stir to distribute. Pour in enough olive oil to cover and let stand at room temperature, loosely covered, for at least 1 week and up to 3 months before serving.

PICKLED TURNIPS

MAKES ABOUT 1½ PINTS

A traditional tangy nibble, these pretty pickles are usually included in plates of radishes, carrots, and hot peppers put out before a Middle Eastern meal. The beet is only included for its color, a divine hot pink it imparts to the turnip slices.

4 medium turnips (about 1 pound), peeled, cut in half, and sliced thin

1 small beet, peeled and quartered

2 garlic cloves, bruised

2 tablespoons coarse salt

2 teaspoons sugar

1 tablespoon distilled white vinegar

1. Put the turnips and beet in a large glass jar. Tuck in the garlic cloves. Stir together 2 cups water, the salt, and sugar to dissolve the salt and sugar. Add the vinegar and pour over the vegetables. Let stand in a cool place for 3 days. Then cover and refrigerate for up to 2 weeks.

2. Drain the turnips and discard the beet before serving.

ORANGE-RADISH SALAD

16 SERVINGS

Paula Wolfert, author of *The Slow Mediterranean Kitchen,* produces some of the tastiest food I have ever eaten. This attractive, unusual salad from her *Couscous and Other Good Food from Morocco* is a refreshing accompaniment to other more highly seasoned dishes.

8 bunches of red radishes

⅓ cup sugar

⅔ cup fresh lemon juice

3 tablespoons orange flower water, optional but authentic

½ teaspoon salt

8 navel oranges

½ teaspoon ground cinnamon

1. Wash and trim the radishes. Using the shredding disk on a food processor (or the large holes on a box grater), finely shred the radishes. Squeeze them gently to remove excess liquid. Put the radishes in a glass serving bowl and sprinkle with the sugar, lemon juice, orange flower water, and salt. Toss to mix, cover, and refrigerate for up to 3 hours.

2. Using a sharp paring knife, cut away the orange peel, removing all the bitter white pith. Holding the oranges over a bowl to catch the juices, slice down along both sides of each membrane to remove the orange sections. Put them in the bowl with the juice, cover, and refrigerate for up to 3 hours.

3. Shortly before serving, add the oranges and their juice to the radishes. Toss lightly to mix and sprinkle with a dusting of cinnamon.

Noonday Brunch

FOR 16

PASSION FRUIT MIMOSAS

CHEESE STRAWS (PAGE 174)

SOUR CREAM AND TWO-CAVIAR DIP (PAGE 191)
WITH ENDIVE SPEARS AND OTHER CRUDITÉS

RICH LIVER MOUSSE WITH TOASTED HAZELNUTS

BAKED EGGS WITH MUSHROOMS AND BROWNED ONIONS

AVOCADO, STRAWBERRY, AND ORANGE SALAD

ASSORTED SMOKED FISH: SALMON, TROUT,
AND STURGEON

OR

SLICED COLD CUTS, SUCH AS HAM, TURKEY,
AND PASTRAMI

ASSORTED BREADS: BAGELS, CROISSANTS, SLICED
WHOLE-GRAIN, AND SOURDOUGH

MARBLED SOUR CREAM COFFEE CAKE

Though it surprises me, the meal for which most people seek my advice and recipes for is brunch. Daytime entertaining is steadily growing in popularity. For parents and busy professionals, late mornings and afternoons are times when they have extra energy. The hour implies a more relaxed, casual form of entertaining, usually with less alcohol—and brunch ends early.

Planning a menu for brunch is fun, because the meal allows such a wide range of food. It can be a breakfast-brunch, with a major egg dish along with accompaniments; a lunch-brunch, with heavier afternoon food and perhaps more alcohol; or an all-day open house, with a substantial buffet as well as passed hors d'oeuvre. Since you will be serving early in the day, food that can be prepared in advance is all the more important.

Here's an excellent "noonish" menu. You never know who has had breakfast beforehand and who is holding out for brunch, so there is plenty of food at the outset, which allows time for everyone to relax and socialize before sitting down. Greet guests with Passion Fruit Mimosas or Bloody Marys. Pass the Cheese Straws. Have the caviar dip set out, surrounded by spears of Belgian endive and with a basket of assorted crudités next to it. Accompany the liver mousse with toast rounds or crackers. I first encountered the pairing of avocados and strawberries many years ago aboard a 65-foot Swan sailboat moored off Newport, Rhode Island, during the America's Cup race. The pastel combination was served as a composed salad at dinner, and it took us all by surprise. It was delicious and has lost none of its appeal. For a crowd, I've combined the avocados and strawberries here with oranges as well for a colorful and delightful starter.

Baked Eggs with Mushrooms and Browned Onions, a classic French recipe, serves extremely well for early entertaining, because the entire dish can be assembled the night before and baked at the last minute. All the other foods offered are purchased: your choice of smoked fish or cold cuts and a gorgeous basket of breads. To make service easy, slice the bagels beforehand. An easy dessert, the moist Marbled Sour Cream Coffee Cake serves 16 easily and keeps extremely well. If you prefer not to freeze it, you can still bake it 5 days in advance and store it in a cool place.

DO-AHEAD PLANNING

UP TO 2 MONTHS IN ADVANCE: Bake and freeze the Cheese Straws and the Marbled Sour Cream Coffee Cake.

UP TO 3 DAYS IN ADVANCE: Make the liver mousse. Cook the eggs, shell them immediately, and store them in a bowl of cold water to cover in the refrigerator.

THE DAY BEFORE THE BRUNCH: Make the caviar dip. Prepare the endive and other crudités. Assemble the Baked Eggs with Mushrooms and Browned Onions.

UP TO 4 HOURS BEFORE SERVING: Prepare the oranges and strawberries for the salad.

ABOUT 1 HOUR BEFORE SERVING: Arrange the dip and crudités. Pour the orange juice and passion fruit nectar into champagne flutes. Complete the Avocado, Strawberry, and Orange Salad.

ABOUT 30 MINUTES BEFORE YOU PLAN TO SERVE: Bake the egg gratin.

PASSION FRUIT MIMOSAS

Passion fruit has a heady flavor uniquely its own. A splash of the nectar turns an ordinary mimosa into a memorable mimosa.

For each drink:

In a champagne flute, combine 2 tablespoons (1 ounce, or a jigger) of fresh orange juice and the same amount of passion fruit nectar. Add a squeeze of lime to each glass. Fill with brut Champagne and garnish with a thin slice of lime.

RICH LIVER MOUSSE WITH TOASTED HAZELNUTS

MAKES ABOUT 2½ CUPS

With all the to-do about foie gras in recent years, it's easy to forget just how unctuous and flavorful chicken livers are, especially if you can find them fresh, from organically fed, free-range birds.

½ cup hazelnuts

1 pound chicken livers

12 tablespoons (1½ sticks) unsalted butter

3 medium shallots, finely chopped

½ cup Madeira

¾ teaspoon salt

⅜ teaspoon freshly ground pepper

⅛ teaspoon freshly grated nutmeg

1 tablespoon Cognac

1. Heat the oven to 325°F. Spread the nuts out in a small baking pan. Toast in the oven, shaking the pan once or twice, until the skins are cracked and the nuts are golden brown, 10 to 15 minutes. Dump the nuts onto a clean kitchen towel and rub them around to remove most of the outer brown skins. Lift the nuts off the towel, leaving the skins behind, put them in a food processor, and coarsely chop.

2. Trim the livers, cutting off any yellow or green spots and large clumps of veins. Discard any livers that are particularly strong smelling. Cut each lobe in half.

3. Melt 1 stick of the butter. Let cool until tepid.

4. In a large skillet, melt the remaining 4 tablespoons butter over moderately high heat. Add the shallots and sauté, stirring frequently, until softened but not browned, about 1 minute. Add the livers and sauté, tossing, for about 2 minutes, until the livers are browned outside and slightly stiffened but still rosy pink inside; do not overcook. Scrape the livers, shallots, and pan juices into the food processor with the nuts.

5. Add the Madeira to the skillet and boil until reduced by half; remove from the heat. Puree the livers for 10 seconds. With the machine on, slowly pour in the cooled melted butter. Gradually add the Madeira through the feed tube. Scrape down the sides of the bowl. Add the salt, pepper, nutmeg, and Cognac. Puree for at least 1 full minute, stopping several times to scrape down the sides of the bowl, until the mousse is as smooth as it can be.

6. Scrape into small crocks or a serving dish, cover, and refrigerate for up to 3 days before serving.

BAKED EGGS WITH MUSHROOMS AND BROWNED ONIONS

16 SERVINGS

In France, this dish is called *oeufs à la tripe.* Since there is no tripe anywhere, I can only assume someone once thought the dish *looked* a bit like tripe. In any event, it tastes heavenly, if you're partial to mushrooms and caramelized onions, as I am. Because the dish can be prepared completely in advance, it is ideal for entertaining.

2 dozen eggs

8 tablespoons (1 stick) plus 6 tablespoons unsalted butter

3 tablespoons olive oil

1 pound mushrooms, sliced

1¼ teaspoons salt

½ teaspoon freshly ground black pepper

1 teaspoon fresh lemon juice

5 medium onions, sliced

⅛ teaspoon saffron threads

⅔ cup all-purpose flour

1 quart milk

⅛ teaspoon *each* freshly grated nutmeg, dried thyme, cayenne pepper

⅔ cup heavy cream or additional milk

⅔ cup shredded Gruyère or imported Swiss cheese

1. Put the eggs in a large saucepan or flameproof casserole. They needn't be in a single layer, but don't pile them high either. Add cold water to cover by at least ½ inch. Bring to a boil, reduce the heat, and simmer for 12 minutes. Remove from the heat and let stand for 5 minutes. Pour off the water and fill the pan with cold water. Peel the eggs immediately to avoid a dark ring around the yolk. (The eggs can be cooked and peeled up to 3 days in advance and refrigerated in a bowl of cold water.)

2. In a large skillet, melt 2 tablespoons of the butter in 1 tablespoon of the oil over moderately high heat. Add the mushrooms and sauté, tossing frequently, until lightly browned, about 10 minutes. Season with ¼ teaspoon of the salt, ¼ teaspoon of the black pepper, and the lemon juice. Set aside.

3. In a large heavy saucepan or flameproof casserole, melt 1 stick of the butter in the remaining 2 tablespoons olive oil over moderately low heat. Add the onions, cover, and cook slowly for 5 minutes. Uncover, increase the heat to moderate, and cook, stirring occasionally, until deep golden brown, about 30 minutes.

4. Crumble the saffron over the onions. Add the flour and cook, stirring, for 2 minutes. Gradually whisk in the milk. Bring to a boil and cook, whisking, for 1 to 2 minutes, until thickened. Reduce the heat to a simmer and cook, stirring frequently, for 3 minutes. Season with the nutmeg, thyme, cayenne, and the remaining 1 teaspoon salt and ¼ teaspoon black pepper. Thin the sauce with the cream. Remove from the heat and set aside.

5. Use 2 tablespoons of the remaining butter to grease 2 large gratin or shallow baking dishes (or use a single dish if you have one large enough). Slice the eggs. Spread a thin layer of the onion-cream sauce over the bottom of each dish. Cover with a layer of half the egg slices, overlapping as necessary. Season the eggs lightly with additional salt and freshly ground pepper to taste. Spoon half the sauce over the eggs and cover with half the sautéed mushrooms. Arrange a layer of the remaining egg slices, season with salt and pepper, and top with the remaining mushrooms and the remaining sauce. Sprinkle the cheese evenly over the top and dot with the remaining 2 tablespoons butter. (The recipe can be completely assembled to this point up to a day ahead. Set aside at room temperature for up to 3 hours or cover and refrigerate overnight.)

6. Preheat the oven to 375°F. Bake the gratins until bubbling hot and lightly browned on top, 15 to 20 minutes. Serve hot.

AVOCADO, STRAWBERRY, AND ORANGE SALAD

16 SERVINGS

I first tasted the combination of avocados and strawberries aboard a yacht somewhere off the coast of Newport, Rhode Island. The cook was British and Cordon Bleu trained, and her specialty was a very pretty avocado salad with a tart strawberry dressing. Here, with the addition of fresh oranges, I've turned it into more of a fruit salad, with the same delightful colors and tastes.

4 navel oranges

3 pints strawberries

3 tablespoons balsamic vinegar

¼ cup avocado oil or sunflower oil

1 teaspoon coarsely cracked black pepper

4 ripe California avocados, preferably Hass

2 to 3 tablespoons fresh lemon juice

1. Cut the ends off the oranges and cut off the peel, removing all of the bitter white pith. Cut the oranges crosswise into ½-inch slices and then cut the slices into ½-inch pieces.

2. Hull the strawberries and halve or quarter them, depending on their size. In a medium bowl, combine the strawberries and oranges with the balsamic vinegar, avocado oil, and pepper. Toss gently. (The recipe can be prepared to this point up to 4 hours ahead. Cover and refrigerate.)

3. Up to 2 hours before serving, peel the avocados and cut them off the pit lengthwise into ½-inch slices. Arrange around the rim of a large platter and brush all over with the lemon juice to prevent discoloration. Mound the strawberries and oranges in the center, cover with plastic wrap, and let stand at room temperature until serving time.

MARBLED SOUR CREAM COFFEE CAKE

16 SERVINGS

This recipe is from the first cookbook I ever wrote, *Tailgate Parties*, but it has proved so popular, keeps so well, and serves so many that I am repeating it here.

- **½ pound semisweet or sweet dark chocolate, broken into pieces**
- **3 cups all-purpose flour**
- **1½ teaspoons baking powder**
- **1½ teaspoons baking soda**
- **8 tablespoons (1 stick) unsalted butter, at room temperature**
- **1½ cups sugar**
- **3 eggs**
- **1 tablespoon vanilla extract**
- **2 cups (1 pint) sour cream**

1. Position a rack in the center of the oven and heat the oven to 325°F. Grease a 10-inch tube pan with a removable bottom. In a double boiler, melt the chocolate over hot water, stirring until smooth. Remove from the heat and set aside.

2. In a bowl, combine the flour, baking powder, and baking soda. Whisk gently to mix.

3. In a large bowl, beat the butter and sugar together with a hand mixer until light and fluffy. Beat in the eggs, 1 at a time, blending well after each addition. Beat in the vanilla and sour cream until blended. Gradually beat in the dry ingredients. The batter will be very thick.

4. Stir about 1 cup of the batter into the melted chocolate. Turn half of the remaining vanilla batter into the tube pan. Spoon half of the chocolate batter on top. Repeat with the remaining vanilla batter and then top with the remaining chocolate. Stick a kitchen knife or spatula straight down into the center of the batter and pull it around the pan, weaving back and forth to swirl the chocolate through the cake. Smooth the top with a rubber spatula.

5. Bake in the center of the oven for 1 hour, or until the cake begins to pull away from the sides of the pan and a cake tester inserted in the center comes out clean, except perhaps for a little melted chocolate. Let stand for 5 minutes. Remove the outside of the pan. Let cool for 10 minutes. Then unmold and let cool completely on a rack before slicing. (Wrapped well, the cake will keep in a cool place for up to a week, or it can be frozen for months.)

PASSOVER SEDER

FOR 12 TO 16

CHICKEN SOUP WITH MATZOH BALLS

GEFILTE FISH

DILLED BEET AND POTATO SALAD

HAROSET WITH DATES AND APPLES

SWEET-AND-SOUR BRISKET WITH APRICOTS AND PRUNES

GINGERED CARROTS

MUSHROOM-MATZOH BAKE

ROASTED ASPARAGUS (PAGE 193)

HAZELNUT TORTE WITH MIXED BERRY COMPOTE

PESADIC CHOCOLATE CANDIES

Because Passover is a joyous, food-oriented holiday, the Seder meal deserves to preserve tradition and, at the same time, offer a fresh culinary approach. Many people who are not otherwise kosher adhere to stricter dietary guidelines for the Seder, so the feast offered here conforms to religious standards. In keeping with a more contemporary outlook, butter is not replaced with margarine but with extra-virgin olive oil. Fresh vegetables are exploited, and seasonings are tailored to a sophisticated palate.

For starters, heirloom recipes are gently tweaked. Rich chicken soup is served with matzoh balls flavored with browned onions and parsley. Gefilte fish, rather than made from scratch, is dressed up with a dilled roasted beet and potato salad. And haroset is sweetened with apples and dates, blended with walnuts, cinnamon, and red wine.

A sumptuous brisket of beef—slow-braised to tenderize and remove all fat, flavored sweet-sour almost like a sauerbraten, smothered with dried apricots and prunes—makes a perfect main course for a crowd, whether it's Passover or not. Best of all, the dish can be prepared up to 3 days in advance and refrigerated or sliced and frozen in its sauce up to a month in advance. It's one of those dishes that improve with reheating. With a nod to the holiday, mushrooms and golden onions are bound with matzoh farfel for a savory bake. Easy roasted asparagus, appropriately fresh this time of year, and gingered carrots, a much simpler preparation than the traditional *tzimmes,* round out the meal. You can add oven-roasted potatoes—tossed with olive oil, garlic, and herbs—if you feel you need them.

For dessert, a flourless hazelnut cake adorned with a mixed berry compote adds just the right note of sweetness. Pesadic chocolates are nice with coffee.

Note: While the do-ahead tips that follow will help with advance preparations, so many dishes are needed at a Seder that I strongly urge you to splurge this one night and get help serving and cleaning up. Just do the math for the number of courses and the number of people and you'll see what I mean.

DO-AHEAD PLANNING

UP TO 1 MONTH IN ADVANCE: Bake and freeze the Hazelnut Torte. Make Matzoh Balls through Step 3. Freeze on sheet pans, then seal in plastic bags.

UP TO 3 DAYS IN ADVANCE: Make the Chicken Soup. Make the brisket; let cool, then slice the meat and refrigerate in its sauce. Or cook the meat up to a month in advance and freeze it (the flavor will be good, but it will lose some texture).

UP TO 2 DAYS IN ADVANCE: Make the haroset. Roast the egg and shank bone for the Seder plate. Roast the beets.

THE DAY BEFORE THE SEDER: Prepare the Gingered Carrots; refrigerate. Make the Mushroom-Matzoh Bake; let cool, then wrap in foil and refrigerate. Cook the potatoes for the Dilled Beet and Potato Salad and finish the salad. Make the berry compote and refrigerate it. Transfer the matzoh balls and hazelnut cake to the refrigerator to thaw.

THE MORNING OF THE SEDER: Chop the parsley and peel and slice the carrots for the chicken soup. Hard-cook the eggs, peel them, and return to the refrigerator in a bowl of lightly salted water.

ABOUT 2 HOURS BEFORE THE SEDER: Slowly bring the chicken soup to a boil. Remove from the heat and cover to keep warm. Reheat the brisket. Rinse the asparagus, shake dry, and spread out on 1 or 2 large baking sheets. Follow the recipe so that they are all ready to roast. Put the grated horseradish in bowls. Place the eggs in a couple of serving bowls and prepare small bowls of salt water for dipping.

ABOUT 1 HOUR BEFORE THE SEDER: Reheat the matzoh bake in the oven.

JUST BEFORE THE SEDER BEGINS: Set the soup over low heat and add the matzoh balls.

AFTER YOU SERVE THE GEFILTE FISH: Roast the asparagus. Reheat the carrots in a microwave or over low heat.

CHICKEN SOUP WITH MATZOH BALLS

12 TO 16 SERVINGS

The only difference between traditional chicken soup and ordinary chicken stock is the flavorings; the basic preparation is the same. I make mine with a large roaster and pick out the meat of one of the breasts in the middle of cooking for salad, sandwiches, or hash. A dusting of parsley and/or a few slices of cooked carrot are all this soup needs for garnish.

1 roasting chicken or stewing hen, 7 to 8 pounds

3 medium onions, halved

2 whole cloves, stuck into a couple of the onion halves

3 inner celery ribs with leaves

4 medium carrots, peeled and quartered

1 medium parsnip, peeled and quartered

1 medium turnip, peeled and quartered

½ bunch parsley stems

2 teaspoons black peppercorns

1 imported bay leaf

1 small head of garlic, cut crosswise in half

Coarse salt

Matzoh Balls (opposite page)

Sliced cooked carrots and chopped parsley, for garnish

1. Remove the giblets and pull all big globs of fat from the chicken cavity; render this fat and reserve it for the matzoh balls. Rinse the chicken inside and out under cold running water until no more blood appears. If you use a kosher chicken, there will be little or no blood, and you can just rinse it briefly. Put the chicken in a very large stockpot and cover with 8 quarts cold water. Bring to a boil, skimming off all the foam as it appears.

2. Add all the remaining ingredients up to and including the garlic, 6 more cups water, and 1 tablespoon coarse salt. Partially cover and simmer for 2 hours. At this point, you can remove the meat from one of the breasts and reserve it for chicken salad or sandwiches. At least one breast has to remain for flavor. Continue to simmer the soup for 3 to 4 hours longer, adding more water as necessary to maintain the level. (There should be at least 3 quarts of liquid.)

3. When the soup is done and very flavorful, ladle it through a fine-mesh sieve into another stockpot. Let cool, then chill overnight in the refrigerator. The next day, skim the congealed fat off the top.

4. If the soup is not used in 3 days, boil it up with the cover on and continue to boil for 5 to 10 minutes, then let cool and refrigerate again for up to 3 more days. Alternatively, the soup can be frozen in covered containers for at least 2 months.

5. Before serving, reheat the soup and season with salt to taste. Add the matzoh balls and sliced carrots and simmer just until heated through. Ladle into bowls and garnish each with a few slices of cooked carrot and a pinch of chopped parsley.

MATZOH BALLS

MAKES 24

Some like them hard, some like them soft, but almost everyone loves matzoh balls. This version adds a little extra flavor by adding bits of onion browned in chicken fat and oil as well as a little chopped parsley.

1 medium onion, minced

2 tablespoons rendered chicken fat

2 tablespoons peanut oil or other vegetable oil

6 eggs

2 teaspoons salt

¼ teaspoon freshly ground pepper

2 tablespoons chopped parsley

⅓ cup chicken soup or seltzer

1½ cups matzoh meal

1. Cook the onion in the chicken fat and peanut oil in a heavy medium skillet over moderate heat, stirring often, for 10 to 15 minutes, until the onion is uniformly golden brown. Remove from the heat and let cool.

2. In a large bowl, beat the eggs until blended with the salt, pepper, parsley, and chicken soup. Beat in the browned onions, scraping all the fat from the skillet into the bowl. Stir in the matzoh meal until well blended. Cover and refrigerate overnight.

3. The next day, bring a large pot of salted water to a boil. Roll the matzoh meal mixture between your hands into 24 balls the size of large walnuts. (If the paste begins to stick, rinse off your hands.) Add the matzoh balls to the pot, cover, and boil for 30 minutes.

4. With a skimmer, transfer the matzoh balls to a baking sheet lined with a clean kitchen towel. Transfer the matzoh balls to plastic bags or a covered container and refrigerate for up to 3 days. Or freeze on sheet pans; when the matzoh balls are hard, transfer them to containers and freeze for up to 2 months.

DILLED BEET AND POTATO SALAD

12 TO 16 SERVINGS AS AN ACCOMPANIMENT, 6 TO 8 SERVINGS AS A SIDE SALAD

Like many, I consider gefilte fish a delivery vehicle for plenty of strong horseradish, but this lovely salad dresses up the plate and complements the fish nicely. It's a dish that would also go beautifully with a range of tastes, from pickled herring to cold roast chicken or grilled flank steak.

6 medium beets

¼ cup red wine vinegar or cider vinegar

½ teaspoon sugar

6 medium-large Yukon gold potatoes

1 medium shallot, minced

¼ cup extra-virgin olive oil

Coarse salt and freshly ground pepper

½ cup coarsely chopped fresh dill

1. Heat the oven to 375°F. Cut off the tops of the beets, leaving just a couple of inches of stem. Wrap each beet or 2 together in heavy-duty foil and place directly on the rack of the oven. Roast for 45 to 60 minutes, until the tip of a small knife pierces the beets easily. Remove and let cool, then rub off the skin and cut the beets into ¼- to ⅜-inch dice. Toss with the vinegar and sugar to mix; let stand for at least 15 minutes.

2. Meanwhile, put the potatoes in a large pot of salted water, bring to a boil, and cook until tender, about 20 minutes. Drain and rinse under cold running water. Peel the skins, which will slip right off, and cut the potatoes into ⅜-inch dice.

3. In another bowl, toss together the warm potatoes with the shallot and olive oil until evenly coated. Season with salt and pepper to taste. Add the beets with the vinegar and the dill and toss gently to mix.

HAROSET WITH DATES AND APPLES

MAKES ABOUT 3 CUPS

The dates in haroset suggest a Lebanese origin, but in fact, there are as many recipes for this fruit and nut condiment as there are cooks. Today's food processor makes this ancient dish extremely easy to prepare. Just be sure when you pulse the apples and walnuts to leave some texture.

1 pound eating apples, such as McIntosh

5 ounces pitted dates (about 1 cup)

¾ to 1 cup Concord grape wine

5 ounces walnut pieces (1¼ cups)

2 teaspoons ground cinnamon

1. Peel and core the apples. Cut them into large chunks.

2. Put the dates and ¾ cup wine in a food processor and puree to a coarse paste. Add half the apples, two-thirds of the walnuts, and the cinnamon. Pulse to chop coarsely and blend with the date paste.

3. Add the remaining apples and walnuts and pulse until chopped. If the haroset tastes too dry, add a bit more wine. Cover and refrigerate for up to 2 days. Let return to cool room temperature before serving.

SWEET-AND-SOUR BRISKET WITH APRICOTS AND PRUNES

16 SERVINGS

Savory and satisfying, this sumptuous dish offers a nice change from the usual turkey. Look for the best-quality brisket you can buy and trim off all excess fat before seasoning the meat. More fat is removed after cooking and chilling, and it's good to know that this is one of those dishes that improve if allowed to stand overnight.

1 whole brisket, 8 to 9 pounds

Coarse salt and freshly ground pepper

3 tablespoons olive oil

3 medium onions, thinly sliced

¾ cup dry red wine

⅓ cup red wine vinegar or cider vinegar

2 tablespoons brown sugar

2 tablespoons tomato paste

½ teaspoon dried thyme

¼ teaspoon ground allspice

½ cup ketchup

12 ounces dried apricots (1½ cups), cut in half

12 ounces prunes (1½ cups), cut in half

1. Heat the oven to 275°F. Trim all excess fat from the brisket or ask your butcher to do this. Season each side with ½ teaspoon salt and ⅛ teaspoon pepper.

2. In a very large Dutch oven, preferably enameled cast iron, heat the olive oil over moderately high heat. Add the brisket and cook for about 5 minutes on each side, until nicely browned. (If you have to trim off a bit or even cut the brisket in half, don't worry; the meat is sliced before serving.) Remove to a plate.

3. Add the onions to the pan and stir to coat with the fat. Cover and cook for 7 to 10 minutes, stirring several times, until soft and lightly browned.

4. Stir in the wine and bring to a boil, scraping up any brown bits from the bottom of the pan with a wooden spatula. Add the vinegar, brown sugar, tomato paste, thyme, allspice, 1½ teaspoons salt, ½ teaspoon pepper, and ½ cup water. Stir to dissolve the tomato paste. Return the brisket to the pan. Spoon some of the sauce and onions up on top of the meat. Cover and braise in the oven for 2 hours.

5. Turn the meat over. Stir the ketchup into the sauce on the bottom of the pan and add half the apricots and prunes; scatter the remainder of the fruit over the brisket. Cover and braise for 2 hours longer. Let the meat stand in the covered casserole for 30 minutes. Then let cool and refrigerate until cold, preferably overnight.

6. Scrape any congealed fat off the top of the sauce. Slice the meat and cover with the sauce and fruit. Either reheat gently or freeze.

GINGERED CARROTS

12 TO 16 SERVINGS

Roll-cutting the carrots into triangular pieces (see Step 1) exposes the most surface area for even cooking and produces a nice chunky shape that is more attractive than slices. It's the spice of the ginger and slight hit of heat from the cayenne providing a counterpoint to the sweetness of the carrots and honey that makes this simple vegetable such a pleasing dish.

3 pounds carrots, preferably organic

⅓ cup olive oil

2 tablespoons minced shallots

2 tablespoons minced fresh ginger

½ teaspoon powdered ginger

¼ teaspoon freshly grated nutmeg

Salt and cayenne pepper

3 tablespoons honey, preferably wildflower

1. Trim and peel the carrots. Roll-cut them as follows: Slice down on a 45° angle to make a piece of carrot about ¾ inch long. Roll the carrot over a half-turn and make another cut. Repeat to produce triangular-shaped pieces of carrot. Alternatively, thickly slice the carrots.

2. In a large, heavy flameproof casserole, heat the oil over moderately low heat. Add the shallots and fresh ginger and cook for 2 minutes. Add the carrots and stir to coat. Season with the powdered ginger, nutmeg, a light dusting of salt, and a dash of cayenne. Pour in ⅓ cup water. Cover and cook slowly, stirring occasionally, for 15 to 20 minutes, until the carrots are just tender.

3. Stir in the honey and season with additional salt and cayenne to taste. Raise the heat slightly and cook until the carrots are tender and nicely glazed, about 5 minutes. Since the carrots will be reheated before serving, do not overcook them. Let cool, then refrigerate. Reheat gently before serving.

MUSHROOM-MATZOH BAKE

14 TO 16 SERVINGS

With one less egg, this mixture would make a great stuffing for a Passover turkey.

5 cups matzoh farfel

1½ cups chicken stock or chicken soup

2 pounds mushrooms, all white or a mix of white, cremini, and/or shiitake

½ cup plus 1 tablespoon extra-virgin olive oil

2 large shallots, minced

3 tablespoons fresh lemon juice

1½ teaspoons dried thyme

Salt, freshly ground black pepper, and cayenne pepper

⅓ cup chopped parsley

3 eggs, lightly beaten

1. In a large bowl, toss the matzoh farfel with the chicken stock. Let stand to soften.

2. Meanwhile, trim the very ends off the mushroom stems. If using shiitakes, remove the stems. Thinly slice half the mushrooms. Put the remaining mushrooms in a food processor and pulse until finely chopped.

3. Heat ¼ cup of the olive oil in a large skillet over moderately high heat. Add the shallots and cook for about 30 seconds. Add the chopped mushrooms and cook, stirring occasionally, for 5 minutes. Season with 1 tablespoon of the lemon juice, 1 teaspoon of the thyme, 1 teaspoon salt, ¼ teaspoon pepper, and about ⅛ teaspoon cayenne. Continue to cook, stirring often, until some of the mushroom liquid evaporates and the mixture begins to mass together, 7 to 10 minutes. Add to the matzoh farfel, scraping in anything left in the skillet, and blend well.

4. In the same skillet, heat another ¼ cup olive oil. Add half the sliced mushrooms. Season them with ½ teaspoon salt, a generous grinding of pepper, and a dash of cayenne. Sauté until nicely browned, about 10 minutes.

5. Push the cooked mushrooms to one side of the pan. Add the remaining sliced mushrooms, drizzle 1 tablespoon olive oil over them. Sauté for about 3 minutes, until the mushrooms soften. Stir all the sliced mushrooms together, add the remaining ½ teaspoon thyme, and continue to sauté for another 5 to 7 minutes, until all the mushrooms are cooked and some are nicely browned. Stir in the remaining 2 tablespoons lemon juice. Remove from the heat and let cool slightly.

6. Heat the oven to 375°F. Add the parsley and eggs to the matzoh farfel and blend well. Add the sliced mushrooms, scraping all the juices in the skillet into the bowl. Stir lightly to blend. Be sure the mixture is well seasoned. Turn into an oiled 9 × 13-inch baking dish. Bake for 25 minutes. Cut into squares to serve. (If baked ahead, wrap in foil. This dish reheats well.)

HAZELNUT TORTE WITH MIXED BERRY COMPOTE

12 TO 16 SERVINGS

The berry compote adds just the right touch of sweetness to this flourless cake.

Hazelnut Roulade batter (page 64)

2 pints strawberries or 1 bag (1 pound) individually quick-frozen strawberries without added sugar, thawed

½ cup seedless raspberry preserves

1 pint blueberries

½ to 1 pint raspberries

Sugar, optional

1. Prepare the batter for Hazelnut Roulade through Step 4; instead of buttering, lining, and flouring a sheet pan, prepare a 10-inch springform pan, using margarine instead of butter.

2. Turn the batter into the pan and bake for 45 minutes, or until a cake tester inserted in the center comes out clean. Let cool completely in the pan before unmolding.

3. Hull the strawberries, if necessary. Puree half of them in a food processor with the raspberry preserves.

4. Halve or quarter the remaining strawberries. In a bowl, toss them with the blueberries and raspberries. Add the strawberry-raspberry sauce and toss to coat. Taste and add sugar to taste only if necessary. Cover and set aside at room temperature for up to 6 hours or refrigerate overnight.

5. To serve, cut the torte into wedges. Spoon the berry compote over the cake.

THANKSGIVING FOR A CROWD

FOR 16 TO 20

CURRIED CARROT-GINGER SOUP

ROAST TURKEY WITH PECAN-CORNBREAD STUFFING

GIBLET PAN GRAVY

GRATIN OF SWEET POTATOES FLAMBÉED WITH BOURBON

BUTTERED PEAS

WILD RICE RISOTTO

BRAISED FENNEL AU GRATIN

CRANBERRY CHUTNEY (PAGE 18)

EASY CREAM CHEESECAKE

BITTERSWEET CHOCOLATE TORTE (PAGE 170)

Thanksgiving has always been one of my favorite holidays—not surprising since it is one of the great feast days of the year. Increasingly, I find myself host to a groaning board set not only for family and friends but for their children and their children's friends, with all the fun and disarray that such a crowd entails.

Curried Carrot-Ginger Soup is a great starter. It's one of my favorite soups, made easily with canned broth, and its piquant flavor acts like an aperitif to whet the appetite.

A grand turkey is called for, big enough to make everyone gasp with delight as it is hefted into the room. Three different vegetables, chosen for contrast of color, flavor, and texture; a delectable wild rice casserole; cornbread stuffing; thick dark gravy; and a jewel-red cranberry condiment make this a spectacular celebration indeed. It's fun to taste a little bit of a lot of things, and heaping plates are the order of the day.

And for dessert? Surprise, no pumpkin pie! It's a silky cream cheesecake and rich chocolate torte. I'm all in favor of the unexpected, especially when it takes the form of vanilla and chocolate and can be made well in advance. Let someone else bring the pies.

Because there is so much food to follow, I never offer hors d'oeuvre before the Thanksgiving meal. If you serve dinner at 2 P.M., I don't think anything is required. If you celebrate in the late afternoon or early evening, you could put out some nuts, chips, and cheese to hold over the exceptionally hungry and the children, who cannot wait.

Feeding a large group on this scale requires planning and organization. Because of the number of dishes, there is a lot to accomplish, even if most of the preparation has been done in advance. For that reason, I suggest a holiday checklist and a timetable to keep you on track.

DO-AHEAD PLANNING

UP TO 1 MONTH IN ADVANCE: Make the Easy Cream Cheesecake and the Bittersweet Chocolate Torte, if you're making that as well. Freeze the desserts.

UP TO 2 WEEKS IN ADVANCE: Make the Cranberry Chutney; store in the refrigerator. Bake the Sage Cornbread for the stuffing, cut into ¾-inch cubes, and freeze.

UP TO 2 DAYS IN ADVANCE: Make the Curried Carrot-Ginger Soup through Step 3. Make the Wild Rice Risotto. Partially cook the sweet potatoes for the gratin.

UP TO 1 DAY AHEAD: Make the Pecan-Cornbread Stuffing. Make the Turkey Stock for the Giblet Pan Gravy. Assemble the Gratin of Sweet Potatoes. Braise the fennel. Prepare the crumbs for the topping. Transfer the desserts to the refrigerator.

THANKSGIVING DAY—ABOUT 8 HOURS BEFORE YOU PLAN TO START SERVING: Take the turkey out of the refrigerator and rub it with the seasoning paste.

ABOUT 6 HOURS BEFORE YOU PLAN TO START SERVING: Stuff the turkey and put it into the oven to roast.

30 MINUTES BEFORE THE TURKEY IS DONE: Put the Gratin of Sweet Potatoes into the oven. Bake the extra stuffing. If your oven is not large enough, bake these while the turkey rests.

AS SOON AS THE TURKEY COMES OUT OF THE OVEN: Cover loosely with foil and set aside. (The turkey will stay warm for at least 45 minutes.) Increase the oven temperature to 450°F and finish the Gratin of Sweet Potatoes. Gratinée the fennel. Make the Giblet Pan Gravy. Reheat, finish, and serve the soup.

WHILE SOMEONE ELSE CARVES THE TURKEY AT TABLE: Reheat the Wild Rice Risotto in a microwave (or set it in the oven earlier). Make the peas, using 3 or 4 packages of "tiny tender peas" and cooking them 1 minute less than directed on the package before tossing them with butter. Flambé the Gratin of Sweet Potatoes as you carry it to the table.

CURRIED CARROT-GINGER SOUP

18 TO 20 SERVINGS

Root vegetables sound humble, but this blend of sweet carrots, pungent fresh ginger, and flavorful spices makes an exceptionally delicious soup. My only advice is: Get help peeling the carrots! The type of curry powder you use will make an enormous difference in flavor. I use Sun Brand Madras.

8 tablespoons (1 stick) unsalted butter

3 tablespoons olive oil

4 medium onions, sliced

½ cup coarsely chopped fresh ginger

2 tablespoons Madras curry powder

1½ tablespoons ground cumin

½ cup all-purpose flour

1 large can (32 ounces) plus 1 small can (13¾ ounces) chicken broth (about 10 cups)

3 pounds carrots, peeled and thickly sliced

3 dashes of cayenne pepper

Salt

1 cup sour cream

1 cup plain yogurt

1. In a large flameproof casserole, melt the butter in the oil over moderate heat. Add the onions and cook, stirring occasionally, until golden brown, about 10 minutes. Add the ginger, curry powder, and cumin and cook, stirring, for 1 minute. Add the flour and cook, stirring, for 1 to 2 minutes without browning.

2. Add the chicken broth and bring to a boil, stirring frequently. Add the carrots, cayenne, and 4 cups water. Simmer, partially covered, for 20 minutes, or until the carrots are tender. Remove from the heat.

3. Puree the soup, in batches, in a blender or food processor. (The recipe can be made to this point up to 2 days ahead. Cover and refrigerate.)

4. Reheat the soup. If it is too thick for your liking, thin with a little more water. Season with salt and additional cayenne to taste.

5. In a small bowl, blend the sour cream and yogurt. Ladle the hot soup into bowls and top with a dollop of the yogurt cream. Garnish with a sprinkle of cumin.

ROAST TURKEY WITH PECAN-CORNBREAD STUFFING

16 TO 20 SERVINGS

Order a fresh turkey from a good butcher if you can. This is a big bird, which will take a long time to roast. Allow at least 20 minutes after cooking for the juices to return to the meat. Since turkey can easily stay warm for 45 minutes before serving, play it safe and allow 5½ to 6 hours from the time the turkey goes into the oven until serving time.

1 turkey, 16 to 20 pounds, preferably fresh

1 large onion, coarsely chopped

1 tablespoon imported sweet paprika

1 tablespoon coarse salt

1 teaspoon freshly ground black pepper

¼ teaspoon cayenne pepper

⅓ cup extra-virgin olive oil

Pecan-Cornbread Stuffing (page 128)

8 tablespoons (1 stick) unsalted butter, cut into pieces

1. Remove the turkey from the refrigerator 1½ hours before roasting. If you haven't removed them earlier, set the giblets aside for the stock and gravy. Pull out any excess fat from the large cavity. Rinse the turkey inside and out with cold running water and dry well with paper towels.

2. In a food processor, combine the onion with the paprika, salt, black pepper, cayenne, and 2 tablespoons of the olive oil. Puree to a paste. Rub this seasoning paste all over the turkey, inside and out. Set the turkey in its roasting pan and let stand at room temperature, uncovered, for 1½ hours. When it's time, heat the oven to 425°F.

3. Fill the turkey loosely with the stuffing; it will hold 6 to 7 cups. Pack the remainder into a buttered baking dish, cover, and refrigerate. Truss the turkey.

4. In a small saucepan, melt the butter in the remaining olive oil. Dip a doubled-up rectangle of cheesecloth (at least 4 layers thick) into the melted butter. Drape over the turkey breast.

5. Roast the turkey for 30 minutes. Baste the legs and thighs with some of the butter left in the saucepan. Reduce the oven temperature to 325°F and roast the turkey for 3 to 4 hours, or until the meat in the thickest part of the thigh registers 155° to 160°F on an instant-read thermometer. Remove the cheesecloth, baste the turkey all over, and roast, basting every 20 minutes, for about 1 hour longer, or until the thigh registers 175° to 180°F.

6. Remove the turkey to a carving board. Loosely cover with foil and let stand for at least 20 minutes before carving. Reserve the drippings for the pan gravy on page 130.

PECAN-CORNBREAD STUFFING

MAKES ABOUT 12 CUPS

Fill the turkey loosely with as much stuffing as it will hold (stuffing expands as it cooks). Spoon any extra into a buttered baking dish and bake it during the last 30 minutes the turkey roasts. Bake the cornbread a day before you prepare the stuffing so it has time to dry out.

1 recipe Sage Cornbread (opposite page) or your favorite packaged cornbread

1½ cups broken or coarsely chopped pecans

8 tablespoons (1 stick) unsalted butter

⅓ cup olive oil

4 medium onions, chopped

3 celery ribs with leaves, chopped

5 garlic cloves, chopped

3 eggs

½ cup chopped parsley

1 teaspoon crumbled dried sage leaves

1 tablespoon salt

1 teaspoon coarsely cracked black pepper

⅛ teaspoon cayenne pepper

1½ teaspoons grated orange zest

½ cup fresh orange juice

1 to 1½ cups turkey or chicken stock

1. Cut the cornbread into ¾-inch cubes. Put them and any crumbs into a large bowl and let stand, tossing occasionally, for at least 6 hours or overnight, to dry out.

2. Heat the oven to 325°F. Spread out the pecans on a baking sheet and toast in the oven for 8 to 10 minutes, or until lightly browned and fragrant. Pour onto a plate and let cool.

3. In a large skillet or flameproof casserole, melt the butter in the oil over moderate heat. Add the onions, cover, and cook for 5 minutes. Uncover, add the celery, and cook, stirring occasionally, until the onions are golden, 15 to 20 minutes. Add the garlic and cook for 1 to 2 minutes longer, until fragrant. Scrape the vegetable mixture over the cornbread.

4. In a small bowl, beat the eggs with a fork until blended. Beat in the parsley, sage, salt, black pepper, cayenne, and orange zest. Pour over the cornbread. Add the pecans and toss to mix. Add the orange juice and ½ cup of the stock and toss again. Add enough remaining stock so that the stuffing is moist but not soggy. Cover and refrigerate for up to a day before stuffing and roasting the turkey.

SAGE CORNBREAD

16 TO 20 SERVINGS

Sage is a traditional seasoning for turkey, so I assumed it would go well with cornbread meant for stuffing a turkey, and it does. The herb is surprisingly assertive, so you don't need too much, but it does contribute a pleasant, almost piney undercurrent.

4 cups stone-ground cornmeal

1½ cups all-purpose flour

¼ cup sugar

1 tablespoon plus 1 teaspoon baking powder

¾ teaspoon baking soda

1½ teaspoons salt

⅔ cup loosely packed parsley sprigs

5 fresh sage leaves, cut up, or 1½ teaspoons dried

8 tablespoons (1 stick) unsalted butter

4 eggs

2 cups milk

1 cup half-and-half or light cream

1. As far ahead as you feel like it, combine the cornmeal, flour, sugar, baking powder, baking soda, and salt in a large bowl. Whisk to blend well.

2. Put 1 cup of the cornmeal mixture, the parsley, and sage in a food processor and process until the herbs are minced. Add to the remaining dry ingredients and whisk to blend.

3. Heat the oven to 425°F. Melt the butter and let cool to tepid.

4. Just before you're ready to cook the cornbread, whisk the eggs to blend them. Gradually beat in the milk and half-and-half. Add the liquid to the dry ingredients. Add the melted butter and mix just until blended.

5. Pour the batter into a buttered 13 × 18-inch half-sheet pan and bake for 25 minutes, or until the cornbread is browned on top and a tester comes out clean.

GIBLET PAN GRAVY

MAKES ABOUT 3 CUPS

Some people are stymied by making gravy, but as long as you have your stock on hand, it's really very simple. Minced shallots contribute a lovely aromatic note, but shallots can burn quickly, so watch closely when you cook them.

Turkey giblets (heart, gizzard, and neck), reserved from Turkey Stock (opposite page)

Drippings from Roast Turkey (page 127)

2 large shallots, minced

⅓ cup all-purpose flour

3½ cups Turkey Stock (opposite page)

3 tablespoons unsalted butter

Salt and freshly ground pepper

1. Cut the cooked heart and gizzard into ¼-inch dice. Pull the meat off the neck bone and cut it into small pieces if the shreds are long. (Do this ahead of time.)

2. As soon as your turkey is done, set it aside on a carving board, loosely covered with foil to keep warm. Pour off and reserve the juices, leaving about ¼ cup of fat in the roasting pan. Set the pan on top of the stove, add the shallots, and cook over moderate heat for 1 to 2 minutes, until softened. Sprinkle on the flour and cook, stirring frequently, for 2 minutes. Pour in the stock and bring to a boil, scraping up the brown bits from the bottom and sides of the pan with a wooden spoon. Add the diced giblets, reduce the heat, and simmer for 2 to 3 minutes, stirring occasionally.

3. Remove from the heat and whisk in the butter, 1 tablespoon at a time. Season with salt and pepper to taste. Pour into a sauce boat and pass with the turkey.

TURKEY STOCK

MAKES 3½ CUPS

Making your own stock will transform the entire Thanksgiving meal, since it is used for both the stuffing and the gravy and its flavor is greatly superior to canned stock. Very likely, you'll already have the ingredients on hand, so just try to find a couple of free hours a day or two before the meal to allow them to render their flavors.

Turkey neck, heart, gizzard, and wing tips

1 large onion, thickly sliced

1 large carrot, peeled and thickly sliced

2 garlic cloves, smashed

1 celery rib, quartered

8 parsley stems

2 ounces fresh mushrooms, sliced, or mushroom trimmings, optional

12 black peppercorns

¼ teaspoon dried thyme

1 imported bay leaf

1. Rinse off the turkey neck; cut it into 1- to 1½-inch pieces. Trim off the fat from the heart and gizzard.

2. Put all the ingredients in a heavy medium saucepan. Add 6 cups of water, or more, to cover. Bring to a boil over moderately high heat, skimming off the foam occasionally. Reduce the heat to low and simmer, adding water as needed to keep the ingredients covered, for 2 hours. Strain and skim off the fat.

3. Pour the stock into a clean saucepan and boil until reduced to 3½ cups.

GRATIN OF SWEET POTATOES FLAMBÉED WITH BOURBON

16 TO 20 SERVINGS

This easy dish is formed just like a French apple tart—minus the pastry. It is only slightly sweet and can make a grand entrance if you choose to flambé it in front of your guests. For best presentation, use a very large, round ovenproof dish—I use my 15-inch paella pan—though it can be prepared in one or even two baking dishes of any sort.

6 pounds large sweet potatoes

10 tablespoons unsalted butter, at room temperature

½ teaspoon salt

½ teaspoon freshly ground pepper

¼ cup sugar

½ to ⅔ cup bourbon, to taste

1. Put the sweet potatoes in a large pot of cold water. Bring to a boil over moderately high heat and cook for about 20 minutes, until about 1 inch of the potatoes is tender around the edges but they are still firm in the center. Drain and rinse with cold water. When they are cool enough to handle, peel the potatoes with a knife—the skins will come off easily. (The potatoes can be cooked a day ahead. Wrap in plastic wrap and refrigerate.)

2. Use 1 tablespoon of the butter to grease a large baking dish, preferably 15 inches round. Cut the sweet potatoes into ¼-inch rounds. Arrange the slices, overlapping, in the dish in concentric circles, as you would a French apple tart. The finished arrangement should look something like a rose. Smear the remaining softened butter all over the potatoes, covering them as well as you can. Season with the salt and pepper. Sprinkle the sugar evenly over the potatoes. (The recipe can be prepared ahead to this point. Set aside at room temperature for up to 3 hours or cover and refrigerate overnight. Let return to room temperature before proceeding.)

3. Heat the oven to 325°F. Bake the sweet potatoes, uncovered, for 30 minutes. Increase the heat to 450°F and bake for 15 to 20 minutes, or until the potatoes are tender and lightly glazed.

4. Pour the bourbon into a small nonreactive saucepan. Warm over low heat for 20 to 30 seconds. Carefully ignite the bourbon with a match and drizzle the flaming liquid over the sweet potatoes.

WILD RICE RISOTTO

18 TO 24 SERVINGS

Sometimes you want a side dish that's a little out of the ordinary, and this one serves well. Wild rice adds a slightly luxuriant note, while the earthiness of the mushrooms and saltiness of the ham and soy provide pleasant contrast to some of the sweeter elements of the Thanksgiving meal.

3 ounces imported dried mushrooms

1½ pounds wild rice (3¼ cups)

4 tablespoons unsalted butter

1½ tablespoons olive oil

2 medium onions, chopped

2 medium celery ribs with leaves, finely diced

2 medium carrots, peeled and finely diced

3 garlic cloves, minced

⅓ pound thickly sliced Black Forest or baked ham, finely diced

2 cans (13¾ ounces each) chicken broth

1 can (13¾ ounces) beef broth

1½ tablespoons soy sauce

¾ teaspoon dried thyme

½ teaspoon freshly ground pepper

1. Put the mushrooms in a medium bowl. Pour on 4 cups boiling water and let soak for 20 minutes, or until soft. Remove the mushrooms from the liquid, squeeze dry, and finely dice. Strain the soaking liquid through a double layer of dampened cheesecloth and reserve 2½ cups.

2. Rinse the wild rice well. Boil in a large saucepan of salted water for 10 minutes; drain.

3. Heat the oven to 350°F. In a large flameproof casserole, melt the butter in the oil over moderate heat. Add the onions and cook for 5 minutes. Add the celery, carrots, garlic, and ham and cook, stirring occasionally, until the onions are golden and the other vegetables are softened, 5 to 10 minutes longer.

4. Add the wild rice and diced mushrooms; stir to blend with the oil and vegetables. Add the chicken broth, beef broth, reserved mushroom liquid, soy sauce, thyme, and pepper. Cover and bake for 50 minutes. (The rice can be made ahead up to 2 days in advance. Transfer to a bowl and refrigerate, covered. Before serving, microwave to heat through or reheat in a covered casserole in a 350°F oven for 20 to 30 minutes.)

BRAISED FENNEL AU GRATIN

16 SERVINGS

This dish combines the deep, toasted flavor of long-braised fennel with the pleasant crunch of a crisp browned topping.

½ cup plus 2 tablespoons extra-virgin olive oil

5 large fennel bulbs, cut lengthwise into ½-inch slices, plus ½ cup coarsely chopped fennel fronds

8 garlic cloves, unpeeled

Salt and freshly ground pepper

2 cups chicken stock or water

3 slices firm-textured white bread

¼ cup freshly grated imported Parmesan cheese

1. Heat the oven to 375°F. In a large heavy skillet, heat ¼ cup of the oil. Fry the fennel slices with the garlic in batches over moderately high heat until the fennel is lightly browned, 1½ to 2 minutes per side. Leave the garlic in until it is softened but do not let it brown. Add more oil as needed; it will probably take another ¼ cup. Transfer the fennel and garlic to a large gratin or baking dish and season with salt and pepper.

2. Pour the stock into the skillet. Bring to a boil, scraping up any browned bits from the bottom of the pan, and pour over the fennel. Cover the dish tightly with foil and bake for 10 minutes. Uncover the pan and bake for 15 to 20 minutes, basting once or twice with the liquid in the pan, until the fennel is just tender. (The recipe can be prepared to this point up to a day ahead. Let cool to room temperature, cover, and refrigerate.)

3. Tear the bread into a food processor. Add the fennel fronds and the cheese. Process until the bread is ground into crumbs and the mixture is well blended.

4. Heat the oven (or increase the temperature) to 450°F. Sprinkle the bread crumb topping all over the fennel and drizzle on 2 tablespoons olive oil. Bake until the fennel is heated through and the topping is crisp and golden brown, 15 to 20 minutes.

EASY CREAM CHEESECAKE

12 TO 16 SERVINGS

No doubt, you've tasted this elementally simple dessert before but probably never realized it was quite this easy to make. Serve it plain or with any fruit topping of your choice.

⅓ box (⅓ pound) graham crackers, broken up

1¼ cups plus 2 tablespoons sugar

8 tablespoons (1 stick) unsalted butter, cut into pieces

4 packages (8 ounces each) cream cheese, at room temperature

6 eggs

1¾ teaspoons vanilla extract

1 pint (2 cups) sour cream

Fresh raspberries or strawberries, for garnish, optional

1. Heat the oven to 375°F. In a food processor, grind the graham crackers to crumbs along with 2 tablespoons of the sugar.

2. Melt the butter. Add the graham cracker crumbs and mix to moisten evenly. Dump this mixture into a 10-inch springform pan. With your fingers, pat it evenly all over the bottom and about 1 inch up the sides.

3. In a large bowl, beat the cream cheese with an electric mixer until light and fluffy. Gradually beat in 1 cup of the sugar. Beat in the eggs, 1 at a time, until well blended. Beat in 1½ teaspoons of the vanilla. Pour into the springform pan and smooth the top.

4. Put on a baking sheet or place a piece of foil under the pan to catch any drips and bake for 15 minutes. Reduce the oven temperature to 325°F and bake for 25 minutes longer.

5. Meanwhile, in a bowl, blend together the sour cream with the remaining ¼ cup sugar and ¼ teaspoon vanilla.

6. Remove the cheesecake from the oven and let cool on a rack for 10 minutes. Leave the oven on. Spoon the sour cream topping over the cheesecake, spreading evenly to the edges. Return to the oven and bake for 10 minutes. Let the cheesecake cool completely in the pan. Cover the pan and refrigerate until chilled, at least 6 hours or overnight.

7. Before serving, run a knife around the edge of the cake and remove the side of the springform. Garnish the cheesecake with fresh berries, if desired.

Christmas Dinner

FOR 16 TO 20

MAPLE-BUTTERNUT BISQUE

HAM BRAISED IN PORT

POTATOES AU GRATIN

GLAZED CARROTS AND SNOW PEAS

ZUCCHINI BREAD FROM THE INN AT THORN HILL

PINEAPPLE AND CHERRIES JUBILEE

OLD-FASHIONED SUGAR COOKIES

OTHER ASSORTED CHRISTMAS COOKIES

Irving Berlin's "White Christmas" left me with an indelible childhood impression of what Christmas should be like. I don't care if the sun is shining, if I find myself blinking at date palms strung with colored lights across a harbor in San Diego or poinsettias grown to 12 feet in height on a remote island in the Bahamas. Come December 25, I hear sleigh bells ringing and see evergreen treetops glistening in the snow: Christmas is always in New England . . . and here are the dishes to prove it.

Soup is the easiest first course to have ready and waiting, and this one, lightly sweetened with maple syrup, is lovely and perfect for the season. A dash of cayenne adds a sophisticated counterpoint to the subtle sweetness. If you have an immersion blender, you can even prepare it all in one pot.

Marinate the ham 2 days before you plan to serve it. Since the meat is precooked, it is braised only for the time it takes to heat through—about 1½ hours for an 8-pound ham—with another half hour to glaze the outside. In terms of scheduling, the easiest way is to put up the ham so that it is completely finished and out of the oven before you begin serving the soup. Just set it aside, loosely covered with foil. It will stay hot for at least 45 minutes, and ham is just as good, if not better, at room temperature.

Potatoes au Gratin are best made with the sharpest aged Vermont Cheddar you can find. Snow peas and carrots, lightly glazed with butter and sugar, make a colorful accompaniment that is slightly different. The Inn at Thorn Hill in Jackson, New Hampshire, looks as if Bing Crosby slept there—or maybe it was Irving Berlin. Originally designed by famous architect Stanford White, it fits my image of a Christmas setting to a tee. So I couldn't resist including their excellent recipe for Zucchini Bread. If you prefer to get your baking done well ahead, the bread freezes perfectly.

Plum pudding represents the traditional Christmas dessert, but its dense sweetness is not to everyone's contemporary taste. Since the drama of a flaming dessert remains so appealing, though, especially in winter, here you get the flames without the weight: cherries jubilee updated with fresh pineapple—a Colonial symbol of welcome and warm hospitality. How perfect for the Christmas season. For the full effect, dim the lights and flambé the dessert in front of your guests. It sounds corny, but everyone loves it. The dessert can be served over vanilla ice cream or with a square of pound cake thrown in as well. Old-Fashioned Sugar Cookies, or your favorite Christmas cookies, will add a pleasing crispness over tea or coffee.

DO-AHEAD PLANNING

UP TO 2 MONTHS IN ADVANCE: Prepare the dough for the Old-Fashioned Sugar Cookies through Step 4; freeze.

UP TO 3 DAYS IN ADVANCE: Bake the Zucchini Bread.

NO LESS THAN 2 DAYS BEFOREHAND: Marinate the ham.

THE DAY BEFORE CHRISTMAS: Make the Maple-Butternut Bisque. Prepare the Potatoes au Gratin. Prepare the pineapple and cherry base for the jubilee through Step 3.

ABOUT 2½ HOURS BEFORE YOU PLAN TO BEGIN SERVING CHRISTMAS DINNER: Bake the ham. Blanch the snow peas and carrots.

ABOUT 30 MINUTES BEFORE DINNER: Reheat the soup. Bake the Potatoes au Gratin.

SHORTLY BEFORE SERVING: Finish the snow peas and carrots. Complete the Pineapple and Cherries Jubilee and flambé just before carrying it in. Ladle over scoops of ice cream at the table.

MAPLE-BUTTERNUT BISQUE

16 TO 20 SERVINGS

This is one of my favorite winter soups. Baking the squash whole keeps them moist and flavorful.

6 pounds butternut or acorn squash

12 tablespoons (1½ sticks) unsalted butter

3 large onions, coarsely chopped

½ cup all-purpose flour

3 cups milk

3 cans (13¾ ounces each) chicken broth

⅜ teaspoon cayenne pepper

1½ teaspoons salt

1½ cups heavy cream

⅓ cup plus 1 tablespoon pure maple syrup

1½ cups pecans, toasted and coarsely chopped

1. Heat the oven to 350°F. Pierce each squash in several places with the tip of a knife and bake until soft, 45 minutes to 1 hour. Remove and let cool slightly, then cut in half, scoop out and discard the seeds and stringy membranes, and scoop the squash into a bowl.

2. In a large flameproof casserole or heavy stockpot, melt the butter over moderately low heat. Add the onions and cook, stirring occasionally, until golden brown, about 30 minutes.

3. Sprinkle the flour over the onions, increase the heat to moderate, and cook, stirring, for about 2 minutes to make a roux. Whisk in the milk and chicken broth. Bring to a boil, stirring frequently. Season with the cayenne and salt.

4. In batches in a blender or food processor, puree the baked squash with the soup base until smooth. Return to the pot, add the cream and maple syrup, and simmer for 10 minutes to blend the flavors. Check the seasoning; if there is not a little bite to contrast with the slight sweetness of the squash and maple syrup, add more cayenne to taste. (The soup can be made a day ahead and refrigerated or weeks ahead and frozen.) Serve hot, garnished with a sprinkling of toasted pecans.

HAM BRAISED IN PORT

16 TO 20 SERVINGS

Ham has such a strong flavor that anything you add to it still plays second fiddle. However, I love the touch of sweetness and nuttiness that port imparts, and the resulting sauce is a nice addition to the holiday table.

1 boneless ham, about 8 pounds

1 bottle of port, such as Sandeman Tawny Port or Croft Distinction

1 cup packed dark brown sugar

2 tablespoons Dijon mustard

Whole cloves

1 tablespoon cornstarch

1 to 2 teaspoons lemon juice

Freshly ground pepper

1. With a barbecue skewer, poke the ham all over at 1½- to 2-inch intervals. Put the ham in a heavy oval casserole or nonreactive roasting pan. Pour the port over the ham, cover, and marinate in the refrigerator, turning occasionally, for 2 days. Let stand at room temperature for 1 to 2 hours before cooking.

Christmas Baskets

There's no gift as special as a homemade one, and every year I try to give Christmas baskets to those friends and associates I really care about. The best baskets are filled with little goodies, buried here and there with one or two larger gifts. I like to include some store-bought items and some homemade, some edible and some ornamental. The trick is to begin early in the year and collect things as you find them.

I use all kinds of baskets—woven rush, wicker, wooden mushroom crates. I collect them whenever I see them, often in antiques shops, country stores that sell dried flowers as well as fruits and vegetables, at five-and-dime stores, and in markets that sell baskets from the Orient. I line them with a printed napkin or with colored tissue paper. Inside may go a bar of scented soap, a nutmeg grater with a few whole nutmegs inside, a bunch of cinnamon sticks tied with a ribbon, always at least one unusual handmade Christmas ornament.

Something should be personalized. One year we included little notebooks, which my husband hand painted, a different design on the cover of each. I make decorated cookies and candies and sometimes preserves. If the basket is being personally delivered, you could include the Cranberry Chutney (page 18) in a small jelly jar with a piece of gingham tied around the top with a ribbon. Label "Refrigerate upon receipt" and mention there is something that needs refrigerating when you hand it over.

Rich Chocolate Sauce (page 31) would also make a lovely gift, or bake mini loaves of Zucchini Bread (page 142). Individually wrapped brownies (pages 178 and 186) and Butter Pecan Turtle Squares (page 218) are guaranteed to be a hit. When everything is assembled, I fill in with found objects—pinecones, sprigs of evergreen, holly, tiny toys. Colored tissue paper is tucked around everything, the basket covered with paper, and a bow and card attached to the top. Merry Christmas!

2. Heat the oven to 325°F. Put the ham in the oven and braise, covered, basting with the port every 15 to 20 minutes, until the ham is just heated through, about 1½ hours. The internal temperature should measure about 125°F. Remove from the oven.

3. Increase the oven temperature to 375°F. Transfer the ham to a shallow roasting pan; reserve all the cooking juices. In a small bowl, combine the brown sugar, 1 cup of the cooking juices, and 1 tablespoon of the mustard; blend well.

4. Score the ham in a diamond pattern and stud with cloves. Baste with the brown sugar mixture and return to the oven. Roast, basting frequently, for 30 minutes, or until the ham is heated through and nicely glazed. Remove to a carving board and cover with foil to keep warm.

5. Pour 3 cups of the cooking liquid into the roasting pan and bring to a boil on top of the stove, scraping up any brown bits from the bottom of the pan. Pour the juices into a small nonreactive saucepan. Boil until the juices are reduced to 2 cups. Whisk in the remaining 1 tablespoon mustard. Dissolve the cornstarch in 2 tablespoons water and stir into the sauce. Bring to a boil, stirring until thickened and smooth. Season with the lemon juice and pepper to taste. Pour into a gravy boat and serve with the ham.

POTATOES AU GRATIN

16 TO 20 SERVINGS AT A SIT-DOWN DINNER, 30 SERVINGS AS PART OF A BUFFET

Old-fashioned and classic, these creamy potatoes are guaranteed to be a hit. As with all recipes that use a lot of cheese, the better the quality, the better the results.

8 pounds red-skinned or Yukon gold potatoes

12 tablespoons (1½ sticks) unsalted butter

⅔ cup all-purpose flour

6 cups milk

3 garlic cloves, crushed through a press

2½ teaspoons salt

½ teaspoon freshly ground black pepper

¼ teaspoon cayenne pepper

1 pound sharp well-aged Cheddar cheese, shredded

1. Put the potatoes in 1 or 2 large pots, cover with cold salted water by at least an inch, and bring to a boil over high heat. Boil for 15 to 20 minutes, or until tender but not mushy; drain. When the potatoes are cool enough to handle, peel them and cut into ½-inch dice. Put in a large bowl.

2. Heat the oven to 475°F. In a large saucepan or flameproof casserole, melt 1 stick plus 2 tablespoons of the butter over moderate heat. Add the flour and cook, stirring, for 2 minutes without allowing the flour to color. Whisk in the milk. Bring to a boil, whisking constantly, until smooth and thickened. Add the garlic, salt, black pepper, and cayenne. Reduce the heat to low and simmer, whisking occasionally, for 10 minutes. Stir in all but ½ cup of the cheese and cook, whisking, until the cheese is melted and the sauce is smooth. The sauce should be the consistency of thick molasses. If it seems too thick, thin with a little additional milk. Add the cheese sauce to the potatoes and toss to mix.

3. Turn the potatoes into 2 large buttered gratin or shallow baking dishes. Sprinkle the remaining cheese evenly over the top and dot with the remaining 2 tablespoons butter. (The recipe can be made to this point up to a day ahead. Cover and refrigerate. Remove from the refrigerator about 1 hour before baking.)

4. Bake the potatoes, uncovered, for 20 to 25 minutes, or until they are bubbling hot and the top is lightly browned.

GLAZED CARROTS AND SNOW PEAS

16 TO 20 SERVINGS

Once the vegetables are prepared, which can be done hours in advance, this colorful dish can be thrown together in minutes. While I suggest finishing them off in two batches, if you prefer, you could do them all at once in two pans.

2 pounds carrots

1 pound snow peas

8 tablespoons (1 stick) unsalted butter

3 tablespoons sugar

1 teaspoon powdered ginger

Salt and freshly ground pepper

1. Peel the carrots and cut them into sticks about 2 inches long, ½ inch wide, and ¼ inch thick. Trim the snow peas and pull off the strings.

2. In a large pot of boiling salted water, cook the carrots until just barely tender, about 5 minutes. Add the snow peas and drain immediately into a colander. Rinse under cold running water; drain well. (The vegetables can be prepared to this point up to 4 hours in advance. Set aside at room temperature.)

3. In a wok or large skillet, melt 4 tablespoons of the butter over moderately high heat. Add half the carrots and snow peas. Sprinkle on 1½ tablespoons of the sugar and ½ teaspoon of the ginger; cook, tossing, until the sugar dissolves and the vegetables are hot, 2 to 3 minutes. Season with salt and pepper to taste. Turn into a large serving bowl; cover to keep warm. Repeat with the remaining ingredients.

ZUCCHINI BREAD FROM THE INN AT THORN HILL

MAKES 2 LOAVES

This scrumptious batter bread has just the perfect balance of sweetness, vanilla, and spice. Serve as you would a cranberry or nut bread or enjoy it with coffee for breakfast or at teatime. For good results, you must use a metal loaf pan; heatproof glass will not yield the same results, with this or any other quick bread recipe.

3 medium zucchini

4 eggs

2⅔ cups sugar

1⅓ cups corn oil or other neutral-flavored vegetable oil

1 tablespoon vanilla extract

4 cups all-purpose flour

1 teaspoon baking powder

1½ teaspoons baking soda

1½ teaspoons ground cinnamon

⅛ teaspoon salt

1 cup walnut halves, broken into large pieces, optional

1. Heat the oven to 350°F. Grease and flour 2 metal loaf pans, 5 × 9 × 3 inches.

2. Shred the zucchini; I use the grating disk on my food processor. Measure out 2⅔ packed cups.

3. In a large bowl, whisk the eggs. Gradually beat in the sugar, then slowly whisk in the oil and vanilla. Stir in the zucchini.

4. In another bowl, gently whisk the flour, baking powder, baking soda, cinnamon, and salt to mix evenly. Add the dry ingredients to the egg mixture and beat with a wooden spoon for 2 minutes, or until well blended. Stir in the nuts.

5. Pour the batter into the 2 loaf pans and rap on the counter to settle any air bubbles. Bake for 1 hour 15 minutes, or until a tester comes out clean. Let cool in the pan for 10 minutes, then unmold and let cool completely on a rack. Wrap well and refrigerate for up to 2 days or freeze for up to 2 months.

PINEAPPLE AND CHERRIES JUBILEE

ABOUT 24 SERVINGS

Dramatically carried to the table with blue flames licking the edges of the bowl, this old-fashioned standby, updated with fresh pineapple, proves why it's always been a favorite. Serve over scoops of vanilla ice cream.

2 bags (20 ounces each) individually quick-frozen sweet cherries without added sugar

⅔ cup kirsch (cherry brandy)

⅔ cup sugar

1 large ripe pineapple

2 tablespoons cornstarch

½ cup Cognac or brandy

½ to 1 gallon French vanilla ice cream

1. Up to 3 days before you plan to serve the fruit, thaw the cherries in the refrigerator. Dump them with their juice into a large bowl. Add the kirsch and sprinkle on ⅓ cup of the sugar; toss gently to mix. Cover and refrigerate.

2. Cut the top off the pineapple. Using a large sharp stainless steel knife, cut down along the sides to remove the thick skin and the spiny brown "eyes." Lay the pineapple on its side and cut into ½-inch-thick slices. Cut down around the core of each slice to make strips and then cut the strips into ½-inch dice. Add the pineapple to the cherries. Cover and refrigerate overnight.

3. Drain the fruit, reserving the juice. Return the fruit to a heatproof glass serving bowl. Cover and refrigerate. Pour the juice into a small nonreactive saucepan. Add the remaining ⅓ cup sugar and bring to a boil over moderate heat, stirring to dissolve the sugar. In a small bowl, combine the cornstarch with 2 tablespoons water; stir to dissolve. Stir the dissolved cornstarch into the sauce and boil, stirring, until thickened and smooth, 1 to 2 minutes. (The sauce keeps well in the refrigerator for up to 3 days. Bring it back to room temperature before proceeding.)

4. Just before serving, reheat the sauce and pour over the fruit. Add the Cognac to the same saucepan and heat for a few seconds, until just warm. Ignite with a match and pour over the fruit. Carefully make a grand entrance with the dramatic blue flames dancing over the fruit.

5. Scoop the ice cream into serving dishes and ladle the fruit and sauce on top.

OLD-FASHIONED SUGAR COOKIES

MAKES ABOUT 90 COOKIES

I call these old-fashioned because the recipe was given to me many years ago by Ruth Smith, a local Pennsylvania baker who was then in her 80s. It was her idea—rather than repeatedly rolling out the dough, which is the hard part—to form it into wide logs that could be stored in the refrigerator or freezer and then sliced and baked off fresh whenever you wanted some cookies. There is nothing old-fashioned about the taste, consisting as it does of pure sweet butter, which gives these their lovely crispness, and real vanilla extract. If you want to go the extra mile, or if you have some eager young bakers who want to help, these are perfect cookies for decorating with crystal sugar or royal icing for Christmas.

3⅔ cups all-purpose flour

2 teaspoons baking powder

½ teaspoon salt

2 sticks (½ pound) unsalted butter, at room temperature

2 cups sugar

3 eggs

¾ teaspoon baking soda

1½ teaspoons vanilla extract

1. Sift together the flour, baking powder, and salt. Set the dry ingredients aside.

2. In a large mixing bowl, cream the butter with an electric mixer until light and fluffy. Gradually beat in the sugar. Beat in the eggs, 1 at a time, beating after each addition until well blended. Add the baking soda and vanilla. Beat well.

3. Add the dry ingredients to the butter mixture and stir with a wooden spoon until thoroughly blended. Cover and refrigerate the dough until it is firm.

4. Form the dough into 3 logs 2½ to 3 inches in diameter. Wrap the logs well and refrigerate for up to a week or freeze for up to 2 months.

5. When you're ready to bake cookies, heat the oven to 375°F. Using a large sharp knife, cut the frozen dough into slices about ⅜ inch thick. Place them 1 inch apart on a buttered cookie sheet. Bake the cookies until lightly browned, 10 to 12 minutes. Let cool on a wire rack before serving.

Southwestern Buffet

FOR 16 TO 20

CAVIAR NACHOS

SPICED NUTS

TACO BEAN DIP (PAGE 237) WITH TOSTADITOS
AND CRUDITÉS FOR DIPPING

MARGARITAS BY THE BATCH AND COLD BEER,
PREFERABLY MEXICAN, SUCH AS DOS EQUIS,
CORONA EXTRA, OR EL SOL

BARBACOA OF LAMB

FRESH TOMATO SALSA

WARM FLOUR TORTILLAS

CHICKEN-CHEESE TORTILLA CASSEROLE

CARROT AND JICAMA SALAD

CORN, RICE, AND BEAN SALAD WITH CHILE VINAIGRETTE

TOASTED COCONUT FLAN

FRESH BERRIES

Like so many people, I've become addicted to the flavors of the American Southwest. This is food that truly deserves its popularity. Chock-full of taste, the piquancy of hot chiles, the herbal astringency of fresh coriander, the dusty pungency of toasted cumin, and the sweet tang of barbecue sauce satisfy our newfound craving for spices and seasonings. Mesquite-grilled meats and refreshing salads are all a part of this regional cuisine, borrowed from Mexico to the south and marked by the cattle country in which it was developed. Above all, it is cheerful food, reflective of the sun under which it was born, and perfect for a large party.

Caviar Nachos are a lot of fun. There is nothing serious about them. They are delicious and something of a conversation piece. Set out spiced nuts around the room, or store-bought highly seasoned pumpkin seeds, which are always good with cocktails.

Guests will roll chunks of the Mexican-style barbecued lamb and salsa in tortillas, to be eaten like a taco. The lamb has to marinate for 3 days. It cooks very slowly in a low oven, so remember to put it in 3 or 4 hours before you plan to serve. You cannot overcook it; the meat is roasted until it is meltingly tender and falling off the bone. If you can manage to make up your salsa no more than a couple of hours in advance, do so, because tomatoes are always more flavorful if they're not refrigerated.

Flour tortillas are now available in the refrigerated section of almost all supermarkets. Warm them just before you bring them to the table. Serve them, Mexican style, in a basket covered with a brightly colored cloth to keep them warm.

Chicken-Cheese Tortilla Casserole, a guaranteed favorite, is one of those quintessentially Tex-Mex dishes that no one can stop eating. Completely assembled in advance, it's a great party dish. After so much highly seasoned food, the cool, crisp Carrot and Jicama Salad provides a welcome contrast.

My Toasted Coconut Flan is a creamy soft, light custard, unlike the traditional version made with condensed milk, and is pleasingly chewy. With its caramel sauce, it stands well on its own, but fresh berries always add a nice touch.

DO-AHEAD PLANNING

3 DAYS IN ADVANCE: Marinate the lamb. Make the Spiced Nuts. Make the Taco Bean Dip.

UP TO 2 DAYS AHEAD: Assemble the Chicken-Cheese Tortilla Casserole. Make the Toasted Coconut Flan.

THE DAY BEFORE THE PARTY: Make the guacamole for the Caviar Nachos. Prepare the crudités. Make the Corn, Rice, and Bean Salad with Chile Vinaigrette. Shred the vegetables for the Carrot and Jicama Salad.

ABOUT 4 HOURS BEFORE SERVING: Roast the lamb.

UP TO 2 HOURS BEFORE THE PARTY STARTS: Squeeze the lime juice for the margaritas. Make the Fresh Tomato Salsa.

ABOUT 30 MINUTES BEFORE SERVING: Bake the Chicken-Cheese Tortilla Casserole. Complete the Carrot and Jicama Salad.

CAVIAR NACHOS

MAKES 48

The idea for these came from—who else?—a Texan, Ray Hertz of Dallas. Use inexpensive lumpfish or golden whitefish caviar for this whimsical hors d'oeuvre. Make the guacamole base up to a day ahead if you wish, but assemble the nachos, assembly-line fashion, shortly before serving, so the tortilla chips remain crisp.

2 ripe California avocados, preferably Hass

¼ cup minced onion

¼ cup fresh lime or lemon juice

1 tablespoon plus 1 teaspoon minced, seeded jalapeño peppers (if you can't get fresh jalapeños, substitute hot pepper sauce to taste)

½ teaspoon salt

¼ teaspoon freshly ground black pepper

1 bag (12 ounces) round corn tortilla chips (tostaditos)

1 cup sour cream

2 to 4 ounces salmon roe or red lumpfish or golden whitefish caviar

1. Mash the avocado in a bowl until fairly finely pureed. Add the onion, lime juice, jalapeño pepper, salt, and black pepper. Blend well. (Guacamole is best fresh, but you can make this up to a day ahead. Cover with a piece of plastic wrap directly on the surface of the guacamole and refrigerate.)

2. To assemble the nachos, spoon about ½ tablespoon guacamole onto each of 48 tortilla chips. Top with a teaspoon of sour cream and garnish with ¼ to ½ teaspoon caviar.

SPICED NUTS

MAKES ABOUT 7 CUPS

Make these spicy nuts up to 3 days ahead and store in a tightly covered jar in a cool dark place or refrigerate for up to a week.

2 pounds mixed shelled raw nuts, such as cashews, almonds, walnuts, and pecans (available in health food stores)

1½ tablespoons vegetable oil

2 tablespoons chili powder

2 teaspoons ground cumin

½ teaspoon cayenne pepper

2 teaspoons salt

1. Heat the oven to 350°F. In a large bowl, toss the nuts with the oil until they are evenly coated.

2. In a small bowl, combine the chili powder, cumin, cayenne, and salt. Sprinkle this spice mixture over the nuts and toss to mix well.

3. Spread out the seasoned nuts on 2 large baking sheets and bake for 5 to 7 minutes, until lightly toasted. Let cool on paper towels. Serve at room temperature.

MARGARITAS BY THE BATCH

16 SERVINGS

It's easy to remember the proportions for a perfect margarita: one, two, three. That's one part fresh lime juice to two parts dry orange liqueur (Cointreau, Triple Sec, or Curaçao) to three parts tequila. White tequila, with its distinctive peppery flavor, is the liquor of choice for a great margarita, though if all you have is gold, the drink will, of course, be consumed with little lack of gusto. The following amounts make a pitcherful to serve one (3-ounce) drink to 16 people. If you remember the proportions, you can adjust this to your needs for any number.

1 cup fresh lime juice

2 cups Cointreau, Triple Sec, or Curaçao

3 cups white or silver tequila

In a pitcher filled with ice, combine the lime juice, Cointreau, and tequila. Stir for 1 to 2 minutes. Serve over plenty of ice (I use 3 cubes per glass).

BARBACOA OF LAMB

12 TO 16 SERVINGS

In Mexico, a whole lamb would be rubbed with seasonings and buried in a barbecue pit, much like our clam bake. A much easier home version marinates whole leg of lamb and then braises it very slowly in a low oven. Because of the acidity of the marinade, an enameled cast-iron casserole or ceramic pot is the best choice here. Buttery, tender meat, moistened with a dollop of tomato salsa, with chunks of avocado and plenty of chopped cilantro, is perfect for rolling up in a nice warm tortilla.

1 whole leg of lamb or 2 shank halves (see Note)

5 large ancho chiles

¾ pound fresh tomatillos (Spanish green tomatoes), papery husks removed, or 1 can (13 ounces) whole tomatillos, drained

2 medium onions, quartered

3 large garlic cloves, crushed

2 teaspoons ground cumin

1½ teaspoons salt

Flour tortillas and Fresh Tomato Salsa (opposite page), for serving

1. Trim off all excess fat from the meat. With a narrow knife, prick the meat deeply all over at 1- to 2-inch intervals. Place the leg of lamb in a heavy nonreactive casserole with a tight-fitting lid, preferably enameled cast iron.

2. Lightly toast the ancho chiles on a dry griddle or over a gas flame for about 30 seconds per side, just to soften them. Cut open and remove the stem, seeds, and ribs. Put in a bowl and pour on boiling water to cover. Let soak for about 15 minutes, until soft; drain.

3. Put the ancho chiles, tomatillos, onions, garlic, cumin, and salt in a food processor or blender. Puree until smooth. Lift up the lamb and smear some of the tomatillo-chile puree over the bottom. Pour the remainder over the lamb and smooth it around to cover the meat entirely. Cover the pot and refrigerate for 3 days.

4. Heat the oven to 275°F. Place the covered casserole of lamb in the oven and roast for 3 hours. Remove the lamb and let stand, covered loosely with foil, for at least

15 minutes. Skim the fat off the liquid in the casserole; there will be a lot.

5. Thickly slice the meat from the bone and then cut or pull with a fork into large shreds. Pour the pan juices over the meat. If made ahead, refrigerate, then reheat gently. Serve with warm tortillas and fresh tomato salsa.

Note: It doesn't matter if you use a whole leg of lamb or 2 shank halves, but I find the 2 halves are often easier to fit into the proper casserole.

FRESH TOMATO SALSA

MAKES ABOUT 3 CUPS

A mix of canned and fresh tomatoes and pickled and fresh chiles makes a large batch of excellent salsa.

1 medium white onion, finely diced

2 tablespoons fresh lime juice

1 teaspoon coarse salt

1 can (14½ ounces) diced peeled tomatoes, drained

2 large ripe tomatoes, finely diced

2 fresh jalapeño peppers, minced

2 tablespoons minced pickled jalapeño peppers, plus 1 tablespoon juice from jar

½ teaspoon sugar

¼ cup chopped fresh cilantro, optional

1. In a medium bowl, combine the onion, lime juice, salt, canned and fresh tomatoes, fresh and pickled jalapeños, and sugar. The salsa should be piquant.

2. The salsa can be refrigerated, covered, for up to a day. Just before serving, stir in the cilantro, if desired.

CHICKEN-CHEESE TORTILLA CASSEROLE

16 TO 20 SERVINGS

Over the years, I've experimented with making this casserole more simply with prepared green salsa, and it's not bad, but this combination of ingredients makes sure you hear the mariachis sing. Do try to find fresh tomatillos; the quality of canned varies hugely from absolutely fine to awful.

6 skinless, boneless chicken breast halves, about 2 pounds total

1½ teaspoons salt

½ teaspoon freshly ground black pepper

3 dozen corn tortillas, 6 inches in diameter

About ½ cup corn oil

¾ pound Monterey Jack cheese

½ pound sharp white Cheddar cheese

2 pounds fresh tomatillos or 3 cans (13 ounces each) tomatillos enteros

1 jar (10¼ ounces) whole pickled jalapeño peppers, drained, tops trimmed off

4 large garlic cloves, crushed

2 medium white onions, cut into eighths

4½ cups sour cream

2 cups milk

Sliced black olives, for garnish

1. Rinse the chicken breasts. Put them in a large saucepan or flameproof casserole and add water to cover by at least 1 inch. Add ½ teaspoon of the salt. Bring to a simmer over moderately high heat, reduce the heat, and barely simmer for 20 to 30 minutes, until the chicken is just white throughout but still moist. Let cool in the water for 30 minutes. Remove the chicken and let cool completely; reserve the liquid for stock, if desired. (The chicken can be poached a day ahead. Wrap and refrigerate.)

2. Shred or very coarsely chop the chicken. Toss with the remaining 1 teaspoon salt and the black pepper.

3. Heat a medium skillet, preferably nonstick, over moderate heat. One at a time, lightly brush each tortilla with oil and cook for 15 to 20 seconds on each side, until softened. Stack as they are cooked and set aside.

4. In a food processor fitted with the shredding disk, grate the Monterey Jack and Cheddar cheeses. Toss them together and set aside.

5. Husk the fresh tomatillos and blanch them in a large pot of boiling salted water for 2 minutes; drain. If using canned, simply drain them. In the processor fitted with the metal blade, combine the tomatillos, pickled jalapeños, and garlic. Puree until smooth. Add the onions and turn the machine quickly on and off about 10 times, or until the onions are chopped. Scrape the green sauce into a bowl.

6. Rinse the work bowl of the processor and add the sour cream. With the machine on, add the milk through the feed tube, blending until smooth.

7. Using 2 large shallow baking dishes about 9 × 13 inches, or 1 very large dish, spread a thin film of green sauce over the bottom of each dish. Cover with a layer of tortillas. Scatter half the chicken over the tortillas. Drizzle on about one-third of the green sauce. Sprinkle on half of the cheese and then spoon about one-third of the sour cream sauce over that. Repeat with another layer of tortillas, the remaining chicken, and half the remaining green sauce, cheese, and sour cream sauce. Top with the remaining tortillas. Spread the remaining green sauce on top of them, cover with the rest of the sour cream sauce, and sprinkle what's left of the cheese on top of everything. Garnish with some sliced black olives. (The dish can be assembled up to a day ahead. Cover and refrigerate.)

8. Heat the oven to 350°F. About half an hour before you plan to serve, bake the casseroles, uncovered, 30 to 40 minutes, or until the cheese is melted and the dishes are sizzling hot throughout.

Chiles

Peppers are notoriously promiscuous, and hot chiles are no exception. They breed like rabbits, and there's no telling what kind of a hybrid you'll end up with. To make matters worse, the same pepper can vary in hotness from field to field, and even from one end of the pepper to the other. On top of all that, people have a bad habit of giving the same pepper different names, depending on whether it's fresh or dried or where it comes from. Such confusion aside, the following are descriptions of some of the most common chile peppers you're likely to come across. Some of the heat of these hot chiles can be reduced by removing the seeds and inner ribs.

Poblano This large, dark green pepper, bell shaped with a tapering bottom, is the largest and one of the mildest of the chiles. With a deep aromatic flavor that is greatly enhanced by roasting, this is the pepper traditionally stuffed to make chiles rellenos.

Ancho Brick red, the ancho is a dried poblano. Used as the basis for red enchilada sauce and mole, it is very flavorful, with an earthy taste. Usually mild, it can kick upon occasion.

Anaheim Also called California chile, chile verde, long green chile, Big Jim. For all practical purposes, you can consider these chiles the same. They are usually semi-hot and, though frequently green, are sometimes red. Narrow and somewhat twisted, the long green chile is often chopped and added to dishes for hotness and flavor. It is probably the most common large chile found in American markets.

Pasilla This long, brownish pepper, known as chile chilaca in its fresh state, is usually used dried. Because of its dark color, the pasilla is sometimes called chile negro, or black chile. It is usually quite hot, with a dusky flavor, and is often used in combination with the ancho.

Jalapeño A small, blunt-nosed dark green chile, the jalapeño is very hot and flavorful. It is used fresh and pickled.

Chipotle When fully ripened, dried, and smoked, the jalapeño becomes the chipotle chile—light brown and wrinkled. It is extremely hot and has a distinctive smoky flavor, which adds a wonderful depth of flavor to sauces. The chipotle is frequently found canned in adobo sauce.

Serrano The very small, narrow, dark green chile is extremely hot. It is usually very finely minced and should be used with discretion.

CARROT AND JICAMA SALAD

16 TO 20 SERVINGS

I learned to make this salad from a wonderful Mexican cook, Luisa (Lula) Bertran. It is pretty, crisp, and refreshing. Served with spicy hot food, it provides contrast and relief.

2 pounds carrots, peeled

2 pounds jicama, peeled

2 tablespoons fresh lime juice

½ cup corn oil, light olive oil, or other vegetable oil

½ teaspoon salt

Cayenne pepper

⅔ cup chopped cilantro

1. Cut the carrots and jicama into very fine julienne strips. I use the fine julienne disk of my food processor or a mandoline; you can cut them by hand, but it is a lot of work. Rinse the jicama in a bowl of cold water, changing the water until the liquid runs clear. Soak the carrot and jicama in a bowl of ice water for at least 30 minutes or overnight; drain well.

2. Shortly before serving, put the vegetables in a large serving bowl, preferably glass. Toss with the lime juice, corn oil, salt, 2 dashes of cayenne, and all but 2 tablespoons of the cilantro. Sprinkle the remaining cilantro on top.

CORN, RICE, AND BEAN SALAD WITH CHILE VINAIGRETTE

16 SERVINGS

I love this salad in summer when fresh sweet corn is in season, but I make it all year in a flash with canned corn niblets. It has a nice sweet-sour tang, with a bite that adds zest without scorching. A fine accompaniment to barbecued chicken or any kind of Mexican or southwestern-style meat, this is a great picnic salad, because there is nothing to spoil.

2 cups converted rice

1 tablespoon salt

2 cans (16 ounces each) pink beans, rinsed and drained

1 can (12 ounces) vacuum-packed corn niblets or 3 cups cooked fresh corn kernels

1 bunch of scallions, chopped (about ¾ cup)

⅔ cup safflower oil or corn oil

¼ cup fresh lime juice

2 tablespoons cider vinegar

2 tablespoons brown sugar

4 pickled jalapeño peppers, stemmed, seeded, and quartered

2 teaspoons chili powder

1 teaspoon ground cumin

1. Cook the rice as directed on the package, using 5 cups of water and 1 teaspoon of the salt. (The rice can be made ahead.)

2. In a large bowl, combine the rice, beans, corn, and scallions. Toss lightly to mix.

3. In a food processor, combine the oil, lime juice, vinegar, brown sugar, jalapeños, chili powder, cumin, and the remaining 2 teaspoons salt. Process until the peppers are finely minced.

4. Pour the dressing over the salad and toss to coat. Let stand at room temperature, tossing occasionally, for up to 4 hours or cover and refrigerate for up to 2 days. Serve at room temperature.

TOASTED COCONUT FLAN

16 TO 20 SERVINGS

This is a rich custard that forms a nice creamy finale to a spicy meal. Though you could make the entire flan in one large baking dish, I find two pie plates are easier in terms of unmolding and serving. This is a do-ahead dessert that should be served well chilled.

1 package (7 ounces) sweetened shredded (flaked) coconut

1½ cups sugar

1 quart milk

2 cups heavy cream

8 whole eggs

4 egg yolks

1 tablespoon vanilla extract

1. Heat the oven to 300°F. Spread out the coconut on a large baking sheet and toast in the oven, tossing frequently, until light brown, 8 to 10 minutes. Don't worry if there is unevenness of color, but don't let the coconut burn. Turn out onto a plate or shallow bowl and let cool. (The coconut can be toasted several days before you make the flan and stored in the refrigerator in a covered container.)

2. Heat the oven to 325°F. In a small heavy saucepan, combine 1 cup of the sugar with 3 tablespoons of water. Melt the sugar over moderate heat and continue to cook until the syrup turns a deep golden brown, 6 to 8 minutes. Immediately remove from the heat and pour half the syrup into each of two 10-inch glass pie plates. Swirl to coat the pie plates evenly with the caramel.

3. Heat the milk and cream together until hot but not boiling. In a large bowl, whisk the eggs and egg yolks until blended. Beat in the remaining ½ cup sugar. Very gradually at first and then in a slow stream, beat the hot milk and cream into the eggs. Reserve ½ cup of the toasted coconut for garnish. Mix the remainder of the coconut and the vanilla into the custard.

4. Divide the coconut custard between the 2 pie plates. Set them in a larger pan (remember those aluminum roasters if you have nothing else) with enough hot water to reach halfway up the sides and bake for 1 hour, or until the custard is set. Remove the flans from the water bath and let cool. Cover and refrigerate until chilled. (The coconut flans can be made up to 2 days in advance.)

5. To serve, unmold the flans onto 2 round platters with lips. The caramel will form a sauce. Garnish the top of each with the reserved toasted coconut. Cut into wedges to serve.

Après-Ski Soup Party

FOR 18 TO 24

PEEL-AND-EAT SHRIMP WITH TWO DIPPING SAUCES

SOY-WASABI DIPPING SAUCE

SEAFOOD COCKTAIL SAUCE

ROMESCO SAUCE (PAGE 39) WITH CRUDITÉS

CRISPY CHEESE PUFFS

CHUNKY CHICKEN CORN CHOWDER

CHEDDARED BROCCOLI SOUP

ITALIAN PASTA AND BEAN SOUP

ONE-POT RICH FUDGE BROWNIES WITH DRIED CHERRIES AND HAZELNUTS (PAGE 186)

APPLES, GRAPES, AND CLEMENTINES

HOT CHOCOLATE AND COFFEE

One of the biggest challenges of cooking for a crowd is service. Here's one solution that creates a lively ambience and allows you to relax, because guests help themselves, sampling and tasting, which makes the meal participatory and a lot of fun. The entire menu is designed to avoid plates and utensils, except for spoons. There's a whole lot of dipping and sipping going on, though, so be sure to put out plenty of napkins.

Shrimp in the shell, purchased already cooked or boiled at home, are eaten with the fingers. Multiple bowls of both dipping sauces will ensure there are no long lines in any one place. Your pick of raw vegetables, cut into bite-size pieces, get drenched in that irresistible Spanish toasted almond and red pepper sauce I am so fond of, Romesco. Short of time? Substitute your favorite blue cheese dip or thick dressing. Gougères are crisp, savory cheese puffs, and they are real crowd-pleasers. Best of all, they freeze perfectly after baking and are reheated right from the freezer.

All these soups can be made in advance. An electric slow-cooker provides an excellent tool for keeping at least one of these hearty potions hot. Chunky Chicken Corn Chowder is a meal in a bowl, which will appeal to every palate. Classic Italian Pasta and Bean Soup, *pasta e fagioli,* is made even more substantial with bacon and chunks of pork. Cheddared Broccoli Soup offers a universally popular vegetarian option.

Serve the soups ladled into mugs and coffee cups. Let guests know they get one cup, and they'd better hold onto it. They can move around and sample as they wish. Borrow as needed, buy a supply of cheap mugs at a kitchen supply house, or use a mix of what you already own and augment, if necessary, with sturdy, heatproof paper cups. Do provide spoons.

There's nothing wrong with serving any of these soups right from their cooking pots. Just be sure you space out the soups or place them on different tables to spread out. You'll notice that each soup serves 12 to 16, but the party is for 18 to 24. The assumption is that everyone will have less than a full portion of the three soups. In fact, you may have leftovers, all of which freeze well.

Even dessert is designed to be eaten out of hand, with just a napkin—irresistibly rich brownies and a big bowl of fruit, which can serve as a decorative centerpiece earlier in the meal.

DO-AHEAD PLANNING

UP TO SEVERAL WEEKS IN ADVANCE: Bake and freeze the cheese puffs.

UP TO 4 DAYS IN ADVANCE: Make the Romesco Sauce.

UP TO 3 DAYS IN ADVANCE: Soak the beans overnight; cook them the next day. Be sure to reserve the cooking liquid. Bake the brownies.

UP TO 2 DAYS IN ADVANCE: Make the Chicken Corn Chowder. Make the Seafood Cocktail Sauce.

THE DAY BEFORE: Make the Cheddared Broccoli Soup through Step 4. Make the Italian Pasta and Bean Soup through Step 4. If you've purchased raw shrimp, cook and chill them.

THE MORNING OF THE PARTY: Make the Soy-Wasabi Dipping Sauce for the shrimp. Prepare the raw vegetables for dipping; store them in cold salted water in the refrigerator.

SHORTLY BEFORE SERVING: Reheat the frozen cheese puffs. Reheat the soups, stirring the cheese into the broccoli soup and finishing the pasta and bean soup.

PEEL-AND-EAT SHRIMP WITH TWO DIPPING SAUCES

18 TO 24 SERVINGS

Using shrimp with the shell on makes life a lot easier for the cook. It turns eating into an activity and is also economical. However, if you have the budget and/or prefer easier eating, simply substitute peeled cooked shrimp or cook them yourself and peel and devein before serving. The easiest and most economical choice is "uncooked peel-and-eat shrimp" about 36 count to the pound. Though smaller, they will allow more pieces per person. Be sure to put out plenty of napkins and small plates.

3 pounds shrimp in the shell
Soy-Wasabi Dipping Sauce (opposite page)
Seafood Cocktail Sauce (opposite page)

1. Bring a stockpot of lightly salted water to a rolling boil. Add the shrimp and cook until the water returns to a boil and the shrimp are pink and curled. Drain and rinse under cold running water. Transfer the shrimp to a bowl of ice water to cool completely and firm up. Drain, then refrigerate in a covered container or plastic bags. The shrimp can be cooked a day or two in advance.

2. Pile up the shrimp in 1 or 2 bowls, over crushed ice if you have it. Be sure to put out bowls for the shells. Set out the sauces, dividing each into several bowls so people don't have to duel with each other to dip their shrimp.

SOY-WASABI DIPPING SAUCE

MAKES 1⅓ CUPS

Wasabi, Japanese sinus-clearing horseradish, comes in several different forms. Consumers rarely see the fresh root, though top chefs covet it when they can find it. On the other hand, fine wasabi powder and a premixed paste are readily available. The powder is easier to find, and it has a very long shelf life with no refrigeration needed, so that is what I call for here.

2 tablespoons wasabi powder

2 tablespoons rice vinegar

1 teaspoon sugar

1 cup soy sauce, such as Kikkoman

1½ tablespoons Asian sesame oil

Stir together the wasabi powder, rice vinegar, and sugar to form a smooth paste. Blend in the soy sauce and sesame oil.

SEAFOOD COCKTAIL SAUCE

MAKES ABOUT 3 CUPS

There's nothing unusual about this classic sauce, but making it yourself lets you season it, with more or less horseradish and Tabasco to taste.

2½ cups ketchup

½ cup prepared white horseradish, or to taste

¼ cup fresh lemon juice

1 tablespoon Worcestershire sauce

1 teaspoon Tabasco sauce, or to taste

½ cup chopped cilantro or parsley, optional

Stir together all the ingredients. Cover and refrigerate until serving time.

CRISPY CHEESE PUFFS

MAKES ABOUT 110 BITE-SIZE PUFFS

Gougères **is the formal name for these French savory pastries from the region of Burgundy. If you've never had them, you're in for a treat—puffs of crisp golden pastry loaded with a mix of nutty Gruyère cheese and flavorful Parmesan. Here the dough is formed into small puffs for an easy hot hors d'oeuvre. Traditionally, the dough paste is baked into a large, golden brown ring; or the puffs can be dropped by tablespoons rather than teaspoons to create dinner roll–size rounds, which are terrific for stuffing or eating out of hand (this recipe will make about 3 dozen). For this quantity of dough, a food processor is a great arm-saver, though you can beat the eggs into the dough with an electric mixer or even a wooden spoon if you prefer.**

2 sticks (½ pound) plus 2 tablespoons unsalted butter, cut into tablespoons

2½ teaspoons salt

½ teaspoon freshly ground black pepper

¼ teaspoon cayenne pepper

3 cups all-purpose flour

12 eggs, at room temperature

2 cups finely diced Gruyère cheese (about 8 ounces)

1 cup freshly grated imported Parmesan cheese

1. Heat the oven to 425°F. Butter 3 large, heavy baking sheets.

2. In a medium saucepan, combine 3 cups of water, the butter, salt, black pepper, and cayenne. Bring to a rolling boil over moderately high heat, melting the butter completely. Add the flour all at once and beat with a wooden spoon over heat until the dough is completely blended and masses together in the center of the pan. Remove from the heat.

3. Scoop one-third of the hot dough into the food processor. With the machine on, add 4 of the eggs through the feed tube, 1 at a time. Blend until smooth and satiny. Turn into a bowl. Repeat 2 more times with the remaining dough and eggs. (There's no need to wash the bowl in between batches.)

4. Add the Gruyère and Parmesan cheeses to the dough and mix well with a wooden spoon to blend. Drop the dough by heaping teaspoons onto the buttered baking sheets, leaving about 1 inch in between. (If you have only 2 sheets, or room in your oven for only 2 sheets, bake 1 sheet after the others.)

5. Bake for 15 to 20 minutes, until crusty and golden brown. Serve warm or at room temperature. (Gougères can be baked up to 2 months in advance and frozen. Reheat until thawed and hot in a 350°F oven.)

CHUNKY CHICKEN CORN CHOWDER

12 TO 16 SERVINGS

For simplicity, I use precooked chicken here, so all you have to do is pull the meat off the bone. On the other hand, I like to use everything I buy, so I turn the bones into a quick, easy stock. If you prefer, you can omit Step 1 and just use 6 cups of purchased reduced-sodium chicken stock in Step 4. Or you can buy 2 to 3 pounds of skinless, boneless breasts and poach them in a pot of lightly salted water (see page 150, Step 1). That liquid can then be used for the stock.

2 rotisserie chickens, 3 to 3½ pounds each

2 cups chicken stock

1 large leek

2 medium onions

3 tablespoons unsalted butter

2 tablespoons olive oil

½ cup all-purpose flour

6 cups milk

2 pounds Yukon gold potatoes, peeled and cut into ¾-inch dice

2 teaspoons dried winter savory or thyme

Salt and freshly ground pepper

3 cups corn kernels

2 cups light cream or half-and-half

1 tablespoon Worcestershire sauce

2 tablespoons fresh lime juice

1 teaspoon Tabasco sauce

1. Remove and reserve the chicken skin. Pull all the meat off the bones, tearing it into chunks and large strips and setting it aside in a bowl. Save all the bones and put them in a large pot along with the chicken skin. Add the chicken stock, 6 cups of water, and the dark green top of the leek, well rinsed. Bring to a boil over high heat, reduce the heat to a simmer, and cook uncovered for 30 to 45 minutes, skimming any foam that rises to the top. Strain and measure; you want 6 cups. Either reduce further or add water to adjust. Let the stock cool, then skim as much fat as possible off the top of the stock. If you make it ahead and refrigerate it, the fat will lift right off.

2. Cut the remainder of the leek in half or quarters lengthwise, then cut crosswise into thick slices. Swish in a bowl of cold water to remove any grit. Dice the onions.

3. In a large stockpot, melt the butter in the olive oil over moderate heat. Add the onions to the pot. Lift the leeks out of the water with your hands and add them, too; don't worry about any water clinging to the leeks. Cover the pot and cook for 5 minutes. Uncover and cook, stirring occasionally, until the onions are golden and beginning to brown, 5 to 7 minutes.

4. Sprinkle the flour over the onions and leeks and cook, stirring, for 1 to 2 minutes without allowing the flour to brown. Gradually whisk in the 6 cups chicken stock. Bring to a boil, whisking until the liquid thickens. Stir in the milk. Add the potatoes, savory, 2 teaspoons salt, and ¼ teaspoon pepper. Bring to a simmer and cook until the potatoes are barely tender, about 5 minutes.

5. Add the corn, pieces of chicken, cream, and Worcestershire sauce. Simmer for 5 to 10 minutes longer. Stir in the lime juice and Tabasco. Season with additional salt to taste.

CHEDDARED BROCCOLI SOUP

12 TO 16 SERVINGS

Go to any of the ubiquitous soup and salad bars studding cities and this flavor always pops up as one of the most sought after. Well, here it is . . . easy as pie. You could make the soup with all water, but some stock gives better flavor. Buttermilk is low in fat and adds a nice tangy note, but if all you have on hand is regular milk, that can be substituted. Don't skimp on the cheese, though. Buy the best, well-aged American or Canadian Cheddar you can find, because that is what adds pizzazz to the soup.

2 large bunches of broccoli

⅓ cup olive oil

3 medium onions, chopped

2 large celery ribs, chopped

⅓ cup all-purpose flour

6 cups chicken or vegetable stock or water

½ teaspoon freshly grated nutmeg

¼ teaspoon cayenne pepper

2 cups buttermilk

Salt and freshly ground black pepper

8 ounces sharp Cheddar cheese, shredded (about 2½ cups)

1. Rinse the broccoli well. Trim off the very bottoms of the stems. Using a paring knife, grasp the edge of the tough outer skin from the stem bottom and pull it off, much as you would if you were stringing celery. Continue all the way around the stalk until you have removed most of the outer skin. Slice the stems and separate the crowns into florets.

2. In a large stockpot or flameproof casserole, heat the olive oil over moderately high heat. Add the onions and sauté for 5 minutes. Add the celery and cook, stirring occasionally, until the onions are soft and golden and beginning to brown, about 10 minutes. Sprinkle on the flour and cook, stirring, for 1 to 2 minutes without allowing the flour to color.

3. Stir in the stock and bring to a boil over high heat, stirring until the liquid is smooth and thickened. Reduce the heat to moderately low. Add the broccoli stems, nutmeg, and cayenne along with 4 cups of water. Slowly bring to a boil. Cook for 7 minutes. Add the broccoli florets and cook for 3 minutes longer.

4. Stir in the buttermilk and season with salt and pepper to taste. Either use an immersion blender to puree the soup right in the pot or transfer the soup in batches to a blender or food processor and puree until smooth. Return to the pot or cover and refrigerate overnight.

5. When you're ready to serve, reheat the soup. Stir in the Cheddar cheese and check your seasonings.

ITALIAN PASTA AND BEAN SOUP

12 TO 16 SERVINGS

You could easily call this the ultimate comfort soup, and nobody would argue with you. *Pasta e fagioli* is a delectable cross between a soup and a stew. The longer it sits, the thicker it gets. You can make the dish ahead through Step 4, but it's best to add the pasta no more than an hour before serving. If the soup becomes too thick, simply add more stock or water and adjust the seasonings.

1 pound dried white beans (cannellini, navy, or Great Northern)

2 imported bay leaves

⅓ cup extra-virgin olive oil

4 ounces lean pancetta or bacon, coarsely chopped

1 pound boneless pork chops, trimmed of excess fat and cut into ½-inch dice

2 medium onions, chopped

3 medium celery ribs, chopped

2 large carrots, peeled and chopped

6 garlic cloves, chopped

½ teaspoon crushed hot red pepper

Salt and freshly ground black pepper

6 cups meat or chicken stock

1 can (28 ounces) Italian peeled tomatoes, with their juices

12 ounces ditalini pasta or elbow macaroni

½ cup chopped parsley

Freshly grated imported Parmesan or Pecorino Romano cheese

1. Rinse the dried beans and pick over to remove any grit. Soak overnight in enough cold water to cover by at least 2 inches. The next day, drain the beans and rinse again. Put the beans in a large pot with the bay leaves and enough fresh cold water to cover by about 2 inches. Bring to a boil, skimming any foam off the water as the beans begin to cook. Simmer the beans until they are tender, 45 minutes to 1 hour 15 minutes, depending upon the freshness of the beans. Drain the beans, reserving 4 cups of the cooking liquid. Pick out and discard the bay leaves. (The recipe can be prepared to this point up to 2 days in advance.)

2. In a large flameproof casserole or stockpot, heat the olive oil over moderately high heat. Add the pancetta and sauté, stirring often, until most of the fat has been rendered, about 3 minutes. Add the pork to the pot and sauté until lightly browned, about 5 minutes. Remove the meats with a slotted spoon and set aside.

3. Add the onions to the fat in the pot, cover, and cook over moderate heat for 5 minutes. Return the heat to moderately high and add the celery, carrots, and garlic. Sauté, stirring occasionally, for 5 minutes longer. Return the meats to the pot, stirring to mix everything together. Season with the hot pepper, 2 teaspoons salt, and ½ teaspoon black pepper.

4. Pour in 4 cups of the stock and bring to a boil, scraping up any browned bits from the bottom of the pot. Puree a generous cup of the beans with 2 cups water and add to the pot. Squeeze the tomatoes through your hands into the pot to break them up. Pour in the reserved 4 cups bean cooking liquid, the tomato juices, and 2 more cups water. Simmer for 20 minutes. (The recipe can be prepared to this point up to a day in advance.)

5. Add the pasta and cook until just tender, 7 to 9 minutes. If you have time, let the soup stand for 30 to 60 minutes. Then add the remaining 2 cups stock and return to a simmer. Stir in the parsley and season with additional salt, black pepper, and hot pepper to taste. Serve with a bowl of grated cheese on the side.

Elegant Evening Buffet

FOR 20 TO 24

NIÇOISE SWORDFISH SALAD IN ENDIVE CUPS (PAGE 247)

CORIANDER CHICKEN ROLLS

RICH LIVER MOUSSE WITH TOASTED HAZELNUTS
(PAGE 110)

OLIVES AND NUTS

SESAME-GINGER GRILLED SALMON

HALF RECIPE COLD FILLET OF BEEF
WITH SHERRY WINE VINAIGRETTE (PAGE 250)

ROASTED ASPARAGUS (PAGE 193)

ROMAINE, RADICCHIO, AND FENNEL SALAD

WILD RICE SALAD WITH CURRANTS AND PEPPERS

FRENCH BREAD

TRUFFLED BRIE

WALNUT OR WHOLE-GRAIN BREAD
OR YOUR FAVORITE CRACKERS

BASKET OF GRAPES

BOURBON-PEACH TRIFLE

BITTERSWEET CHOCOLATE TORTE

Buffets are frequently the butt of bad jokes. There's something about that endless overburdened table laden with platters of garishly garnished food that brings out the beast in people. We've all been there, dressed in evening clothes, standing in line, balancing plate, napkin, silverware, and wineglass like a trained seal, while fending off friends who begin jockeying for position as soon as dinner is announced.

There is, however, nothing quite as breathtaking as a glorious display of food, and a buffet can be not only the most practicable way to serve a crowd but the best way. All you need are a few tricks to avoid traffic jams and turn what could be a free-for-all into an elegant, civilized way for guests to help themselves. There are a few dos and don'ts that I guarantee will make a spectacular, smooth-flowing buffet.

This particular menu for an elegant evening buffet is especially easy on the cook. It offers one individual cold hors d'oeuvre—Niçoise Swordfish Salad in Endive Cups—and one hot hors d'oeuvre—Coriander Chicken Rolls, little filo packets filled with an Asian-flavored, coriander-flecked chicken. They are fabulous and can be prepared and frozen well before the party. They're so good, in fact, that you may want to make a double recipe. These and a simple liver mousse spread and nuts and olives are all you need to accompany cocktails.

Because the flavorful sesame-ginger salmon is excellent at room temperature, you can broil or grill it shortly before guests arrive or earlier in the day and refrigerate it. Just be sure it is close to room temperature when it is served. Simple fillet of beef, served with a tart Sherry Wine Vinaigrette loaded with fresh herbs, offers a delightful choice. I think you'll find most of your guests opting for both. Since the salmon is richly flavored, I've chosen wild rice as an accompaniment. This delicious salad, studded with diced red and yellow peppers, improves when made a day ahead. Also colorful, the Romaine, Radicchio, and Fennel Salad is shredded so that it is easy to serve and relatively compact on the plate. And roasting asparagus, my favorite way of cooking this lovely and elegant vegetable, is simple and doesn't take up space on the stove.

For a crowd of this size, make a double recipe of the Wild Rice Salad; likewise, the Romaine, Radicchio, and Fennel Salad. Obviously, this menu halves easily to serve 12.

Cheese courses are becoming more and more popular in this country. Here, it stretches out the festivities and offers a pleasing interlude after dinner and before dessert.

No matter how much food you put out, everyone will still be looking forward to dessert, and a double offering of Bourbon-Peach Trifle and Bittersweet Chocolate Torte won't disappoint them. While fresh peaches are, of course, a tremendous treat, I make the trifle year-round, using individually quick-frozen peach slices with no added sugar when fresh are out of season. If you want to make only one dessert, go for the chocolate. The cake makes two, anyway, so you only need to double the syrup and chocolate ganache frosting.

DO-AHEAD PLANNING

UP TO 1 MONTH IN ADVANCE: Assemble and freeze one or two recipes of the Coriander Chicken Rolls. Bake and freeze the cakes for the Bittersweet Chocolate Torte.

4 DAYS BEFORE THE PARTY: Prepare the Truffled Brie.

UP TO 3 DAYS AHEAD: Make the Rich Liver Mousse with Toasted Hazelnuts.

UP TO 2 DAYS IN ADVANCE: Make the frosting for the Bittersweet Chocolate Torte and assemble the dessert. Refrigerate, covered, until 1 hour before serving.

THE DAY BEFORE THE PARTY: Make the swordfish salad. Roast the fillet of beef. Let cool and refrigerate, well wrapped. Separate the endive spears; rinse and dry them and refrigerate in a plastic bag. Make two recipes of Wild Rice Salad. Prepare a double amount of romaine, radicchio, and fennel for the salad. Prepare the peaches and the pastry cream for the trifle.

THE MORNING OF THE PARTY: Assemble the Bourbon-Peach Trifle.

ABOUT 4 HOURS IN ADVANCE: Assemble the Niçoise Swordfish Salad in Endive Cups, arrange on a platter, cover, and refrigerate. Roast the asparagus; set aside at room temperature. Remove the Truffled Brie from the refrigerator.

ABOUT 2 HOURS AHEAD: Marinate the salmon. Remove the beef from the refrigerator.

JUST BEFORE GUESTS ARRIVE: Broil or grill two sides of salmon. Let stand at room temperature for up to 1½ hours before serving.

SHORTLY BEFORE SERVING: Bake the frozen Coriander Chicken Rolls. Toss the Romaine, Radicchio, and Fennel Salad.

Buffet Dos and Don'ts

Choose attractive, colorful food. A buffet should be as inviting to look at as it is to eat. Avoid dishes with fancy little garnishes in the center that will be destroyed as soon as guests help themselves. Decorate around the rims of platters.

Replenish platters when they start looking depleted. Always carry them out to the kitchen and refill them out of sight of the guests.

Don't put all the food in one place. Allow at least one station for every 10 or 12 guests so that lines are kept to a minimum. Divide recipes between two bowls or platters where appropriate.

Put the bar in a separate place. If possible, help guests to drinks after they are seated with their food.

Be sure that there is somewhere for everyone to perch or to set his or her glass.

Don't serve a lot of hot food. Limit yourself to one or two hot dishes, perhaps as the centerpiece of the meal. Choose accompaniments that are appropriate chilled or at room temperature.

Select recipes that can be prepared ahead.

CORIANDER CHICKEN ROLLS

MAKES ABOUT 50

Rosa Ross, New York author, cooking teacher, and caterer (Wok on Wheels), gave me this terrific recipe. It is based on the classic Chinese paper-wrapped chicken, which Rosa used to serve. But when she saw too many people popping the paper into their mouths, she realized it was time for a change and cleverly chose filo dough, thin as parchment but edible. Provided you keep the dough covered so it doesn't dry out, filo is easy to work with. Don't open the package until you are ready to begin wrapping, keep the sheets covered with a damp towel or sheet of plastic wrap, and pull them out as you need them. Don't worry about tears and rips; they can be patched with a little oil.

¾ pound skinless, boneless chicken breasts

2 tablespoons hoisin sauce

1 tablespoon Chinese dark soy sauce

1 tablespoon dry sherry

1 tablespoon cornstarch

2 teaspoons Asian sesame oil

2 garlic cloves, smashed and minced

¼ cup minced scallion

¼ cup finely chopped cilantro or parsley

⅛ teaspoon salt

¼ teaspoon freshly ground pepper

1 box (8 ounces) filo pastry sheets, thawed in the refrigerator

About ⅓ cup safflower or corn oil

1. Trim any fat or gristle from the chicken. With the knife at an angle, cut the chicken crosswise into thin slices. (This is easier to do if the chicken is partially frozen.) Then stack the slices and cut the chicken into very thin slivers.

2. In a bowl, combine the slivered chicken, hoisin sauce, soy sauce, sherry, cornstarch, sesame oil, garlic, scallion, cilantro, salt, and pepper. Toss to mix well.

3. Remove one-third of the filo dough from its package. Reroll the remainder and keep it wrapped. Cut the filo sheets lengthwise in half to measure rectangles about 10 inches long and 3 to 4 inches wide. Stack the strips and keep them covered with plastic or a damp kitchen towel. One by one, remove a strip of filo and set it down lengthwise with one of the short ends facing you. Brush the top half of the pastry with safflower oil, fold up the bottom to double the sheet and scoop a scant teaspoon (use a measuring spoon) of the chicken filling onto the center of the bottom edge. Roll up twice, fold in the sides about ½ inch at each edge, and paint the top ½ to 1 inch of the pastry with oil. Roll up all the way to form a packet about 1 × 2 inches; it will self-seal. Repeat to use up all the filo and filling. (The recipe can be prepared to this point up to 3 months in advance. Layer the packets in an airtight container with waxed paper between the layers and freeze.)

4. Heat the oven to 350°F. Bake the chicken packets (unthawed, if frozen) on an ungreased baking sheet for 10 to 15 minutes, until golden brown. Serve hot.

SESAME-GINGER GRILLED SALMON

16 TO 20 SERVINGS

This dish is based on a recipe given to me by caterer, cooking teacher, and cookbook author Karen Lee. Delicious at room temperature, the fish can also be reheated and served hot. To do so, simply grill or broil as directed in Step 3 for 5 minutes only. Just before serving, pop into a 400°F oven for about 10 minutes, until the salmon is heated through and just opaque throughout.

2 sides of salmon, skin on, about 3 pounds each

1 cup medium-dry sherry

½ cup soy sauce

⅓ cup Asian sesame oil

¼ cup minced fresh ginger

1 cup thinly sliced scallions

1 tablespoon minced garlic

Lemon slices and parsley sprigs, for garnish

1. Rinse the salmon under cold running water; pat dry.

2. Put the salmon, skin side down, into 2 shallow nonreactive roasting pans, roughly 12 × 17 inches each. Combine the sherry, soy sauce, sesame oil, ginger, scallions, and garlic and pour half over each piece of fish. Let marinate at room temperature for 1 hour.

3. Adjust your broiler so that the rack is about 4 inches from the heat. Heat the broiler for at least 10 minutes. Place one side of salmon on the broiler rack, skin side down, and broil without turning for 10 to 12 minutes, or until it is just cooked through but still moist and juicy. Set aside loosely covered with foil and repeat with the remaining side of salmon. (If the salmon is so thick that it doesn't cook in this time, transfer to a 450°F oven for about 5 minutes to finish off.) Serve garnished with lemon slices and parsley sprigs.

ROMAINE, RADICCHIO, AND FENNEL SALAD

12 TO 16 SERVINGS

Pretty with its strips of red, white, and green, this salad looks especially nice in a glass bowl. Because it's shredded, it is easy to serve and eat at a buffet.

Double the recipe for this party.

2 heads of romaine lettuce

1 large head of radicchio

2 large fennel bulbs

¼ cup sherry vinegar

¾ cup extra-virgin olive oil

Salt and freshly ground pepper

1. Separate the lettuce leaves and rinse well. Drain and dry.

2. Stack the lettuce and radicchio leaves and shred fine. Sliver the fennel bulbs as fine as possible. You can prepare this a day in advance. Refrigerate the lettuce and radicchio together wrapped in a clean white kitchen towel inside a sealed plastic bag or covered container. To keep it crisp, store the fennel in a covered container of lightly salted cold water.

3. In a large salad bowl, combine the romaine, radicchio, and fennel. Drizzle on the vinegar and then the oil. Toss to coat with the dressing. Season with salt and pepper to taste and toss again.

WILD RICE SALAD WITH CURRANTS AND PEPPERS

12 SERVINGS

This terrific party salad, the creation of Ila Stanger, former editor-in-chief of *Food & Wine* magazine, tastes much better if made the day before (and lasts well for a day after that). It just needs an hour out of the refrigerator to allow it to return to room temperature before serving.

Double the recipe for this party.

1 pound (2⅓ cups) wild rice

1 cup dried currants

4 carrots, peeled and finely diced

5 celery ribs, finely diced

1 small red bell pepper, finely diced

1 small yellow pepper (or use another red), finely diced

1 large red onion, finely diced

⅔ cup chopped parsley

1 large shallot, minced

1 cup extra-virgin olive oil

¼ cup balsamic vinegar

½ teaspoon freshly ground pepper

1. Rinse the rice well under cold running water. Place it in a large saucepan with 10 cups of water. Cover and bring to a boil. Remove the cover, reduce the heat, and simmer until the rice is tender but still pleasantly chewy, about 40 minutes. Drain and let cool.

2. Meanwhile, put the currants in a bowl and cover with warm water for 20 to 30 minutes, until they are plump; drain.

3. In a large bowl, combine the wild rice, currants, carrots, celery, bell peppers, red onion, and parsley, tossing to mix. In a small bowl, combine the shallot, olive oil, vinegar, and pepper; whisk to blend the dressing well. Pour the dressing over the salad and toss to coat. Serve at room temperature.

TRUFFLED BRIE

24 TO 30 SERVINGS

This dish is expensive but worth it. Choose the best brie you can, ripe but not ammoniated. The rind should have some light brown striations, and, even when cold, it should be no harder than a grapefruit.

1 wheel (8½ inches) of brie, about 2 pounds

8 ounces mascarpone

1 fresh white truffle (1 to 1½ ounces), finely minced, or 1 tube (2 ounces) white truffle paste

1. With a long, sharp knife, split the brie horizontally in half. In a small bowl, blend the mascarpone and white truffle. Spread it in an even layer over the cut side of the bottom half of the brie to about ¼ inch from the edge. Set the top of the brie back in place and press gently to sandwich the layers. If any filling squeezes out, use your finger or a narrow spatula to smooth it in place.

2. Wrap the brie in plastic wrap. If you've saved the wooden container it came in (I always do), set it back in the container. Refrigerate for 4 days to allow the flavors to develop. Let stand at room temperature for at least 3 hours before serving.

BOURBON-PEACH TRIFLE

24 SERVINGS

Made with store-bought pound cake, a trifle is one of the easiest desserts to serve to a large group. When peaches are out of season, opt for the individually quick-frozen ones without sugar rather than a rock-hard tasteless fruit.

4 pounds ripe peaches or 5 packages (12 ounces each) individually quick-frozen peach slices without added sugar

⅓ cup bourbon

2 tablespoons peach schnapps or Pecher Mignon

1 tablespoon plus ½ teaspoon fresh lemon juice

1⅔ cups plus 3 to 4 tablespoons granulated sugar

9 egg yolks

⅔ cup all-purpose flour

3 cups hot milk

1 tablespoon plus 1 teaspoon vanilla extract

2 pound cakes (12 ounces each)

2½ cups heavy cream

1 tablespoon confectioners' sugar

1 cup chopped or slivered toasted almonds

1. In a large pot of boiling water, blanch the peaches for 2 minutes, or until the skins peel off easily; drain. Peel and pit the peaches and cut them into ½-inch wedges over a bowl to catch the juices. (If using frozen peach slices, just let them defrost and be sure to include all their juices.) Put the fruit with any of its juices into a large bowl. Add the bourbon, peach schnapps, 1 tablespoon of the lemon juice, and 3 to 4 tablespoons of the granulated sugar, depending on the sweetness of the peaches. Toss gently and let stand for at least 3 hours; the peaches will exude more juice. (The peaches can be prepared a day ahead. Cover and refrigerate; toss occasionally.)

2. In a medium bowl, whisk the egg yolks to break them up. Gradually beat in ⅔ cup of the sugar. Whisk until the mixture turns pale yellow and forms a slowly dissolving ribbon when the whisk is lifted, 2 to 3 minutes. Beat in the flour. Gradually whisk in the hot milk and ½ cup of the juices from the peaches.

3. Pour the custard mixture into a heavy saucepan, preferably enameled cast iron. Cook over moderately high heat, whisking frequently, until the pastry cream is smooth and thick, 3 to 5 minutes. Reduce the heat to moderate and continue to boil, whisking, until the mixture relaxes and thins out slightly and loses any trace of a raw flour taste, about 3 minutes longer. Scrape into a bowl and whisk in 1 tablespoon of the vanilla. Cover with a piece of plastic wrap directly on the surface to prevent a skin from forming. Refrigerate until chilled. (The pastry cream can be made a day in advance.)

4. Trim the brown edges off the pound cakes. Cut them into ½-inch slices and then into pieces about 2 × 1 inch. Set aside.

5. Up to 6 hours before serving, whip the cream in a large bowl until it forms soft peaks. Transfer half to a medium bowl. Whisk about one-third of the remaining whipped cream from the large bowl into the pastry cream to lighten it. Turn the lightened pastry cream into the large bowl and fold in the remaining whipped cream in that bowl. Cover and refrigerate.

6. Add the confectioners' sugar and remaining 1 teaspoon vanilla to the whipped cream in the medium bowl and beat until stiff peaks form. Cover and refrigerate.

7. When you are ready to assemble the dessert, have on hand a large (5-quart) glass serving bowl, the peaches, pastry cream, and nuts; then make the caramel. In a small saucepan, combine the remaining 1 cup sugar and ½ teaspoon lemon juice with ⅓ cup water. Cook over moderately low heat, swirling the pan, until the sugar melts and the liquid is clear. Increase the heat to moderate and boil without stirring until the syrup caramelizes to a golden brown. It will continue to cook after you remove it from the heat, so don't wait too long. (You'll only use about two-thirds of the caramel, but I find it easier to work with a larger amount.)

8. Immediately arrange a layer of cake pieces in the bottom of the glass bowl. Cover with a single layer of the peach slices and their juices and, with a spoon, drizzle the hot caramel in a thin lacy pattern over the peaches; if you're heavy-handed, you'll end up with hard globs of caramel. Add a light sprinkling of almonds and spoon on about a 1-inch layer of the pastry cream. Repeat the layers until you use all the ingredients except a little caramel, 5 or 6 peach slices, and a couple of tablespoons of the nuts, which should be reserved for garnish. When you're through, spoon or pipe the whipped cream onto the top, drizzle on a little caramel, and garnish with the reserved peaches and almonds. Cover and refrigerate for up to 6 hours before serving.

BITTERSWEET CHOCOLATE TORTE

12 TO 16 SERVINGS

Bittersweet rather than cloying and just a little bit different from any other deep-chocolate dessert you've tasted. This rich creation is from one of Jean-Georges Vongerichten's former pastry chefs, Jean-Marc Burillier.

3 eggs

1 cup sugar

¼ cup all-purpose flour

2 tablespoons cake flour

2½ tablespoons unsweetened Dutch-process cocoa powder, preferably imported

½ cup fraise de Bourgogne (strawberry liqueur), framboise (raspberry eau-de-vie), or Grand Marnier liqueur

9 ounces best-quality bittersweet, sweet, or semisweet chocolate

2½ ounces unsweetened chocolate

2 cups heavy cream

Cocoa powder, for garnish

1. Heat the oven to 375°F. Butter an 8½- or 9-inch cake pan or springform pan. Dust with flour and tap out any excess.

2. In a metal bowl, beat the eggs with ½ cup of the sugar. Place over a pan of barely simmering water and whisk until the mixture is very warm, 3 to 5 minutes. Remove from the heat and beat with an electric mixer until the mixture is cold and falls back in a slowly dissolving ribbon, 3 to 5 minutes.

3. Sift together the all-purpose flour, cake flour, and cocoa. One-third at a time, fold the cocoa and flour into the egg mixture. Turn the batter into the cake pan and bake for 15 to 20 minutes, until a cake tester comes out dry and the edges are just beginning to pull away from the sides of the pan. Unmold onto a rack and let cool completely. The cake is best made a day ahead or bake it weeks or even months ahead and freeze; it is supposed to be dry.

4. To assemble the torte, cut the cake horizontally in half; you need only one half for this recipe. (Freeze the second half or make two tortes if you need them. You will need to double the ingredients for the syrup and ganache for two tortes.) Put the cake, cut side up, in the center of the bottom of a 10-inch springform pan. If you don't like to serve off the bottom of the springform, line it with a round of cardboard first.

5. In a small saucepan, combine the remaining ½ cup sugar with ½ cup water. Bring to a boil, stirring to dissolve the sugar. Boil for 1 minute; remove from the heat. Add the liqueur. Brush this syrup all over the cake; it will be very moist.

6. In a small heavy saucepan, melt the bittersweet and unsweetened chocolate in ⅓ cup of water over low heat, stirring frequently, until smooth. Remove from the heat and let cool until almost room temperature and slightly thickened.

7. In a large bowl, beat the cream until fairly stiff. Whisk about one-third of the cream into the chocolate to lighten it. Fold the chocolate into the remaining cream just until no streaks show. Pour this ganache, or chocolate cream, over the cake, filling in the gap around the edge of the springform. Smooth the top. Cover and freeze for 1 to 2 hours, until set, or refrigerate overnight. To unmold, run a knife around the edge; remove the side of the springform. Dust with cocoa before serving.

Southern Shrimp Boil

FOR 20 TO 24

PESTO DEVILED EGGS

CHEESE STRAWS

SOUR CREAM AND TWO-CAVIAR DIP (PAGE 191)
WITH SUMMER CRUDITÉS

LOUISIANA SHRIMP BOIL

CREOLE BUTTER DIPPING SAUCE

24-HOUR SALAD

CORN ON THE COB

RED AND YELLOW GRAPE TOMATOES

PORTUGUESE OR FRENCH BREAD

BROWNIE SUNDAES

MARGARET HESS'S BEST FUDGE BROWNIES

FRESH STRAWBERRY SUNDAES
WITH STRAWBERRY SAUCE

When I was young, we spent summers in a big stone house on a hill overlooking the ocean. Our neighbor's rock garden, a patchwork of brilliant colors abuzz with dragonflies and bees, led down to the beach path, lined with milkweed and wild roses. Above, a line of white pine and Seckel pear trees hemmed in our lawn. During the week, when we were there alone, the yard seemed as vast as the shore. But on weekends, with company milling all about, it barely contained the crowd. Anyone with a country house or even a comfortable backyard knows this phenomenon. Wherever you are, summer weekends bring guests—usually lots of them—and they're not always expected.

For those times when you're entertaining a couple of dozen good friends and you'd rather be outdoors in the sun than indoors cooking, here's a delightful backyard spread that's perfect for large-scale casual entertaining—a down-home, Southern-style shrimp boil. A combination of Cajun spice, Mediterranean freshness, and good old-fashioned food highlights this menu, which is easy to serve and fun to eat. Just spread out plenty of newspapers all over your backyard picnic table, set down a tall pile of paper napkins at either end, dump these tasty shrimp in the middle, place several bowls of butter strategically around the table, and let everyone have at 'em.

The appetizers range from frozen-ahead to easy-to-make to store-bought. Tangy cheese and a bit of hot pepper make cheese straws that are irresistible nibbles. Fresh basil and toasted pine nuts bring the flavor of pesto to a traditional deviled egg. For the crudités, scour your local farmers' market or raid your own garden for the prettiest, most unusual seasonal vegetables you can find. Serve them raw or lightly blanched, as their texture dictates, with the easy Two-Caviar Dip.

You'll need at least two big pots—10 gallons or more—for the shrimp and corn (borrow or rent an extra if you need it). Both cook quickly at the last moment. Allow ⅓ to ½ pound shrimp and 2 ears of corn per person and get help shucking. Guests shell their own shrimp as they eat them. Pile up the cherry tomatoes in large baskets, lined with dark green grape leaves if you have any vines growing near you.

The 24-Hour Salad, a classic American recipe found at more than one family reunion and church supper, is called that because it is assembled a day ahead. There's nothing fancy about it, but everyone loves it. Be sure you have a garage full of iced beer before you start and one or two large, clean, plastic-lined garbage cans for easy cleanup.

For dessert, just set out the components for the sundaes—brownie squares, vanilla ice cream, chocolate sauce, walnuts, sliced strawberries, strawberry sauce, and whipped cream—and let all your guests help themselves. It is, after all, the informal, self-serve aspect of this food that makes it so lighthearted.

DO-AHEAD PLANNING

UP TO A MONTH IN ADVANCE: Make the Cheese Straws and freeze them. Bake the brownies and freeze them.

UP TO 2 DAYS IN ADVANCE: Cook the eggs, shell them immediately, and store them in the refrigerator in a bowl of cold water to cover. Make the Creole Butter Dipping Sauce and refrigerate.

THE DAY BEFORE THE PARTY: Stuff the Pesto Deviled Eggs; cover and refrigerate. Prepare the crudités. Make two recipes of the 24-Hour Salad, except for the bacon. Make the Strawberry Sauce for the sundaes.

SEVERAL HOURS IN ADVANCE OF THE PARTY: Arrange the crudités on platters or in baskets; cover with a damp cloth. Make the Two-Caviar Dip. Make the court bouillon for the Shrimp Boil. Cook the bacon for the 24-Hour Salad. Slice the berries for the Strawberry Sundaes. Whip the cream for the sundaes; cover and refrigerate.

SHORTLY BEFORE SERVING: Boil the shrimp. Reheat the Creole butter sauce. Cook the corn on the cob. Add the bacon to the salad and toss. Reheat the Hot Fudge Sauce.

PESTO DEVILED EGGS

MAKES 48

For my taste, any deviled egg is a good egg. This version imparts a touch of sophistication to the standard classic with a few alternative ingredients: toasted pine nuts, fresh basil, and olive oil in place of mayonnaise.

⅓ cup pine nuts

2 dozen extra-large eggs

1 large bunch of basil

1 tablespoon plus 1 teaspoon Dijon mustard

1 tablespoon red wine vinegar

1 teaspoon hot pepper sauce

½ teaspoon salt

½ teaspoon freshly ground pepper

3 garlic cloves, crushed through a press

½ cup extra-virgin olive oil

1. Heat the oven to 300°F. Put the pine nuts on a small baking sheet and toast in the oven for about 8 minutes, until golden brown. Immediately transfer to a plate to cool. (The nuts can be toasted up to 3 days ahead and stored in the refrigerator in a covered container.)

2. Put the eggs in a large heavy pot and add water to cover by at least 1 inch. Bring to a simmer over moderately high heat, reduce the heat, and simmer for 12 minutes. Drain and rinse under cold water until cool. Peel the eggs immediately to avoid a dark ring around the yolk. (The eggs can be cooked and peeled up to 2 days in advance. Put in a bowl, cover with cold water, and refrigerate.)

3. Split the eggs in half lengthwise and remove the yolks. Wash and dry the basil. Set aside 48 small leaves for garnish. Coarsely cut up enough basil to measure ⅔ cup loosely packed. (Reserve the remainder for another use.)

4. In a food processor, combine the egg yolks, basil, mustard, vinegar, hot sauce, salt, pepper, and garlic. Pulse quickly until the mixture is blended and the basil is coarsely chopped. Add the pine nuts to the yolk mixture. With the machine on, add the olive oil through the feed tube until it is incorporated and the nuts are coarsely chopped.

5. Fill the egg white halves with heaping teaspoonfuls of the egg yolk–basil filling. Garnish each egg half with a small basil leaf. Cover and refrigerate for up to a day before serving.

CHEESE STRAWS

MAKES ABOUT 12 DOZEN

These are irresistible; there is no way anybody can eat just one . . . or two . . . or . . . This recipe makes a large batch, but you'll be surprised at how fast they disappear. And they freeze beautifully.

12 tablespoons (1½ sticks) unsalted butter

¼ pound extra-sharp white Cheddar cheese

¼ pound imported Parmesan cheese

2 cups all-purpose unbleached flour

1 teaspoon salt

⅛ teaspoon cayenne pepper

1 egg yolk blended with 3 tablespoons cold water

1. Heat the oven to 375°F. Set out 4 tablespoons of the butter to soften.

2. With the shredding disk on a food processor, grate the Cheddar cheese; transfer to a medium bowl.

3. With the metal blade on the processor, break the Parmesan into the bowl and finely grate. Add the Parmesan to the Cheddar and toss to mix.

4. Put the flour in the same processor bowl (no need to rinse). Add the salt and cayenne and process for 5 seconds to blend. Add the 1 stick cold butter, cut into tablespoons. Pulse (turn the machine quickly on and off) 12 times. Add half the mixed cheeses. Pulse 6 times. Add the remaining cheese and pulse 6 more times. The dough should be evenly mixed, but it will remain granular. Add the egg yolk and water and process just until the dough is evenly moistened, about 10 seconds.

5. Divide the dough in half and press each into a ½-inch-thick rectangle. Wrap one half in plastic and refrigerate. On a lightly floured surface, roll out the other half of the dough to an 8 × 12-inch rectangle, about ¼ inch thick. Spread 2 tablespoons of the softened butter over the dough. Fold in thirds like a letter, dust with flour, and roll out again. Fold in thirds a second time. (You can use the dough now or give it a couple more turns if you'd like it to be more puffed. If it becomes too soft to work with, refrigerate it for 10 to 15 minutes until it firms up. This is not a delicate dough, so feel free to pat and patch wherever necessary.)

6. To form the straws, roll out the dough to a rectangle about 8 inches wide and ⅛ to ¼ inch thick. Using a fluted rolling wheel cutter or a small sharp knife, cut the dough into straws 3½ to 4 inches long and ¼ to ⅜ inch wide. Use a pastry scraper or wide spatula to transfer them to lightly buttered baking sheets. Repeat with the remaining dough and butter. Place each sheet in the freezer for 10 to 15 minutes.

7. Bake the straws for 10 minutes, or until they are golden and crisp. Transfer to a rack and let cool. Store in an airtight container at room temperature for up to 5 days or freeze for longer storage.

LOUISIANA SHRIMP BOIL

20 TO 24 SERVINGS

Don't be misled by the long list of ingredients here. Much of it is made up of spices for the "court bouillon" in which the shrimp are boiled. The dish is actually just about the easiest thing you can do with a big pile of shrimp, and it is always hugely popular.

Because you need so much shrimp, and the bigger the better, a shrimp boil can get pricey. For that reason, I suggest you call your local fish market and ask for a wholesale price on volume. When you buy this much, you can usually get a substantial discount.

7 to 8 pounds medium shrimp (25 to 30 per pound) in the shell

⅓ cup mustard seeds

¼ cup coriander seeds

¼ cup allspice berries

2 tablespoons black peppercorns

2 tablespoons crushed hot red pepper flakes

12 whole cloves

6 blades of mace

3 imported bay leaves, broken in half

2½ tablespoons coarse salt

3 onions, thickly sliced

2 celery ribs, thickly sliced

6 garlic cloves, smashed

1 lemon, sliced

½ cup fresh lemon juice

Creole Butter Dipping Sauce (page 176)

1. Rinse the shrimp very well but do not shell. Drain and set aside. Fill a large (at least 10-quart) stockpot with 6 to 8 quarts of water. Add all the remaining ingredients except the dipping sauce. Bring to a boil, reduce the heat, and simmer for 15 minutes. (The court bouillon can be made several hours ahead.)

2. Just before you are ready to serve the shrimp, bring the court bouillon to a boil. Dump about one-third of the shrimp into the pot and boil for 2 to 3 minutes, until pink, loosely curled, and opaque throughout. Remove with a skimmer or slotted spoon and transfer to a bowl. (The shrimp in their shell will stay hot for a good 5 to 10 minutes.) Repeat twice with the remaining shrimp. Serve with the Creole dipping sauce.

CREOLE BUTTER DIPPING SAUCE

MAKES 3 CUPS

6 sticks (1½ pounds) unsalted butter

¼ cup fresh lemon juice

1 tablespoon Worcestershire sauce

2 to 3 teaspoons hot pepper sauce, to taste

1½ teaspoons salt

1. In a heavy medium saucepan, melt the butter over low heat. Skim the white foam off the top. Pour the clear butter into another saucepan or bowl, discarding the thick milky residue at the bottom of the pan. (This clarified butter can be made up to 2 weeks ahead and stored in a covered jar in the refrigerator.)

2. Whisk in the lemon juice, Worcestershire, hot sauce, and salt. (The flavored butter can be made up to 2 days ahead. Refrigerate in a covered jar.) Reheat over low heat until hot before serving.

Crudités

Nothing brightens up a buffet table or is more welcome to a group of nibblers than a colorful assortment of crudités with a tasty dip. Short of flowers, fresh vegetables are the most attractive thing you can put on a table. For that reason, it pays to give them some thought. Which will be more effective, creating large areas of color or a mix of contrasting light and dark together? Plan your design, thinking of your container as well. Will everything be standing up in a basket or piled in mounds on a platter? A lot of what you decide will depend on seasonal availability. Try to choose one or two unusual vegetables, along with the more standard carrots, bell peppers, broccoli, cauliflower, radishes, zucchini, and cherry tomatoes. Perhaps steamed artichokes, asparagus stalks, Belgian endive leaves, sticks of crisp jicama or fresh fennel, or even bunches of tiny white enoki mushrooms.

Though the French word *crudité* implies rawness, I am very opinionated on that subject. Some vegetables are wonderful raw—carrots, peppers, and tomatoes, to name a few. Others, such as broccoli, cauliflower, asparagus, and green beans, require at least momentary blanching in boiling water both to heighten their flavor and to soften them to a pleasing crunch rather than woody toughness. For display purposes, blanching also performs the important service of greatly intensifying the color of the vegetable. The boiling water breaks up tiny air pockets under the skin, brightening the color underneath. After blanching, be sure to rinse vegetables under cold running water to stop the cooking and set the color.

24-HOUR SALAD

12 TO 14 SERVINGS

In Texas, folks do a lot of large-scale entertaining. This ranch recipe, from Betty Jo Conlee of Bryan, Texas, is one she uses frequently at barbecues and picnics. It's a great boon to any busy cook because the salad is prepared a day ahead and just tossed together before serving. I like to add the bacon when I toss the salad with the dressing so that it stays crisp.

Make a double recipe in two bowls for this menu.

1 pound spinach, stemmed, rinsed, dried, and torn into large bite-size pieces, or substitute prewashed baby spinach leaves

1 medium red bell pepper, cut into 1½ × ¼-inch strips

3 scallions, cut into ½-inch lengths

1 large head of romaine lettuce, rinsed, dried, and torn into large bite-size pieces

½ red onion, very thinly sliced

½ pound Swiss cheese, shredded

1 package (10 ounces) frozen peas

4 hard-cooked eggs, sliced

1⅓ cups sour cream

⅔ cup mayonnaise

½ cup chopped parsley

⅓ cup minced fresh chives

2 garlic cloves, crushed through a press

1 tablespoon fresh lemon juice

1 tablespoon red wine vinegar

2 teaspoons Dijon mustard

½ teaspoon salt

¼ teaspoon freshly ground pepper

1 pound sliced bacon, cooked until crisp and crumbled

1. Up to 24 hours before you plan to serve the salad, layer in a large bowl in the exact order given—first the spinach, then the red pepper, scallions, half the romaine lettuce, the red onion, the remaining lettuce and the Swiss cheese. Scatter the frozen peas on top. Cover with a layer of the egg slices.

2. In a bowl, combine the sour cream, mayonnaise, parsley, chives, garlic, lemon juice, vinegar, mustard, salt, and pepper. Whisk to blend well. Spread the dressing over the top of the salad to cover it completely. Cover the bowl with plastic wrap and refrigerate for up to 24 hours.

3. Shortly before serving, toss the salad with the dressing until coated. Save about ½ cup bacon. Add the rest to the salad and toss again. Sprinkle the reserved bacon on top.

BROWNIE SUNDAES

12 SERVINGS

This dessert is a guaranteed crowd-pleaser for guests of all ages. For a dozen sundaes, you'll need only a half-recipe of brownies, but I'd make the whole batch, put them all out, and freeze the extras, if you are fortunate enough to end up with any. For a crowd, it's probably easiest just to put out all the fixings and let guests help themselves.

½ recipe Margaret Hess's Best Fudge Brownies (below), cut into 3-inch squares

2 to 3 pints good-quality vanilla ice cream

Rich Chocolate Sauce (page 31)

Whipped cream and broken walnuts

For each sundae, set a brownie on a plate. Top with a ½-cup scoop of vanilla ice cream. Drizzle a couple of spoonfuls of the fudge sauce over the ice cream and top with a dollop of whipped cream and a sprinkling of walnuts.

MARGARET HESS'S BEST FUDGE BROWNIES

MAKES 2 DOZEN 3-INCH OR 4 DOZEN 1½-INCH BROWNIES

These moist brownies are as rich as they come. The better the quality of chocolate you use, the better the brownies will taste.

2 pounds semisweet chocolate, cut up

4 sticks (1 pound) unsalted butter, cut up

7 eggs

2 cups sugar

1 tablespoon vanilla extract

2½ cups all-purpose flour

1½ teaspoons salt

¾ pound walnuts, optional

1. Heat the oven to 350°F. In a large double boiler or a large bowl placed in a skillet of water, melt the chocolate and butter together over simmering water, stirring until smooth. Remove from the heat.

2. In a mixing bowl, beat the eggs and sugar until they are light in color and begin to form a slowly dissolving ribbon when the beaters are lifted, about 2 minutes. Beat in the chocolate mixture and the vanilla. Mix until well blended, about 1 minute. Add the flour and salt and beat until just blended, 30 to 60 seconds. Stir in the walnuts, if you're adding them.

3. Pour the batter into a 13 × 18-inch half-sheet pan lined with waxed paper. Spread to an even thickness and bang the pan on the table two or three times to release any air bubbles.

4. Bake the brownies for 35 minutes. Let cool on a rack for 15 minutes before cutting into 3- or 1½-inch squares.

FRESH STRAWBERRY SUNDAES WITH STRAWBERRY SAUCE

12 SERVINGS

When fresh strawberries are in their summer prime, they offer a delightful alternative to chocolate. Don't be surprised if many of your guests opt for a small portion of each.

4 pints fresh strawberries

¼ cup sugar

3 tablespoons fraise de Bourgogne (French strawberry liqueur), framboise (raspberry brandy), or kirsch (cherry brandy)

2 teaspoons arrowroot or cornstarch

2 to 3 pints good-quality vanilla ice cream

Vanilla-flavored sweetened whipped cream, optional

1. Rinse the strawberries by dunking them in a bowl of cold water. Lift them out into a colander and drain well. Hull the berries. Reserve 12 of the most attractive berries for garnish. Halve or quarter 3 cups of the berries, depending on their size. Puree the remaining berries in a food processor until smooth; strain through a fine-mesh sieve to remove the seeds.

2. Put the cut berries in a bowl. Sprinkle with the sugar and liqueur and toss gently. Let stand at room temperature to macerate for at least 2 hours.

3. In a small nonreactive saucepan, bring the pureed strawberries to a boil over moderate heat. Drain the juice from the macerated strawberries into a small bowl and stir in the arrowroot until it is smooth and blended. Stir into the hot puree and cook, stirring, until the sauce thickens. Remove from the heat and let cool. Cover and refrigerate until serving time.

4. For each sundae, put a scoop of vanilla ice cream in a dessert bowl. Top with about ⅓ cup of the cut berries. Then spoon on about 3 tablespoons of the strawberry sauce. If you're including whipped cream, spoon a dollop on top and garnish the sundae with a whole strawberry.

Black and Orange Halloween Party

FOR 24

TACO BEAN DIP (PAGE 237) WITH TORTILLA CHIPS AND BABY CARROTS

HALLOWEEN CAVIAR PIE

THINLY SLICED PEPPERONI AND/OR SOPPRESSATA

CHOCOLATE CHILI WITH BEEF, PORK, AND BLACK BEANS

NO-STIR BUTTERNUT-LEEK RISOTTO

FRESH FENNEL SALAD WITH PICKLED RED ONIONS, ORANGE PEPPERS, AND BLACK OLIVES

ONE-POT RICH FUDGE BROWNIES WITH DRIED CHERRIES AND HAZELNUTS

CANDY CORN

CLEMENTINES OR TANGERINES

SANGRIA

BEER

Anyone who knows me well remembers one or another of my annual Halloween parties. Not otherwise noted for dramatic tendencies, on the October bewitching night, I cannot resist dressing up in costume and inviting all my friends over to do the same. Everyone groans at first, but then they get into it and the turnout is astonishingly creative, with the festive crowd looking like a lot of extras on a fantasy movie set.

Finally, though it's taken a bit of time, I think I've gotten the food to match. Some of my experiments in black and orange food have turned out less than appealing, even if they tasted fine. I learned the hard way what an ugly green color lumpfish caviar can turn when mixed with certain orange ingredients. But the theme was irresistible to add to the fun, and I think you'll agree, this is a menu that does, indeed, make the party. Plus, it will make *your* party, because the pace of the cooking will truly leave you enough time to enjoy Halloween along with your friends.

Taco Bean Dip is a cinch, whipped together in a food processor days in advance. Here you don't even need to cut up crudités, assuming you can live with baby carrots and tortilla chips. I didn't hear any complaints. For the Caviar Pie, which is a no-brainer, you need one of two pieces of special equipment: a template of a Halloween cat with an arched back or a friend with the talent to draw one. I opted for a friend.

The biggest production for the main course is the chili, and it does have a lot of ingredients and steps. All I can tell you is that I really believe it's worth the trouble and that it will open your eyes to the possibilities of cooking with dried chiles, as opposed to the prepared powder. To offset the labor involved, know that this fine dish can be made days in advance and refrigerated (it improves upon reheating) or weeks ahead and frozen. While prunes may sound like an odd ingredient, dried fruit is a traditional ingredient in *mole poblano,* and the dried plums add a lovely, mildly sweet deep note as well as dark color. Combined with just a hint of chocolate and some chiles negros, this stew, while a bit reddish, is about as black as you are likely to come, short of squid ink.

On the orange side, No-Stir Butternut-Leek Risotto can serve as a side dish for the meat-eaters at your party and as a main course for any vegetarians. It is one of my favorite risottos, and though you need to time it correctly because it is cooked at the last minute, as the title implies, it cooks on its own, so all you have to do is regulate the heat and serve. A refreshing salad, spiked with no-cook pickled red onions, oranges, and orange bell peppers, is dotted with black olives and completes the Halloween theme.

Dessert is easy: dynamite brownies and a big bowl of clementines or tangerines, which are in season and affordable in late fall. That's the food. Black and orange decorations to match are definitely called for here, and I always use a candlelit jack-o'-lantern as my centerpiece on the buffet table.

DO-AHEAD PLANNING

UP TO 3 DAYS IN ADVANCE: Make the Taco Bean Dip and refrigerate, covered. Make the Chocolate Chili and refrigerate or make it weeks in advance and freeze. Bake the brownies. Wrap well, first in plastic wrap, then in foil, and set aside at room temperature.

UP TO A DAY AHEAD: Roast the butternut squash and prepare the risotto through Step 4. Prepare the base for the Halloween Caviar Pie through Step 1; refrigerate in a covered container. Pickle the red onions for the salad. Prepare the romaine for the salad.

THE DAY OF THE PARTY: Prepare the Caviar Pie through Step 2; cover and refrigerate. Cut up the fennel and bell peppers for the salad.

SHORTLY BEFORE THE PARTY: Finish the Caviar Pie. Reheat the Chocolate Chili very slowly over low heat. Finish the salad.

ABOUT 30 MINUTES BEFORE SERVING THE MAIN COURSE: Finish the risotto.

HALLOWEEN CAVIAR PIE

24 SERVINGS

This simple creamy spread, topped with a black cat, bat, or witch made out of caviar, is perfect for the holiday. I use lumpfish or whitefish roe, but if you have the budget for it, mallosol, which is lightly salted, pressed sturgeon caviar, would work beautifully here. You need to be a little artistic to make this a dramatic presentation. Since I am not, I get the base all ready and then ask a friend to arrange the caviar on top. For others digitally challenged like me, a stencil offers an independent alternative. Garnish the platter, if you like, with lemon wedges and serve with small squares of cocktail rye or pumpernickel.

1 pound reduced-fat cream cheese (Neufchâtel)

1 cup sour cream

1 medium shallot, chopped

½ teaspoon grated lemon zest

⅛ to ¼ teaspoon ground chipotle chile or cayenne pepper

3 to 4 ounces black caviar—lumpfish, whitefish, or the real thing

1. In a food processor, combine the cream cheese, sour cream, shallot, lemon zest, and hot pepper. Puree until smooth.

2. Turn the spread out onto a platter and smooth into a layer about ⅜ inch thick. You can make this a round, a square, or a shape that mimics your top design.

3. If the caviar is runny, and the lumpfish will be, pour off as much liquid as possible or strain it through a fine-mesh sieve. Arrange the caviar on top of the cream cheese in a Halloween shape, such as a cat, bat, or witch.

CHOCOLATE CHILI WITH BEEF, PORK, AND BLACK BEANS

MAKES 3 GALLONS; 24 TO 30 SERVINGS

Calling this chili is a bit of an understatement. It is a complexly flavored stew modeled after an authentic Mexican *mole negro.* Unlike more everyday chilies, it requires no extra garnishes. I guarantee you raves. Three secret ingredients, which are not obvious in the finished dish but contribute to its extraordinary flavor, are: toasted almonds, prunes, and chocolate. The chocolate may sound like a ringer, but it is an essential ingredient in the Mexican dish as well as in certain classic Italian game stews. It sounds a rich, dark note but remains subtle because of all the other flavors.

This dish is not hard, but it does have a number of steps. The good news is that you can make it up to 2 days in advance; the flavor will only improve. Real dried chiles are used in place of chili powder; they are worth the trouble. Chiles are becoming more readily available in many supermarkets; and of course, all Latin markets sell them. They are not expensive; if you can't find them, it is worth mail-ordering a batch and storing them in the freezer.

Coarse ground meat makes a big difference here. Order ahead and ask your butcher to put both the beef and the pork through the coarse grinder only once.

1 box (12 ounces) pitted prunes

½ cup inexpensive dry sherry or Madeira

½ cup vegetable oil

12 ancho chiles

5 chiles negros or pasilla chiles

4 California or New Mexico chiles

1 cup slivered almonds

2 medium onions, coarsely chopped

3 large garlic cloves, coarsely chopped

4 cups chicken stock

4 pounds coarsely ground beef chuck

4 pounds coarsely ground boneless pork loin

Coarse salt and freshly ground pepper

¼ pound bacon, finely diced

3 tablespoons ground cumin

1½ tablespoons dried oregano, Mexican if you have it

2 teaspoons ground cinnamon

2 tablespoons tomato paste

4 ounces bittersweet chocolate

4 cans (15 ounces each) black beans, drained but not rinsed

1. Put the prunes in a glass or ceramic bowl with the sherry and ½ cup of water and microwave for 45 seconds. Stir, cover, and set aside to soften.

2. Toast the chiles: In a large cast-iron skillet, heat about 2 teaspoons of the vegetable oil over moderate heat. Using tongs and working in batches, toast each chile for 10 to 15 seconds on each side. The idea is to soften the dried chiles slightly, not to brown them; some may puff up. When you are through with each batch, transfer the chiles to a large bowl. Reduce the heat if necessary to prevent scorching. When all the chiles are toasted, cover them with boiling water and set aside to soften.

3. Meanwhile, in the same skillet, toast the almonds over moderate heat, stirring often, until they are fragrant and lightly browned, about 5 minutes. Remove to a small bowl.

4. In a food processor, pulse the onions and garlic until very finely chopped; you may need to do this in 2 batches. Set the onions aside. You'll use the processor again, but there's no need to rinse it.

5. When the chiles are soft and cool enough to handle, pull them apart and discard the seeds, stems, and any thick ribs. Put the trimmed chiles in another bowl. Strain the chile soaking water and reserve 2 cups.

6. In the food processor, puree the chiles and toasted almonds in batches with the reserved soaking water and some of the stock, if you need it, to make a smooth paste. Without washing the processor, puree the prunes with their soaking liquid and some of the stock, if you need it, until smooth.

7. At this point, you need to prepare the meat. Season the beef and pork with 4 teaspoons salt and 1 teaspoon pepper. Brown the meat in one of two ways: Either roast it spread out in a very large roasting pan in a 425°F oven, stirring several times, for 30 to 40 minutes, then drain off the fat. Or brown it in the same cast-iron skillet in 3 or 4 batches, stirring occasionally. If you do this, pour off the fat in between batches.

8. In a very large pot (I use a 4-gallon stockpot), heat the remaining oil over moderately high heat. Add the bacon and cook until it just begins to render its fat, 3 to 5 minutes. Add the onions and garlic and cook, stirring often, until the onions are golden and beginning to brown, 10 to 15 minutes.

9. Add the cumin, oregano, and cinnamon and toast the spices for 2 to 3 minutes. Add the tomato paste and chile-almond paste and cook, stirring for 3 to 5 minutes. Add the browned meat, the remaining stock, and 4 cups of water. Bring to a boil, reduce the heat, and simmer, partially covered, for 45 minutes.

10. Stir in the chocolate until melted. Add the beans. Season with salt to taste.

11. You'll find if you make this in advance that it may want more salt after a while. Because this makes such a huge amount of thick chili, allow plenty of time to reheat over moderately low heat, stirring the bottom with a wooden spatula so the sauce doesn't burn. If you make it the same day you plan to serve it, it's probably best to simply reheat it every few hours to prevent spoilage, rather than try to cool it off and then reheat it.

NO-STIR BUTTERNUT-LEEK RISOTTO

24 SERVINGS

I have to give credit for this startlingly simple way of making risotto to Carol Field, whose pumpkin and rice recipe in her marvelous book *Celebrating Italy* inspired this dish. What makes it perfect for entertaining is that the base can be made a day ahead. Let the mixture return to room temperature and then 20 to 30 minutes before serving the main course, simply put the pot on the heat. This savory risotto will be perfectly cooked when you're ready for it.

Tip: If you have some truffle butter in your refrigerator or freezer, this is the place to use it; it will turn what is a delicious dish into something sublime. Alternatively, substitute a couple of tablespoons of white truffle oil for some of the butter at the end.

5 pounds butternut squash (2 medium-large squash)

2 large leeks (white and tender green)

¼ cup extra-virgin olive oil

11 tablespoons unsalted butter

1 large shallot, minced

1½ teaspoons crushed sage leaves

1 teaspoon freshly grated nutmeg

¼ teaspoon cayenne pepper

2 teaspoons coarse salt

2 pounds (32 ounces) Arborio or other risotto rice

8 cups chicken, meat, or vegetable stock

2 cups freshly grated imported Parmesan cheese

1. Heat the oven to 400°F. Poke 4 or 5 holes in each squash with the tip of a small knife. Roast directly on the rack of the oven, turning several times, until the squash are just tender, about 45 minutes. Remove and let cool.

2. When the squash are cool enough to handle, cut them in half, scoop out the seeds and fibrous membranes, and peel off the skin. Cut the squash into 1-inch cubes.

3. To make the risotto base, quarter the leeks lengthwise, then thinly slice. Dump into a large bowl of cold water and swish to remove any sand. Heat the olive oil and 3 tablespoons of the butter in a very large heavy-bottomed pot. (I use an 8-quart Le Creuset casserole.) Lift the leeks out of the bowl with your hands and add them to the pot. Add the shallot, stir to coat with the oil, cover, and cook over moderately low heat for 5 to 7 minutes, or until the leeks and shallot are very soft.

4. Add the sage, nutmeg, cayenne, and salt. Cook, stirring often, for 2 minutes; remove from the heat and let cool slightly. Add the rice and stir to mix with the leeks and oil. Put the squash on top and gently fold once or twice. (The base can be made ahead to this point up to a day in advance. Let return to room temperature before proceeding.)

5. About half an hour before you're ready to serve the risotto, pour in the stock and 2 cups of water, set the pot over moderate heat, cover, and bring to a boil. Reduce the heat to a simmer and cook for 15 minutes. Uncover, stir once, and continue to cook for 3 to 5 minutes, until the rice is just tender but still firm in the center.

6. Stir in the remaining 1 stick butter in bits, then stir in the cheese. Serve at once.

FRESH FENNEL SALAD WITH PICKLED RED ONIONS, ORANGE PEPPERS, AND BLACK OLIVES

24 SERVINGS

Orange peppers are called for here simply because it's Halloween. With red, yellow, or even a mix of colored peppers, this salad is a good choice anytime you need a crisp vegetable for a couple of dozen people.

1 large red onion

¼ cup sherry vinegar

2 teaspoons sugar

2 teaspoons coarse salt

3 large bulbs of fresh fennel

1 lemon

2 medium-large orange bell peppers

1 large head of romaine lettuce

1½ teaspoons Dijon mustard

⅔ cup extra-virgin olive oil

Freshly ground pepper

½ pound Mediterranean black olives—use your favorite, oil- or brine-cured

1. Quarter the onion lengthwise and then cut crosswise into very thin slices. Combine in a bowl with the vinegar, sugar, 1 teaspoon of the salt, and 3 tablespoons cold water. Let stand, tossing occasionally, for at least 3 hours or overnight.

2. Trim the stems and root ends from the fennel bulbs. Halve or quarter them lengthwise and then slice as thinly as possible. I do them on a mandoline (see Note) or in a processor with the thin slicing disk. Fennel discolors after a time, so put the slices in a covered container with the juice from the lemon, the remaining 1 teaspoon salt, and cold water to cover. Put the lid on and refrigerate until you're ready to assemble the salad.

3. Thinly slice the bell peppers and refrigerate them in a sealed plastic bag or covered container. Cut the romaine lengthwise in half or quarters and then cut crosswise into very thin slivers. Soak in a bowl of cold water for at least 10 minutes; then spin dry in batches and store in a sealed plastic bag in the refrigerator.

4. Up to 2 hours before serving, drain the red onions over a bowl to catch the vinegar. Whisk the mustard into the vinegar. Gradually whisk in the oil in a thin stream to make an emulsified dressing. Season with pepper to taste.

5. Up to 45 minutes before serving, toss the romaine with a generous half of the dressing and arrange it on a large platter, making a bed all the way to the edge. Drain the fennel and scatter it over the lettuce, leaving a dark green margin around the rim. Drizzle a couple of tablespoons of dressing over the fennel. Scatter the pickled onions over the fennel and top with the pepper slices. Drizzle the remaining dressing over all. Garnish with the black olives. Cover with plastic wrap and set aside at room temperature until you're ready to serve the salad.

Note: For a special look, if you have a mandoline or Japanese vegetable slicer, slice the fennel bulbs lengthwise paper-thin the day before. Soak them in cold water overnight; they will curl up loosely like ruffles.

ONE-POT RICH FUDGE BROWNIES WITH DRIED CHERRIES AND HAZELNUTS

MAKES 54

I don't care how many brownie recipes you have, if you like moist, fudgy brownies with intense chocolate flavor, these can go head to head with the best. I should add, while kids will scarf them up, these really are an adult confection. Since these have so little filler, the flavor and quality of both the butter and the chocolate really do make a difference. I use sweet butter and a premium baking chocolate, such as Scharffen Berger.

1 cup (4 ounces) dried cherries

2 tablespoons kirsch (cherry brandy), brandy, or orange liqueur

2 sticks (½ pound) unsalted butter

8 ounces unsweetened chocolate, broken up

2¾ cups sugar

6 eggs

1 tablespoon vanilla extract

1⅓ cups all-purpose flour

1 cup chopped hazelnuts

1. Put the dried cherries and kirsch in a glass bowl or measuring cup with 2 tablespoons water. (If you don't want to use any alcohol, simply up the water to ¼ cup or use coffee.) Microwave on high for 45 seconds. Stir, then set aside to let the cherries soften and cool.

2. Heat the oven to 350°F. Butter and flour a 13 × 18-inch half-sheet pan.

3. In a large, heavy-bottomed pot (I use a 5-quart enameled cast-iron casserole), melt the butter over moderately low heat. When it is about half melted, add the chocolate and continue to melt the two together, stirring often. Be sure to scrape the bottom of the pot and lower the heat, if necessary, so the chocolate doesn't scorch. When about three-fourths of the butter is melted, turn the heat off and let the rest of the butter and chocolate melt from the heat of the pan.

4. Gradually stir the sugar into the chocolate mixture. Continue to mix until most of the sugar is melted and the mixture is smooth.

5. Add the eggs, 1 at a time, beating vigorously with a wooden spoon until each is fully incorporated before adding the next. Beat in the vanilla. Add the flour in 2 additions, mixing just until blended. Add the cherries with their soaking liquid and the nuts. Stir to distribute evenly.

6. Turn the batter into the pan and spread out evenly. Bake for 20 to 22 minutes. The top should firm and the brownies just beginning to separate from the edges of the pan. Do not overbake. The insides should still be soft and fudgy.

7. Let cool completely, then cut into 1½-inch squares.

SANGRIA

MAKES ABOUT 6 QUARTS; 20 TO 24 SERVINGS

Besides the fact that this is simply the best sangria you've ever tasted, it is great for a party because it is so inexpensive. The best—and most authentic—wine to use for sangria is Grenache, which costs well under $10 a bottle. Make the sangria early in the morning or preferably a day ahead so it has time to ripen and be sure to have a couple of trays of ice on hand for final service.

2 cups sugar

5 cinnamon sticks

5 oranges

1 lemon

3 flavorful apples, such as McIntosh or Braeburn

2 Bartlett pears

5 bottles (1 liter each) Grenache wine or Grenache blend, preferably Spanish

½ cup Cognac or brandy

1. In a medium saucepan, combine the sugar and cinnamon sticks with 2 cups of water. Bring to a boil, stirring to dissolve the sugar. Remove from the heat and pour in 2 cups of cold water.

2. Prepare all the fruit: Scrub the oranges and lemon with both liquid detergent and water; rinse well and dry. Rinse and dry the apples and pears. Quarter the oranges through the stem ends and then slice them crosswise. Put in a very large bowl or in a large pot. Remove the zest from the lemon in wide strips with a paring knife or swivel-bladed vegetable peeler. Add the zest to the oranges. Squeeze the juice from the lemon into the bowl. Quarter the apples and pears, remove the stems and cores, and slice the fruit. Add to the citrus.

3. Pour the syrup and cinnamon sticks over the fruit and stir to mix. Pour the wine over the fruit, stir in the Cognac, cover, and refrigerate the sangria for up to 2 days.

4. To serve, pour 2 trays of ice into a punch bowl or other serving vessel. Pour the wine and fruit into the bowl. When serving, give everyone some fruit with the wine.

BRIDAL SHOWER

FOR 24

GINGERED EGGPLANT SPREAD

SOUR CREAM AND TWO-CAVIAR DIP

TOASTED FRENCH BREAD

CRISPY CHEESE PUFFS (PAGE 158)

FRUITED CHICKEN AND HAM SALAD
WITH BASIL-WALNUT DRESSING

SESAME-GINGER GRILLED SALMON (PAGE 166), SERVED
CHILLED OR AT ROOM TEMPERATURE

COLD SESAME NOODLES

ROASTED ASPARAGUS

STRAWBERRY CREAM CAKE

CHAMPAGNE OR PROSECCO
NONALCOHOLIC PARTY PUNCH

Since one major delight of a party like this is not only the mingling of friends but the opening of presents, it's an event that tends to stretch out longer than many others. For that reason, early afternoon, around one, offers a leisurely afternoon to socialize and celebrate while letting everyone return home before dark. That means you'll be serving around one-thirty or two, which calls for a celebratory lunch that is not too heavy and pretty food, which will show well in the light.

A selection of dips and bake-ahead cheese puffs ensures that the first part of the meal is easy on the hostess. For the main buffet, a chicken and ham salad—adorned with apples, pears, and grapes as well as walnuts—and ever-popular Cold Sesame Noodles also allow much advance preparation, so all you have to do is grill or broil the salmon and roast the asparagus. Both these last-minute dishes can, in fact, be cooked an hour or two ahead and served at room temperature. That will give you plenty of time to garnish the platters.

The cake, of course, is a star. This eye-catcher, with its striking pink icing, makes a stunning bed for the red strawberries that top it. A cake this colorful needs no further garnish, but if you like, fresh roses would be lovely: pink or red, of course—or both. While I propose this as a shower for an engagement, the same menu would work as well for a baby shower. Don't forget a glass of bubbly to toast the bride-to-be and nonalcoholic punch or another beverage for those who eschew alcohol.

DO-AHEAD PLANNING

UP TO A MONTH IN ADVANCE: Make the Crispy Cheese Puffs. Freeze them in a sealed container or plastic freezer bags.

UP TO 2 DAYS IN ADVANCE: Poach the chicken. Make the Raspberry Buttercream for the cake.

UP TO A DAY AHEAD: Make the Gingered Eggplant Spread and the Two-Caviar Dip. Prepare the Basil-Walnut Dressing for the chicken salad. Cook the Chinese noodles and toss them with half the sesame oil; store them in the refrigerator in a covered container or sealable plastic bags. Bake the cake and frost it, but do not top with the berries.

THE MORNING OF THE PARTY: Finish the Chicken Salad. Broil or grill the salmon. Top the cake with the strawberries. Refrigerate all this food. Make the sauce for the sesame noodles; set aside at room temperature.

SHORTLY BEFORE EVERYONE ARRIVES: Roast the asparagus. Remove all the food from the refrigerator. Toss the sauce with the cold noodles.

JUST AS THE GUESTS BEGIN ARRIVING: Pop the frozen cheese puffs into the oven. Pass them hot.

GINGERED EGGPLANT SPREAD

MAKES ABOUT 5 CUPS

Years ago, Chinese food expert Bruce Cost, author of *Ginger East to West,* gave me the recipe for this rich northern Chinese eggplant, loaded with fresh ginger. For a party, serve it in a pretty bowl, with a basket of toasted French bread slices on the side. It can be made the night before but should be allowed to return to room temperature and stirred up before serving.

3 pounds small, thin Asian eggplants

Peanut oil

3 tablespoons soy sauce, preferably dark

3 tablespoons sugar

1½ tablespoons distilled white vinegar

1 tablespoon pale dry sherry or Chinese rice wine

2 tablespoons finely minced fresh ginger

1 tablespoon finely minced garlic

1 teaspoon Asian sesame oil

⅓ cup toasted sesame seeds

1. Rinse and dry the eggplants but do not peel. Trim off both ends and cut the eggplants crosswise on a diagonal into ½-inch ovals.

2. In a wok or large skillet, heat about 1 inch of peanut oil over moderately high heat to 375°F. Fry the eggplant in batches without crowding, turning, until golden brown, 3 to 5 minutes per batch. As they are cooked, remove the eggplant slices with a skimmer or slotted spoon and spread out on paper towels to drain.

3. In a small bowl, combine the soy sauce, sugar, vinegar, and sherry. In a clean wok or large skillet, heat 2 tablespoons of peanut oil over moderately high heat until it just begins to smoke. Add the ginger and garlic and stir-fry for about 10 seconds, until fragrant. Add the soy sauce mixture and stir briefly. Add the fried eggplant and stir quickly to coat all the slices with sauce. Remove from the heat and transfer to a bowl. Drizzle the sesame oil over the eggplant and stir gently to mix. Let cool to room temperature before serving. (The eggplant can be made a day ahead and refrigerated, covered. Let return to room temperature before serving.)

4. To serve, stir up the eggplant, mashing some of the slices. Stir in 3 tablespoons of the toasted sesame seeds. Mound in a serving bowl. Sprinkle the remaining sesame seeds on top.

SOUR CREAM AND TWO-CAVIAR DIP

MAKES ABOUT 2½ CUPS

This dip is particularly good with Belgian endive leaves, assorted raw or partially cooked vegetables, and even low-salt potato chips.

2 cups (1 pint) sour cream

2 ounces salmon caviar

2 ounces golden whitefish caviar

⅓ cup minced fresh chives

Stir together all the ingredients. Cover and refrigerate until serving time. Serve chilled.

FRUITED CHICKEN AND HAM SALAD WITH BASIL-WALNUT DRESSING

20 TO 24 SERVINGS

It's surprising how refreshing and stylish a good chicken salad can be. This is one of the best, with clean, enticing flavors and wonderful texture. Dark meat is my choice for salad, chunks of poached thighs, which yield silky, moist chicken. If you prefer white meat, though, you can use skinless, boneless breasts or even the meat from a large roast chicken. For best results, cook the chicken in advance but assemble the salad the day you plan to serve it, so the fruit doesn't soften. I like to mound this on a large platter atop a bed of arugula, lightly dressed with white wine vinegar and olive oil. The pungency of the bitter green contrasts nicely with the sweetness of the fruit in the salad.

3 pounds cooked chicken meat

1 pound Black Forest or other flavorful ham, sliced ⅜ inch thick

10 ounces seedless red grapes

3 ripe but firm pears

3 flavorful tart apples

1 cup dried cherries, cranberries, or currants (or use a combination)

Basil-Walnut Dressing (page 192)

1. Cut the chicken into ½-inch dice. Dice the ham. Halve the grapes. Core the pears and apples but leave the peels on; cut into ½-inch dice. If the dried fruit is hard, soak it in hot water to soften, then drain.

2. In a large bowl, toss together the chicken, ham, grapes, pears, apples, and dried cherries. Add the dressing and toss to coat. If not serving soon, cover and refrigerate for up to 6 hours.

Note: To poach chicken breasts or thighs, place them in a saucepan of lightly salted water and slowly bring to a boil. Skim off the foam as it rises to the top. Immediately reduce the heat to a low simmer and cook the breasts for 15 to 20 minutes, the thighs for 20 to 25. Remove from the heat and let the chicken cool in the cooking liquid, then refrigerate, still in the liquid, overnight.

BASIL-WALNUT DRESSING

MAKES ABOUT 3½ CUPS

If walnut oil is not in your cupboard, it's worth seeking out. Just a tablespoon or two is a wonderful addition to almost any vinaigrette. Here it reinforces the flavor of the toasted walnuts. The amount of curry used here is not enough to be fully recognizable, but it boosts the flavor of the fruit in the salad with a mild piquancy.

1½ cups chopped walnuts

1¼ cups mayonnaise

1¼ cups sour cream

3½ tablespoons fresh lemon juice

1½ teaspoons Madras curry powder

⅓ cup walnut oil, preferably French

Sea salt, preferably fleur de sel, and freshly ground pepper

1 cup lightly packed basil leaves

1. Heat the oven to 350°F. Spread out the walnuts in a small baking pan and toast in the oven until lightly browned and fragrant, 7 to 10 minutes. Remove to a dish and let cool.

2. In a food processor, combine the mayonnaise, sour cream, lemon juice, and curry powder. Whirl to blend. With the machine on, slowly add the walnut oil through the feed tube. Season liberally with salt and pepper.

3. Add the basil and pulse until coarsely chopped. Scrape into a bowl and stir in the toasted walnuts. Cover and refrigerate until serving time.

COLD SESAME NOODLES

20 TO 24 SERVINGS AS A SIDE DISH

Easy and irresistible, these noodles are always a hit. The trick is to get the noodles really cold but have the sauce at room temperature when you toss them. If the sauce is refrigerated, it will stiffen up. If you don't have Chinese noodles, substitute 2 pounds thin linguine.

3 packages (10 ounces each) dried Chinese noodles

½ cup Asian sesame oil

1½ cups smooth peanut butter, at room temperature

½ cup soy sauce

⅓ cup rice vinegar

⅓ cup packed dark brown sugar

2 garlic cloves, crushed through a press

1 teaspoon crushed hot red pepper

⅔ cup minced scallions

¼ cup toasted sesame seeds

1. In a large pot of boiling salted water, cook the noodles, carefully separating the strands with a pasta fork or other long fork as they soften, until just tender, about 2 minutes. Drain and rinse under cold running water to cool and stop the cooking; drain well.

2. In a large bowl, toss the noodles with ¼ cup of the sesame oil to coat the strands and prevent sticking. Cover and refrigerate until cold.

3. In a blender or food processor, combine the remaining ¼ cup sesame oil with the peanut butter, soy sauce, vinegar, brown sugar, garlic, and hot pepper. Whirl until blended. Thin with ½ cup hot water.

4. Pour the sauce over the noodles, add ½ cup of the scallions and half the sesame seeds and toss to mix. Sprinkle the remaining scallions and sesame seeds on top. Serve chilled or at room temperature.

ROASTED ASPARAGUS

24 SERVINGS

Roasting, rather than boiling or steaming, intensifies the flavor of asparagus. Plus, there's no big pot of boiling water on the stove to deal with. It also obviates the need to peel the stalks and imparts a faint hint of smoke. The only tricks to success are to be sure the oven is preheated to the proper temperature and to use very shallow pans, such as baking sheets or half-sheet pans. A deep roasting pan will create too much steam.

4 pounds fresh asparagus

6 tablespoons olive oil

2 teaspoons coarse salt

Lemon wedges, for garnish

1. Heat the oven to 425°F. Break or cut off the tough bottom ends of the stalks. Rinse the asparagus well. For smaller amounts, I just run the bunches under the faucet. For this amount, it's probably easier to soak the stalks for a few minutes in a large bowl of cold water. Drain briefly in a colander.

2. Spread out the asparagus on 2 large baking sheets or half-sheet pans, making as close to a single layer as you can. Drizzle half the olive oil over each batch. Toss the stalks with your hands to coat them with the oil. Sprinkle with the salt.

3. Roast the asparagus for 10 to 12 minutes, turning them over with tongs once about halfway through. They are done when the asparagus is bright green with a tinge of brown in spots and the stalk bends just slightly when it is lifted; do not overcook. Transfer to a platter and garnish with lemon wedges. Serve warm or at room temperature.

Note: If you make the asparagus several hours in advance, you might want to line the platter with a white cloth napkin to absorb any juices that seep out.

STRAWBERRY CREAM CAKE

24 TO 30 SERVINGS

By and large, when you're baking a cake for this many people, a sheet cake is the easiest way to go. This calls for a 9 × 13 × 2-inch rectangular pan, a size worth having on hand if you plan to bake for large numbers with any regularity.

Lush, pink raspberry buttercream dresses up an excellent vanilla-almond cake, and the entire package is lavishly covered with fresh strawberries for a gala dessert that is a little like strawberry shortcake taken to the nth degree. Gorgeous on its own, the cake can be further adorned, if you wish, with a small bouquet or two of roses or pansies or with a sprinkling of candied rose petals or violets.

12 tablespoons (1½ sticks) unsalted butter, at room temperature

1½ cups sugar

4 eggs

2 teaspoons vanilla extract

2 cups all-purpose flour

1 cup almond flour (see Note)

1½ teaspoons baking powder

1 teaspoon baking soda

1 cup buttermilk

Raspberry Buttercream (opposite page)

3 pints fresh strawberries

1. Heat the oven to 350°F. Butter a 9 × 13-inch baking pan. Line the bottom with waxed paper. Butter the paper and dust with flour; tap out any excess.

2. With an electric mixer, whip the butter until light and fluffy. Gradually beat in the sugar. Then beat in the eggs, 1 at a time, beating well between additions. Beat in the vanilla.

3. In a medium bowl, combine the all-purpose flour, almond flour, baking powder, and baking soda. Whisk gently to blend. Sprinkle half the dry ingredients over the egg batter and stir until almost blended. Mix in half the buttermilk. Repeat with the remaining dry ingredients and buttermilk and mix just until evenly blended. Scrape the batter into the pan and rap it on the counter to release any air bubbles.

4. Bake the cake for 25 to 30 minutes, or until the edges are just beginning to pull away from the sides of the pan and a toothpick inserted in the center comes out clean. Let the cake cool in the pan for 10 minutes, then unmold onto a rack and peel off the waxed paper. Let cool completely before frosting and garnishing with the berries. I like to cover the entire cake and sides, then pipe a ribbon around the edges and fill in with the berries.

Note: Almond flour, sometimes called almond meal, can often be found in the health food section of your supermarket if you don't see it on the baking shelf. If you cannot find almond flour, which is simply very finely ground almonds, first add 1 cup slivered almonds to a food processor fitted with the shredding disk through the feed tube. Change to the metal blade and process the shredded almonds with ½ cup of the sugar until the almonds are ground as finely as possible.

RASPBERRY BUTTERCREAM

MAKES ABOUT 5 CUPS

Master baker Nick Malgieri, author of many cookbooks, including *Perfect Cakes*, uses unsweetened frozen raspberries to flavor and color an easy Swiss buttercream, made with just egg whites, no yolks.

1 package (10 ounces) individually quick-frozen raspberries without added sugar

1¼ cups granulated sugar

Pinch of salt

5 egg whites

3 sticks (¾ pound) unsalted butter, at room temperature

1. Dump the raspberries into a small nonreactive saucepan. Stir in ¼ cup of the sugar and the salt. Bring to a boil, reduce the heat to moderately low, and boil until reduced and thickened to about ¾ cup puree, about 10 minutes. Strain through a sieve to remove the seeds. Let the raspberry puree cool.

2. In a large heatproof bowl, beat the egg whites until frothy. Gradually beat in the remaining 1 cup sugar. Set over a saucepan or deep skillet of simmering water and whisk until the egg whites are hot and the sugar is dissolved, 3 to 5 minutes.

3. Remove from the heat and beat with an electric mixer until the meringue is cooled and thickened, about 5 minutes. Gradually beat in the butter, a few tablespoons at a time. (If made ahead, cover and refrigerate for up to 3 days; let soften, then beat again until smooth and fluffy.)

4. Just before using, beat in the raspberry puree.

The Ultimate Tailgate Party

FOR 24

BLOODY MARY TOMATO SOUP

CHEESE STRAWS, HOMEMADE (PAGE 174) OR PURCHASED

LENTIL SALAD WITH GOAT CHEESE AND TOMATOES (PAGE 71)

GRILLED MARINATED FLANK STEAK

CHICKEN PASTA SALAD WITH LEMON-SESAME DRESSING

POTATO SALAD WITH SWEET SAUSAGES AND MUSHROOMS

GREEN BEAN SALAD WITH ROASTED RED PEPPERS (PAGE 253)

ITALIAN BREAD

SHARP CHEDDAR CHEESE (BUY A SMALL WHEEL IF YOU CAN) AND TART APPLES

CHOCOLATE CHUNK PECAN COOKIES

A tailgate party is by definition a picnic away from home, traditionally in the parking lot of a football stadium, though the venue could be any place you drive to. Whether the spread is laid out on a blanket, a folding table, or the tailgate of your station wagon or SUV, the nature of the party dictates the style of the food. That is, it must travel well, look pretty without a lot of fussy garnishes, and, preferably, taste good at room temperature.

The meal begins with a nicely spiced—and liberally spiked—tomato soup, aptly called Bloody Mary Tomato Soup, served in cups or mugs. Depending upon the weather, you may offer it hot or cold. Since it uses a mix of fresh and canned tomatoes, it can be made almost any season. Of course, if children are present, set some aside before adding the vodka, thinning it, if necessary, with a little extra stock. Crisp, savory cheese straws will be popular with or without the soup.

For the main event, three substantial international salads and one lighter vegetable salad offer enough choices to please all your guests: a chicken and broccoli pasta salad with a Middle Eastern lemon-sesame dressing; a French-style lentil salad with fresh and sun-dried tomatoes and goat cheese; an Italianate potato salad with chunks of sausage and mushrooms; and a colorful green bean salad with slivers of red bell peppers. Despite the appeal of all these selections, an irresistibly tasty flank steak, marinated in a soy-sesame marinade flavored with star anise, will still be the star of the party.

You have two options with the meat. Either marinate it 2 days before the event, grill it a day ahead, wrap it thinly sliced, and serve just slightly chilled; or as suggested in the do-ahead planning notes that follow, transport it to the picnic in the marinade in a sealed container. Then grill the steak on-site on a small portable grill and serve it hot. Either way, you cannot miss.

Dessert is easy both to carry and to eat. Good Cheddar cheese (the older, the better) and crisp, juicy apples provide a segue to the real crowd-pleasers, giant cookies loaded with everything good: oats, currants, pecans, and, best of all, two kinds of chocolate—dark and white.

DO-AHEAD PLANNING

UP TO 5 DAYS IN ADVANCE: Bake the Chocolate Chunk Pecan Cookies. Store at room temperature in a closed container.

UP TO 3 DAYS AHEAD: Roast and peel the red peppers for the green bean salad. Refrigerate them in a bowl, covered with olive oil.

UP TO 2 DAYS IN ADVANCE: Make the Bloody Mary Tomato Soup through Step 2.

THE DAY BEFORE THE PICNIC: Cook the chicken, pasta, and broccoli and make the lemon-sesame dressing. Make the Lentil Salad with Goat Cheese and Tomatoes. Make the Potato Salad with Sweet Sausages and Mushrooms. Cook the green beans.

THE MORNING OF THE PICNIC: Make the marinade for the steak. Transport the meat in the marinade in a tightly covered container and grill it at the picnic site. (Alternatively, grill the steak the night before and bring it already sliced.) Finish the soup. Toss the Green Bean Salad with Roasted Red Peppers and the Chicken Pasta Salad with Lemon-Sesame Dressing just before leaving the house.

BLOODY MARY TOMATO SOUP

MAKES ABOUT 6 QUARTS; 24 CUP-SIZE SERVINGS

A mix of fresh and canned tomatoes imparts an intense, bright flavor to this zippy soup. Of course, the final splash of vodka is optional. Note the equally delicious variation, which softens the soup with cream and fresh basil. Either way, this is a smooth soup that can be served hot or cold and is easily transported in large beverage thermoses to keep it hot or cold, as you wish.

2 pounds ripe plum tomatoes

3 large leeks (white and tender green)

¾ cup extra-virgin olive oil

1 tablespoon sugar

½ cup flour

6 cups chicken stock

2 cans (35 ounces each) Italian peeled tomatoes, with their juices

1 tablespoon coarse (kosher) salt

2 tablespoons Worcestershire sauce

1½ teaspoons Tabasco sauce, or more to taste

¼ cup fresh lemon juice

2 cups vodka

1. Bring a large pot of water to a boil. Dump in the tomatoes and cook for 10 seconds. Drain in a colander and rinse under cold running water. The peels of the tomatoes will slip right off. Halve or quarter the tomatoes and set aside.

2. Trim the leeks and cut lengthwise in half, then cut crosswise into thick slices. Swish the leeks in a bowl of cold water, then lift out to drain, leaving any sand behind in the bowl.

3. Heat the olive oil in a large pot. Add the leeks, cover, and cook over moderate heat for 5 minutes. Uncover, raise the heat to moderately high, and sauté, stirring, until the leeks are soft and just beginning to color, 5 to 7 minutes longer. Add the cut plum tomatoes and sugar and cook, stirring occasionally, until the tomatoes give up some of their juices and begin to soften, about 5 minutes.

4. Sprinkle the flour over the leeks and tomatoes and cook, stirring, for another minute or two. Whisk in the chicken stock and bring to a boil, whisking several times to blend, until thickened. Add the canned tomatoes with their juices, the salt, Worcestershire sauce, and Tabasco. Return to a boil, reduce the heat to a simmer, and cook partially covered, stirring occasionally, for 20 minutes. Stir in the lemon juice and taste. Puree in the pot with an immersion blender or in batches in a food processor or blender. Adjust the taste with salt and sugar as needed.

5. If serving hot, pour in the vodka and ladle into a thermos or into individual cups. If serving cold, let cool, then stir in the vodka and refrigerate, covered, until chilled.

Creamy Tomato Soup with Fresh Basil

Prepare the soup as described above through Step 4 but omit the Worcestershire sauce and lemon juice. Add 1½ cups heavy cream and simmer for 2 minutes. Stir in 1 cup finely shredded fresh basil with the vodka.

Potluck

These days, potluck makes more sense than ever, especially for entertaining a crowd. No one has as much time as he or she needs, and people enjoy themselves more when they contribute something to the party. For a picnic or tailgate, when the attention is on the out-of-doors and having fun, get the cooking done ahead and spread out the chores. If you are playing host, you might design the menu in detail or outline it and let friends fill in the blanks with their favorite recipes. Just make sure you don't end up with three chicken salads and two chocolate cakes.

Once the menu is planned, consider sending around a sheet with all the recipes listed, as well as where and when you are assembling. It will serve as a reminder and raise enthusiasm for the event. I've been at potluck parties where all the recipes were distributed to everyone who brought something—a nice souvenir and a great way to add to your repertoire. Chances are if a friend loves a recipe and finds it doable, you will too.

People who don't like to cook or who won't be around beforehand can bring bread, cheese, apples, beverages, and the like. As coordinator, make sure there is a grill, if you need one, as well as charcoal and matches. Make sure there are serving utensils, coolers, and plenty of ice. If it's paper plates, cups, napkins, and plastic utensils, make sure you have extra. If you're assigning this responsibility to some of the guests, establish a color scheme so everything matches. And make sure you throw in a couple of large plastic garbage bags for cleaning up.

Potluck suppers can make great charity fundraisers. For a special potluck party—indoors or out—consider a theme (Italian, Chinese, seafood, or something sillier like South Seas, black and white, the Fifties) with appropriate props and dress. Sometimes it's fun to go all out with flowers, silver, china, and evening dress, if you are so inclined.

GRILLED MARINATED FLANK STEAK

20 TO 24 SERVINGS

Nothing is as succulent or satisfying as a perfectly grilled piece of beef, and flank steak is an excellent choice when you're marinating it first. Thinly sliced, with no waste, it feeds a crowd easily. Just be sure not to overcook it; rare or medium-rare is perfect for this cut.

1 cup soy sauce

¼ cup packed dark brown sugar

12 black peppercorns

3 star anise pods

2 imported bay leaves

1 small dried hot red pepper, optional

2 tablespoons vegetable oil

2 tablespoons Asian sesame oil

3 large garlic cloves, crushed through a press

4 to 5 pounds flank steak, trimmed of excess fat

1. In a small nonreactive saucepan, combine the soy sauce, brown sugar, peppercorns, star anise, bay leaves, hot pepper, and vegetable oil. Bring to a boil, stirring to dissolve the sugar. Reduce the heat to low and steep the marinade for 5 minutes. Remove from the heat, add ⅓ cup water, and let cool.

2. Stir the sesame oil and garlic into the marinade. Put the flank steak in 1 or 2 large glass baking dishes (so that the meat lies in a flat layer). Pour the marinade over the meat and turn the steaks to coat. Marinate at room temperature, turning every 20 or 30 minutes, for at least 45 minutes and up to 3 hours.

3. Light a hot fire in the grill or heat the broiler. Grill the steak, turning once, for 3 to 5 minutes per side, until rare (you can cook it longer, but flank steak is best rare—juicy and tender). Let stand, loosely covered with foil, for 5 to 10 minutes before slicing. Serve warm or at room temperature.

CHICKEN PASTA SALAD WITH LEMON-SESAME DRESSING

24 SERVINGS

My friend Irene Thomas is of Lebanese descent, and she taught me how to make the fabulous dressing used in this salad, which is also excellent as a sauce on broiled or grilled fish and on vegetables or as a dip with toasted pita bread.

3 pounds skinless, boneless chicken breasts

2 pounds pasta shells or penne, preferably imported

¼ cup plus 2 tablespoons extra-virgin olive oil

Coarse (kosher) salt and freshly ground pepper

1⅓ cups plus 2 tablespoons fresh lemon juice

2 large shallots, minced

2 large bunches of broccoli (2½ to 3 pounds)

8 garlic cloves, crushed through a press

2 cups tahina (Middle Eastern sesame seed paste)

¼ to ½ teaspoon cayenne pepper

2 large red bell peppers, cut into ½-inch squares

1 cup thinly sliced scallions

1. Rinse the chicken breasts under cold running water and put them in a large saucepan. Add lightly salted water to cover by at least 1 inch. Bring to a simmer, reduce the heat to moderately low, and cook at a bare simmer, partially covered, for 20 minutes, or until the chicken is still juicy but white throughout; do not allow to boil. Let the chicken cool in the cooking liquid.

2. Meanwhile, in a large pot of boiling salted water, cook the pasta until it is tender but still slightly firm to the bite, 10 to 12 minutes. Drain, rinse in a bowl of cold water, and drain well. Put the pasta in a very large bowl and toss with ¼ cup of the olive oil, 1 teaspoon salt, and ½ teaspoon pepper.

3. Remove the chicken from its cooking liquid (which can be saved for stock) and trim off any cartilage or bits of fat. Cut the chicken into ¾-inch cubes. In a large bowl, toss the chicken with the remaining 2 tablespoons olive oil, 2 tablespoons of the lemon juice, the shallots, 2 teaspoons salt, and ½ teaspoon pepper.

4. Separate the tops of the broccoli into 1- to 1½-inch florets. Peel the stems and cut them crosswise on the diagonal into ½-inch-thick slices. Steam the broccoli over boiling salted water until just tender but still bright green, about 5 minutes. Rinse immediately under cold running water; drain well. (The chicken, pasta, and broccoli can all be prepared a day ahead. Cover the bowls, put the broccoli in a plastic bag, and refrigerate separately.)

5. In a medium bowl, combine the crushed garlic with 2 teaspoons salt; mash to a paste. Blend in the tahina and remaining 1⅓ cups lemon juice. Gradually whisk in 2 cups hot water and the cayenne. (The dressing can be made a day ahead. Cover and refrigerate. Thin with additional water if necessary.)

6. To assemble the salad, add the chicken, broccoli, red bell pepper, and scallions to the pasta. Toss lightly to mix. Drizzle on the dressing and toss to coat. Season with additional salt and pepper to taste. (The salad can be assembled up to 6 hours ahead.) Serve slightly chilled or at room temperature.

POTATO SALAD WITH SWEET SAUSAGES AND MUSHROOMS

20 TO 24 SERVINGS

This hearty salad, from Convito Italiano—a chic Chicago Italian food shop, restaurant, and catering firm—is unusual in that it is made with no vinegar. Consequently, it is full of flavor but easy to eat . . . lots of. The salad can be served as a side dish or as one of a number of offerings on a buffet. My favorite way to eat it is as a main-course salad, along with some well-dressed arugula and tomato. As a main course by itself, the dish will serve 12.

3 pounds small red-skinned potatoes or yellow fingerling potatoes, preferably organic

2 pounds sweet Italian sausages

½ cup dry red wine

⅔ cup plus 2 tablespoons extra-virgin olive oil

1 pound mushrooms, sliced

1 teaspoon fresh lemon juice

Salt and freshly ground pepper

¾ cup chopped scallions

1½ tablespoons Dijon mustard

⅓ cup dry white wine

⅓ cup chicken stock or canned broth

1. Put the potatoes in a large saucepan of salted water and bring to a boil. Cook the potatoes until tender, 15 to 20 minutes. Let cool slightly, then slice. Put the potatoes in a large bowl.

2. Meanwhile, heat the oven to 375°F. Put the sausages in a single layer in a baking dish and prick them several times with a fork. Bake for 10 minutes. Turn and bake for 10 minutes. Add the red wine to the baking dish, turn the sausages, and bake for 6 minutes. Turn the sausages once more and bake for 5 minutes longer, or until the wine is evaporated. Remove the sausages to a dish and let cool. Slice into rounds and add to the potatoes.

3. In a large skillet, heat the 2 tablespoons olive oil. Add the mushrooms and sauté over moderately high heat, tossing, until they are nicely browned, 5 to 7 minutes. Sprinkle on the lemon juice and season lightly with salt and pepper. Add to the potatoes and sausages. Add the scallions. Toss lightly to mix.

4. In a food processor or blender, combine the mustard, 1 teaspoon salt, ½ teaspoon pepper, the white wine, and stock. Blend to mix well. With the machine on, slowly add the remaining ⅔ cup olive oil. Pour the dressing over the salad and toss to coat. Serve warm or at room temperature or cover and refrigerate overnight.

CHOCOLATE CHUNK PECAN COOKIES

MAKES 24 LARGE COOKIES

You'll probably want to double this recipe, because these cookies, while quite large, are irresistible. I like big chunks of chocolate, but chips can substitute.

2 sticks (½ pound) unsalted butter, at room temperature

¾ cup packed dark brown sugar

¾ cup granulated sugar

3 eggs

1 tablespoon vanilla extract

2 cups flour

1 teaspoon baking soda

¾ teaspoon salt

2 cups rolled oats

1 cup bittersweet, sweet, or semisweet chocolate chunks

½ cup white chocolate chunks

1 cup pecan pieces

1 cup dried currants or raisins

1. Heat the oven to 350°F. Grease 2 or 3 large cookie sheets for baking the cookies in batches.

2. In a large mixing bowl, cream the butter with the brown sugar and granulated sugar until light and fluffy. Beat in the eggs, 1 at a time, beating well after each addition. Beat in the vanilla.

3. In another bowl, combine the flour, baking soda, and salt. Whisk gently to mix. Add the oats and toss with the flour. Add the dry ingredients to the butter mixture and stir with a wooden spoon until evenly blended. Stir in the bittersweet chocolate, white chocolate, pecans, and currants.

4. Use a ¼-cup measuring cup to scoop up the cookie dough. Drop it onto the cookie sheets, leaving about 2 inches in between. Press lightly on the dough with the back of the measuring cup to flatten slightly. If the dough begins to stick, dip the back of the cup in sugar before pressing.

5. Bake 14 to 16 minutes, or until the cookies are lightly browned around the edges. Transfer to a wire rack to cool.

Texas-Style Barbecue

FOR 24 TO 30

PEPPER-PECAN CORNBREAD

GUACAMOLE FOR A CROWD (PAGE 237)
AND FRESH TOMATO SALSA (PAGE 149)
WITH TACO CHIPS

BARBECUED CARNITAS WITH PINEAPPLE-CHIPOTLE SALSA (PAGE 236)

MESQUITE-SMOKED BARBECUED BRISKET OF BEEF

TEXAS-STYLE BBQ SAUCE

MESQUITE-GRILLED CHICKEN WITH SAUSAGES (PAGE 47)

COOL CABBAGE SALAD WITH CARROTS AND RED PEPPERS (PAGE 242)

EGG AND POTATO SALAD WITH ROASTED RED PEPPERS

BACON AND BRANDY BAKED BEANS (PAGE 229)

STRAWBERRY CORN SHORTCAKES

A "crowd" in Texas can be as oversized as the state. They know how to have a good time out there and don't even blink at a guest list that might fill a football stadium elsewhere. I've scaled things down a bit for this big old barbecue, but I've kept the exuberant flavors and relaxed style that typifies Western outdoor entertaining. It's a menu that works well anywhere and requires nothing more than a barbecue grill and a warm smile to guarantee a great party.

If you look carefully, you'll notice that cornmeal is used three times in this menu. Corn flavors the taco chips, served here with guacamole. It also appears in the slightly unusual cornbread, adapted from a recipe from the San Simeon restaurant in Dallas, and in the cloudlike biscuits for the dessert shortcake.

I must confess, I am proud of this Mesquite-Smoked Barbecued Brisket of Beef. I smoke it for 2 hours, in a smoker or a covered grill, and then bake it slowly in the oven until it shreds with a fork. For a fiesta this size, you'll want to make two of the briskets and a double recipe of the Texas-Style BBQ Sauce. To make things easier with everyone milling about, marinate and grill the chicken and blanch the sausages a day ahead. Then reheat them in the oven or on the grill at the last minute.

While the Egg and Potato Salad can be made a day ahead, it has a fresher, creamier taste if the components are prepared in advance and the salad is assembled only several hours before serving. Remember to begin the Bacon and Brandy Baked Beans 3 days ahead, especially if you plan to soak the beans overnight. With all this food, one recipe should be enough. Likewise, the refreshing Cool Cabbage Salad with Carrots and Red Peppers.

With dessert for this many, I suggest you partially split the light, fluffy corn shortcakes and pile them up in baskets. Put out bowls of the strawberries and whipped cream so guests can help themselves. With a pretty cloth and maybe some wildflowers, it will make a lovely presentation. If you're having more than two dozen guests, make an extra half-recipe of dessert; there will be extras, but I'm sure they'll disappear.

DO-AHEAD PLANNING

UP TO 1 MONTH IN ADVANCE: Bake the Pepper-Pecan Cornbread and the Corn Shortcakes. Freeze both.

UP TO 3 DAYS BEFORE THE BARBECUE: Smoke and bake two beef briskets. Soak the beans overnight. Roast the bell peppers. Make the Bacon and Brandy Baked Beans.

THE DAY BEFORE THE BARBECUE: Make the guacamole. To prevent discoloration, cover the top with a film of mayonnaise thinned with lemon juice, cover the bowl with plastic wrap, and refrigerate. Stir to blend well before serving. Marinate a double recipe of pork for the carnitas. Make the Texas-Style BBQ Sauce. Marinate the chicken (and grill it if you wish). Precook the sausages. Boil the potatoes for the salad.

THE DAY OF THE BARBECUE, UP TO 6 HOURS IN ADVANCE: Make a large bowl of Fresh Tomato Salsa. Assemble the Egg and Potato Salad; cover and refrigerate. Make the Cool Cabbage Salad and refrigerate until serving.

ABOUT 3 HOURS BEFORE GUESTS ARRIVE: Make the Pineapple-Chipotle Salsa; set aside at room temperature. Macerate the strawberries and whip the cream for the Strawberry Corn Shortcakes. Defrost the shortcakes.

SHORTLY BEFORE SERVING: Reheat the Pepper-Pecan Cornbread in the oven. Grill the carnitas. Reheat the mesquite-smoked brisket in the oven and the Texas-Style BBQ Sauce on top of the stove. Adjust the seasoning of the sauce if necessary. Reheat the chicken in the oven if it's precooked or grill it. Grill the sausages until browned. Reheat the baked beans in the oven for 30 to 40 minutes.

PEPPER-PECAN CORNBREAD

MAKES ABOUT 70 SQUARES

A professional trip to Dallas, Texas, led me to this unusually savory cornbread. Sweet peppers impart lovely color and extra flavor without the heat of the usual jalapeños, though you can substitute half a dozen or so of those, minced, for one of the green peppers if you prefer your cornbread spicy.

4 ears of corn, shucked

1 cup plus 1 tablespoon corn oil

2 large red bell peppers

2 large green bell peppers

1 cup pecans, coarsely chopped

4 eggs

1⅓ cups sugar

2½ cups milk

2 teaspoons salt

5½ cups all-purpose flour

2½ cups yellow cornmeal, preferably stone-ground

4 tablespoons baking powder

6 tablespoons honey

1. Brush the corn with 1 tablespoon of the oil. Roast the corn and the red and green bell peppers directly over a gas flame or under a hot broiler as close to the heat as possible, turning, until the corn is roasted to a light brown and the peppers are charred all over, 5 to 10 minutes for the corn and 10 to 15 minutes for the peppers. Put the peppers in a bag and steam for 10 minutes. Remove the blackened skins and the stems, seeds, and ribs and cut the peppers into ½-inch dice. Cut the corn off the cob.

2. Heat the oven to 375°F. Grease 2 rectangular baking pans, 9 × 13 inches.

3. In a large, dry cast-iron skillet, sauté the peppers, corn, and pecans over moderately high heat, stirring often, for about 5 minutes to toast them lightly. Set aside.

4. In a large mixing bowl, beat the eggs with an electric mixer. Gradually beat in the sugar and then the milk and salt. Beat on medium-high speed for 2 minutes. Scrape down the sides of the bowl. Gradually beat in the flour, cornmeal, and baking powder. Beat for 3 minutes. Gradually beat in the remaining 1 cup oil and the honey. Mix until smooth. Reserve ½ cup of the peppers, corn, and pecans; stir the rest into the batter.

5. Turn the batter into the greased pans. Sprinkle ¼ cup of the reserved pepper mixture over the top of each pan. Bake for 30 minutes, or until a tester comes out clean and the cornbread is beginning to pull away from the sides of the pan. Let cool slightly before cutting into squares.

Dry Marinades

Most of us are familiar with oil and vinegar or wine-based marinades for grilling. They tenderize the meat and add moisture as well as extra flavor. Dry marinades, or spice mixtures, are not as commonly used, but they too tenderize and add flavor in a different way. A dry marinade is not completely dry; sometimes it is moistened to a paste with onion and a little oil and vinegar or citrus juice. Rubbed into meat, it is like a short-term curing process, which works extremely well with foods to be barbecued. As demonstrated in the Backyard Barbecue (page 94), it turns chicken into instant barbecue, with no sauce needed. It's also great on roast pork and is a prerequisite for an authentic smoked barbecued brisket.

Any dry marinade begins with salt and pepper. For this purpose, I prefer coarse (kosher) salt. It has no additives and works well for this purpose. Don't be alarmed at the amount of coarse salt called for; because of the size of the crystals, 1 teaspoon of coarse salt is equivalent to about ½ teaspoon of ordinary table salt. The pepper should be freshly ground in a pepper mill. For flavor, I prefer Tellicherry, which can be found in specialty food shops, but any kind will do. Cayenne pepper is another must. Believe it or not, even cayenne pepper can lose its fire if it's old enough. If yours has been on the shelf for over a year and it's a dusty brick brown rather than bright red, buy a new jar. (These days, many spice companies label their hot red pepper as such, rather than calling it cayenne. They can be used interchangeably.)

Other spices and herbs in the dry marinade can vary, but for barbecue I always add a hefty dose of ground cumin and frequently oregano—and I prefer the taste of Mexican oregano. Paprika produces appealing color. I am partial to the imported sweet Hungarian paprika; it has fine flavor as well as a nice color. Experiment, if you like, with your favorite dried herb, perhaps thyme or tarragon in place of oregano, and with different meats and cuts—lamb chops, steaks, pork chops, roasts, and ribs.

Here is my basic dry marinade, which you can mix up and set aside in a covered jar in a cool, dark place for whenever you need it. When you're ready to marinate the meat, for every 5 pounds, put 2 to 3 tablespoons of the Basic Spice Blend in a food processor. Add 1 medium onion cut up, 2 garlic cloves, 2 tablespoons olive oil, and 2 tablespoons fresh lemon or lime juice and puree. Smear over the meat and let marinate in the refrigerator overnight or at room temperature for 2 to 3 hours before grilling.

Basic Spice Blend

½ cup coarse salt

¼ cup sweet Hungarian paprika

2 tablespoons coarsely cracked black peppercorns

1 to 1½ tablespoons cayenne pepper, to taste

1½ tablespoons crumbled dried oregano

1 tablespoon ground cumin

MESQUITE-SMOKED BARBECUED BRISKET OF BEEF

12 TO 16 SERVINGS

Here's my answer to pit-smoked barbecue; it's as close as you can get with most home equipment, and I think it gives excellent results. If meat is smoked all night, it often ends up tasting like wood chips. Here spice-rubbed brisket is smoked over mesquite coals—either in a smoker or with the indirect method over your charcoal grill—for 2 hours to impart that inimitable flavor. Then it's finished in a very low oven, wrapped tightly so that it braises in its own juices. I guarantee this is one of the best barbecued briskets you'll ever taste.

Double the recipe for this party.

1 whole brisket of beef, 9 to 10 pounds

2 tablespoons coarse salt

2 teaspoons coarsely cracked black pepper

2 teaspoons sweet Hungarian paprika

1 teaspoon cayenne pepper

1 teaspoon crumbled dried oregano, preferably Mexican

½ teaspoon ground cumin

Texas-Style BBQ Sauce (opposite page)

1. Ask your butcher to trim the brisket, leaving just a thin layer of fat. The meat will weigh 7 to 8 pounds after trimming. Put the brisket in a large glass baking dish.

2. Combine the salt, black pepper, paprika, cayenne, oregano, and cumin and rub into both sides of the meat. Let stand at room temperature for about 2 hours.

3. If you are using a smoker, follow the manufacturer's instructions for mesquite smoking. If you are using a covered grill, place enough mesquite chunks to cover the bottom of your grill in a bucket; cover with water and soak for 45 minutes. Meanwhile, in a covered grill or smoker, start a charcoal fire. When the coals are covered with white ash, add the mesquite. When the fire is hot, put the brisket on the grill rack. Grill for 5 minutes, then turn and cook for 5 minutes longer.

4. When you are through searing the meat, splash the coals with water so that only a red glow remains. Cover the grill. If it is gas, turn to the lowest setting. If it is a kettle grill, adjust the vents so that the fire is as slow as possible. Smoke the brisket for 1 hour. Turn and smoke for 1 hour longer. Check the grill several times during smoking to be sure the wood is smoking. Splash the fire with water or open the vents or turn up the heat, if necessary, to keep the smoking going without charring the meat (it will finish cooking in the oven).

5. After 2 hours, remove the brisket from the grill or smoker. Wrap well in 2 layers of heavy-duty foil. Place in a preheated 250°F oven and bake for 4 hours. If baked ahead, let cool a bit without unwrapping, then refrigerate for 2 or 3 days before serving.

6. To reheat, place the wrapped brisket in a preheated 300°F oven and bake until heated through, 1 to 1½ hours (if it's coming straight from the refrigerator). Drizzle with a little barbecue sauce and pass the remainder on the side. Thinly slice the brisket, crosswise on the diagonal. It will be so tender, it will almost shred.

TEXAS-STYLE BBQ SAUCE

MAKES ABOUT 2½ CUPS

To obtain the drippings, unwrap the brisket after baking. If it has been chilled, the drippings will be jellied. Double the recipe for this menu.

1¼ cups cider vinegar

¾ cup ketchup

3 tablespoons dark brown sugar

2 tablespoons Worcestershire sauce

2 tablespoons drippings from Barbecued Brisket (opposite page), optional

1 tablespoon soy sauce

1 medium onion, minced

1 teaspoon ground cumin

1 teaspoon powdered mustard

1 to 2 teaspoons hot pepper sauce, depending on whether you like your sauce spicy or hot

In a small nonreactive saucepan, combine all the ingredients. Stir to blend well. Bring to a boil, reduce the heat to low, and simmer uncovered, stirring occasionally, for 45 minutes. The sauce can be made up to 2 days ahead.

EGG AND POTATO SALAD WITH ROASTED RED PEPPERS

24 SERVINGS

This rich salad can be served as a side dish or as a luncheon main course with green salad.

2 dozen eggs

4 pounds red-skinned potatoes

3 medium red bell peppers

2 cups mayonnaise

3 tablespoons white wine vinegar

3 tablespoons tiny (nonpareil) capers

1½ cups finely chopped red onion

2 dozen anchovy fillets (preferably bottled), drained, rinsed, and coarsely chopped

3 tablespoons chopped parsley

3 tablespoons chopped fresh basil

2 tablespoons Dijon mustard

Salt and freshly ground pepper

1. Put the eggs in a large flameproof casserole. Add cold water to cover by 1 inch. Bring to a boil, reduce the heat, and simmer for 12 minutes. Remove from the heat and let stand for 5 minutes. Drain and let cold water run into the pan to cool the eggs. Peel immediately. (The eggs can be prepared up to a day ahead and refrigerated in a bowl, covered with cold water, but I prefer them freshly cooked in this salad.)

2. Put the potatoes in a large pot, cover with cold salted water, and bring to a boil over moderately high heat. Cook for 15 to 25 minutes, or until tender. Drain, let cool, then peel. Cut the potatoes into ½-inch dice.

3. Roast the peppers directly over a gas flame or under a broiler as close to the heat as possible, turning, until charred and blackened all over, 7 to 10 minutes. Seal in a bag and let steam for 10 minutes. Peel the peppers, discarding the stems, seeds, and ribs. Cut the peppers into ½-inch dice.

4. Put the mayonnaise in a large bowl. Blend in the vinegar, capers, onion, anchovies, parsley, basil, and mustard. Coarsely chop the eggs and add to the mayonnaise. Add the potatoes and peppers and toss to mix. Season with salt and pepper to taste. Cover and refrigerate until serving time.

STRAWBERRY CORN SHORTCAKES

24 SERVINGS

Cornmeal adds a little nuttiness and a slight crunch to shortcake biscuits, which I find very appealing. Partially crushing the berries and macerating them with sugar and a little liqueur and orange zest for at least an hour draws out their juice and amplifies their flavor.

5 pints strawberries

¾ cup granulated sugar

¼ cup fraise de Bourgogne (strawberry liqueur) or Grand Marnier liqueur, optional

1 tablespoon grated orange zest

4 cups (1 quart) heavy cream

½ cup confectioners' sugar

1½ tablespoons vanilla extract

24 Corn Shortcakes (opposite page)

1. Set aside 24 perfect berries in a separate bowl for garnish. Hull and thickly slice the remaining berries. With a potato masher or fork, lightly crush the sliced berries. Sprinkle on ½ cup granulated sugar, the strawberry liqueur, if you have it, and the orange zest. Taste and add the remaining sugar if needed. Cover and set aside at room temperature for at least 1 hour.

2. In a chilled bowl with chilled beaters, whip the cream until it mounds softly. Add the confectioners' sugar and vanilla and beat the cream until firm but not stiff. Cover and refrigerate for up to 4 hours before serving.

3. To serve, split the shortcakes horizontally in half. Lay the bottom on a dessert plate or in a shallow bowl and cover with crushed strawberries and their juice. Put the top on, add a generous dollop of the whipped cream, and garnish with a whole berry.

CORN SHORTCAKES

MAKES 24

Partially prepared in a food processor, these take only minutes to assemble. Unless you have an extra-large bowl, make the dough in two batches without rinsing the bowl in between.

You should make another half-recipe if you've invited more than 24 guests. Extras always seem to disappear.

4½ cups all-purpose flour

2¼ cups yellow cornmeal, preferably stone-ground

⅔ cup sugar

¼ cup baking powder

1 teaspoon baking soda

1 teaspoon salt

Zest from ½ orange, removed with a swivel-bladed vegetable peeler

2 sticks (½ pound) cold unsalted butter, cut into tablespoons

3½ cups heavy cream

1. Heat the oven to 450°F. Grease 2 large baking sheets.

2. In a food processor (in two batches if necessary), combine the flour, cornmeal, sugar, baking powder, baking soda, salt, and orange zest. Process until the orange zest is minced.

3. Add the butter and pulse about 20 times, until the mixture resembles coarse meal.

4. Turn the dough into a large bowl. If there are any large clumps of butter, pinch them into the dough with your fingers. Stir in the cream just until mixed. Turn out and knead lightly to complete the blending.

5. If you made all the dough at once, divide in half and form one half at a time. On a lightly floured surface, pat out half the dough to a 9 × 7-inch rectangle. Cut into 2¼-inch squares. Using a pastry scraper or wide spatula, transfer the corn cakes to one of the baking sheets.

6. Bake the corn cakes for 10 to 12 minutes, or until golden brown on top. Repeat with the remaining dough. (You can first form all the cakes and then bake them together, but you'll get more even results with one sheet in the oven at a time.) Let cool for at least 20 minutes before splitting. Store in an airtight container for up to 1 day before serving or freeze for longer storage. Defrost no more than 3 hours before serving.

Dessert and Champagne Party

FOR 36

CRANBERRY-RASPBERRY MOUSSE

BITTERSWEET CHOCOLATE TORTE
(PAGE 170) (USE BOTH HALVES OF THE CAKE
AND DOUBLE THE SYRUP AND FROSTING)

EASY CREAM CHEESECAKE (PAGE 135)

ROSE LEVY BERANBAUM'S CHOCOLATE PARTY CAKE

FRESH LEMON ROULADE

BUTTER PECAN TURTLE SQUARES

FRESH FRUIT BASKET

CHEESE PLATTER WITH WALNUT BREAD
AND CRISP CRACKERS

CHILLED BRUT CHAMPAGNE, PROSECCO,
OR OTHER SPARKLING WINE

COFFEE AND TEA

What could be more elegant than a gorgeous array of glamorous desserts and glittering iced Champagne! Just picture a table—covered with confections of chocolate, raspberry, lemon, caramel, and nuts. To the many who look forward to the end of a meal so they can delve into dessert, a buffet of sweets is the stuff of which dreams are made. Such indulgence provides the perfect excuse for dressing up and putting out your fine china, best linen, bouquets of flowers, cut crystal, and polished silver.

Everything should be made ahead, whether it is frozen, refrigerated, or just set aside in a covered container. Don't worry about each dessert serving every person in the room. Since sampling is de rigueur at a party like this, a dessert that serves 16 will serve at least 32. In total, there will be more than enough to go around. Serving amounts listed with the recipes are for that single dessert alone.

On the invitations, do be sure to indicate that this is a dessert party, so that guests will know to eat dinner beforehand. Unless you hold the party after lunch on a Saturday or Sunday, I recommend that it not begin before eight or eight-thirty at night.

Since some people will eat only a light supper and because a few people in any crowd cannot eat refined sugar, I like to put out a cheese platter with walnut bread and crackers and an attractive fruit basket. Choose appropriate dessert cheeses, such as Bel Paese, walnut-flavored Gourmandise, and perhaps a fresh goat cheese or big chunk of younger Parmesan.

Champagne is a great crowd-pleaser, and these days you can get those tingly bubbles in a variety of styles and prices. Aside from the finest French brut Champagne, there are excellent sparkling wines available from the United States, Spain, and Italy. For a pretty change, consider a pink champagne, fragile as a rose.

You can pour six to eight glasses from one bottle. Allow an average of three glasses per person. For 36 people, that would mean a case and a half. But remember, it's always better to have extra than to run out. About an hour before the party starts, put the Champagne on ice. For this many bottles, I use a tub or plastic trashcan, discreetly hidden away or draped with a tablecloth. Recently I've seen some inexpensive plastic party coolers that are not unattractive. Open each bottle only when you're ready to pour, which means that somebody—you, your spouse, a friend, or hired help—should be delegated this important job. Have a big urn of coffee and a pot of tea as well as plenty of club soda or sparkling water for those who prefer a nonalcoholic beverage.

DO-AHEAD PLANNING

UP TO 1 MONTH IN ADVANCE: Bake and freeze the Easy Cream Cheesecake, the layers for the Chocolate Party Cake, the two cakes for the Bittersweet Chocolate Torte, and the Butter Pecan Turtle Squares.

UP TO 1 WEEK IN ADVANCE: Make and freeze the Fresh Lemon Roulade.

UP TO 2 DAYS IN ADVANCE: Make the frosting for the Bittersweet Chocolate Torte and assemble the dessert. Refrigerate, covered, until 1 hour before serving.

THE DAY BEFORE THE PARTY: Make the Cranberry-Raspberry Mousse. Defrost the chocolate cake layers.

THE MORNING OF THE PARTY: Complete the Chocolate Party Cake. Defrost the cheesecake, lemon roulade, and turtle squares.

ABOUT 3 HOURS BEFORE SERVING: Arrange the fruit basket and cheese platter.

ABOUT 1 HOUR BEFORE THE PARTY STARTS: Put the Champagne on ice. Remove all the desserts from the refrigerator and arrange them on the buffet. Get the coffee urn ready to go.

CRANBERRY-RASPBERRY MOUSSE

30 TO 36 SERVINGS

A glorious rose color, this frothy dessert is as lush to look at as it is to eat. For a smaller group, the recipe can be halved exactly.

1 envelope (¼ ounce) unflavored gelatin

2 packages (12 ounces each) cranberries, fresh or frozen

2½ cups sugar

1 package (12 ounces) individually quick-frozen raspberries without added sugar

6 egg whites

¼ teaspoon cream of tartar

3 cups heavy cream

1. In a small bowl, sprinkle the gelatin over ¼ cup of cold water. Let stand to soften.

2. In a large heavy saucepan, combine the cranberries with 1½ cups of the sugar and 1½ cups of water. Bring to a boil over moderately high heat, reduce the heat to moderate, and cook, stirring frequently, for 5 minutes. Remove from the heat, stir in the softened gelatin, and let cool slightly.

3. Pass the cranberries through the medium disk of a food mill or puree in a food processor and then strain to remove the skins. Let cool to room temperature.

4. Puree the raspberries in a food processor. Work through a mesh sieve with a rubber or plastic spatula to remove the seeds. (There will be about 1¼ cups puree.) Combine the cranberry and raspberry purees in a large bowl and mix well to blend.

5. Beat the egg whites and cream of tartar with an electric mixer on high speed until stiff. Gradually beat in the remaining 1 cup sugar.

6. Beat the cream until fairly stiff. (Tip: The cream will mount much faster if you put the cream, mixer bowl, and beaters in the freezer for 10 minutes before beating.)

7. Fold about one-third of the cream into the berry puree to lighten it a little. Fold in the remaining cream and then the egg whites, until the mousse is even in color and no white streaks show. Turn into a large serving bowl, preferably glass, cover with plastic wrap, and refrigerate until chilled and set, at least 6 hours, or overnight.

ROSE LEVY BERANBAUM'S CHOCOLATE PARTY CAKE

16 TO 20 SERVINGS

Dessert is Rose's middle name, as her cookbooks and articles testify. This deep chocolate double layer cake with its rich dark frosting reminds me of the kind of chocolate cake I used to dream about as a child. Thankfully, some dreams never fade.

If you want to ready this dessert ahead, bake the layers up to 2 months in advance and freeze them. After thawing, frost the cake and store in the refrigerator for up to 3 days before serving.

1 cup unsweetened Dutch-process cocoa powder, such as Droste or Poulain

1⅔ cups boiling water

5 eggs, at room temperature

1 teaspoon vanilla extract

4 cups sifted cake flour

2½ cups sugar

1 tablespoon plus 2 teaspoons baking powder

1¼ teaspoons salt

3 sticks (¾ pound) plus 2 tablespoons unsalted butter, at room temperature

Chocolate Cream Frosting (page 216)

1. Grease two 10-inch round cake pans. Line the bottoms with rounds of parchment or waxed paper and grease the paper. Flour the pans; tap out any excess. Heat the oven to 350°F.

2. In a medium bowl, whisk together the cocoa and boiling water until smooth. Let cool to room temperature.

3. In another bowl, lightly beat the eggs. Whisk in the vanilla and ½ cup of the cooled cocoa mixture.

4. In a large mixing bowl, combine the flour, sugar, baking powder, and salt. Whisk to blend. Add the butter and the remaining cocoa and beat on medium speed with a stationary mixer, or on high speed with a hand mixer, for 2 minutes. Scrape down the sides of the bowl.

5. Gradually beat in the egg mixture, one-third at a time, beating well for about 20 seconds after each addition and scraping down the sides of the bowl as necessary.

6. Divide the batter between the cake pans and smooth the tops. Tap the pans lightly on the counter to settle any air bubbles. Bake the cakes for 25 to 30 minutes, or until a tester inserted near the center comes out clean and the edges of the cake have begun to pull away from the side of the pan. Let cool for 15 minutes, then unmold onto a lightly greased rack and let cool completely. Carefully peel off the paper.

7. To assemble, spread about one-quarter of the frosting over one of the layers. Put the second layer on top and cover the top and sides with the remaining frosting, swirling it decoratively with the back of a spoon.

CHOCOLATE CREAM FROSTING

MAKES ENOUGH FOR ONE 10-INCH DOUBLE LAYER CAKE

When a recipe is this simple, the ingredients have to be the best. There are many excellent chocolate brands. Valhrona and Scharffen Berger are two of my favorites, Lindt Excellence is another fine choice.

1 pound dark chocolate—bittersweet, sweet, or semisweet

1½ cups heavy cream

6 tablespoons unsalted butter, at room temperature

3 tablespoons Cognac or strongly brewed coffee, optional

1. Grate the chocolate in a food processor. Scald the cream. With the machine on, pour the cream through the feed tube; process until blended. Pour the chocolate cream into a large bowl and let cool slightly.

2. Whisk the butter and Cognac into the chocolate cream just until blended. Let stand until the chocolate begins to firm up. Whisk to fluff up the frosting.

FRESH LEMON ROULADE

12 TO 16 SERVINGS

Sometimes a light dessert is the best dessert. This one is melt-in-your-mouth and refreshing with a double dose of tart fresh lemon. You can use any good raspberry jam, but I like the fresh fruit flavor of the low-sugar fruit spreads.

5 eggs, separated

⅓ cup granulated sugar

3 tablespoons fresh lemon juice

Grated zest from 1 large lemon

¼ teaspoon salt

½ cup sifted all-purpose flour

¾ cup raspberry jam, preferably seedless

Fresh Lemon Cream (opposite page)

Confectioners' sugar

1. Heat the oven to 375°F. Butter a 13 × 18-inch jellyroll or half-sheet pan. Line the bottom with a sheet of waxed paper; butter the paper. Dust the pan with flour and tap out any excess.

2. In a large bowl, beat the egg yolks. Gradually beat in the granulated sugar. Add 1 tablespoon of the lemon juice, the lemon zest, and salt. Beat until the mixture is thick enough to fall from the whisk or beaters in a slowly dissolving ribbon, 3 to 5 minutes.

3. In another large bowl, use clean beaters to beat the egg whites until stiff but not dry. Scoop about one-third of the egg whites onto the egg yolk mixture and partially fold in. Return the flour to the sifter and sift about one-third over the batter. Fold until just blended. Scoop half the remaining egg whites onto the batter. Sift half the remaining flour onto the egg whites. Fold into the batter until just blended. Repeat with the remaining egg whites and flour.

4. Turn the batter into the jellyroll pan. With a rubber spatula, spread to fill the pan evenly. Bake for 15 to 20 minutes, until the cake is puffed and lightly browned and the edges have begun to pull away from the sides of the pan. Let cool for 5 minutes.

5. Lay a damp kitchen towel over a rack. Invert the jellyroll pan to unmold the cake onto the towel. Carefully peel off the waxed paper. Combine the remaining 2 tablespoons lemon juice with 2 tablespoons water and sprinkle evenly over the cake. Starting with a long side, fold one edge up about 2 inches. Continue to roll up the cake in the towel, with the material between the layers. Let stand until completely cool, at least 15 minutes but no longer than 1 hour.

6. Unroll the cake. Cover with a thin, even layer of the raspberry jam. Scrape the lemon cream onto the cake and spread evenly. Again roll up the cake (without the towel this time, of course), allowing 2 to 3 inches for the first fold. Wrap in plastic wrap and refrigerate for up to 2 days before serving. (After the filling is completely cold and set, you can freeze the roulade for up to 2 months. Thaw in the refrigerator.)

7. Just before serving, sprinkle confectioners' sugar generously over the roulade to coat.

FRESH LEMON CREAM

3 egg yolks

¼ cup white wine

Grated zest of 1 lemon

¼ cup fresh lemon juice

1 teaspoon unflavored gelatin dissolved in 2 tablespoons of cold water

½ cup heavy cream

1. In a heavy nonreactive saucepan, combine the egg yolks, wine, lemon zest, and lemon juice. Whisk over moderate heat until the mixture is frothy and hot and thick enough to leave a trace as the whisk moves through it, about 10 minutes. Beat in the dissolved gelatin and whisk over the heat for about 30 seconds to blend completely. Strain into a bowl. Cover and put in the freezer for about 10 minutes, stirring twice, or stir over a bowl of ice and water, until cold.

2. Meanwhile, whip the cream until it is stiff. Scrape the lemon mixture onto the whipped cream and fold until blended. Cover and refrigerate until almost set before using. (If too stiff, whisk to soften.)

BUTTER PECAN TURTLE SQUARES

MAKES ABOUT 100

An incredibly decadent recipe from my former editor, Harriet Bell, now publisher of cookbooks at William Morrow, these are guaranteed to disappear . . . fast! The cookie-candies freeze remarkably well.

2 cups all-purpose flour

1½ cups packed dark brown sugar

2 sticks (½ pound) plus 3 tablespoons unsalted butter

1½ cups pecans, coarsely chopped

1½ cups chocolate chips

1. Heat the oven to 350°F. In a food processor, combine the flour, 1 cup of the brown sugar, and 1 stick of the butter. Process until sandy; the dough will not form a ball. Pat the dough firmly into an ungreased 9 × 13-inch baking pan. Sprinkle the pecans evenly over the dough.

2. In a heavy medium saucepan, combine the remaining 1 stick plus 3 tablespoons butter and ½ cup brown sugar. Bring to a boil over moderate heat, stirring to dissolve the sugar. Boil the caramel for 30 seconds, stirring constantly.

3. Pour the hot caramel evenly over the nuts in the baking pan. Bake for 20 minutes. Remove from the oven and immediately sprinkle the chocolate chips evenly over the top. Let melt slightly, then spread lightly, leaving some of the chips whole. Let cool completely before cutting into 1-inch squares.

How to Open a Bottle of Champagne

To my ear, the popping of a Champagne cork is just about the prettiest sound in the world. For many years, I sat back and listened; the idea of opening a bottle myself was unthinkable. I played helpless. To be honest, it scared me. Then one day, at a Champagne tasting I was attending, a sommelier explained exactly how it should be done—for ease, for safety purposes (to avoid shooting the cork across the room), and to preserve all the bubbly. When they asked for volunteers, I impulsively raised my hand. It was with great trepidation that I opened my first bottle, and with great pride, I poured. I was liberated forever. Here's how easy it is.

Set out the glasses in advance of opening the bottle. Tall, narrow flutes are the shape connoisseurs prefer to maximize the effect of the effervescence. Be sure the Champagne has been resting for at least a couple of hours; shaking up the bottle before opening is for locker rooms only. The wine should be well chilled, in the refrigerator or in a bucket of ice and water, for 45 minutes to 1 hour.

First remove the outer foil wrappings from the top of the bottle. Then loosen the wires around the neck. Do not peer over the top as you do this, because occasionally a cork will eject spontaneously. Leaving the wire loose but still over the cap, grip the cork, using a folded kitchen towel to help you, and, holding the bottle at a 45-degree angle, slowly twist, not the cork but the bottle. Continue to hold the cork with the towel to restrain it if necessary as you twist. You'll feel the cork partially ease up out of the bottle before it pops open. Immediately put down the cork and pour, filling the glasses slowly and only partway until the initial foam subsides, then top them off. *Salud!*

Pork-o-Rama

FOR 36

CHEF MICKEY'S PULLED PORK

POOT'S SECRET TENNESSEE BARBECUE SAUCE

HAMBURGER BUNS OR POTATO ROLLS

PAULINE'S DOWN-HOME DOCTORED BEANS

KICK-ASS COLE SLAW

BUTTERMILK CORNBREAD SQUARES

KEGS OF BEER

STRAWBERRY CORN SHORTCAKES (PAGE 210)

Bring on the guitars and bluegrass music. Ice down the beer keg and pray for good weather, because this rollicking good party, starring real Tennessee smoked pork, deserves an outdoor venue. Nothing makes for a better time than a backyard barbecue. My friend, chef Michael Campbell, who hails from Nashville and has the musical vocabulary to prove it, delights us with this great party every summer, often on the Fourth of July.

Here's what you need for a real Tennessee barbecue.

◆ A barrel smoker or other real smoker. You can improvise with a kettle grill, but the results will not be as good.

◆ Chunks of hickory wood—it's the only kind to use. These large pieces do not need soaking ahead of time, but if you are rigging a regular grill to use as a smoker, you will probably use hickory chips, which do need to be wet down beforehand.

◆ A couple of large stockpots. You can probably fit two picnic shoulders in a 4-gallon stockpot, but not three. A second, smaller stockpot will be necessary. Why a stockpot at all?

Traditionally, pulled pork is smoked for at least 16 hours. But Chef Mickey's adult palate found that after such a lot of smoking, the meat was inevitably dry, and it tasted a lot like wood. Spying a big steam kettle next to the smoker at his favorite barbecue joint, legendary in Tennessee, he realized that professionals were braising the pork first to keep it moist and juicy before smoking it for a couple of hours or less, until imbued with hickory flavor and mahogany brown.

◆ Pork picnic shoulders. Ham comes from the back of the pig, picnic shoulder from the front. The shoulders average 7 to 8 pounds, and if you don't see it in your supermarket, it should be no problem for the butcher to order it for you. Butchers sometimes call this cut a "Callie." Each shoulder yields about 12 servings of pulled pork.

Accompaniments to the pork are traditional. The shredded meat, splashed with zesty sauce, is either eaten on a bun with cole slaw or served on a plate with beans, greens, and cornbread. I suggest the buns here, with sides of baked beans, made in a fraction of the time with doctored-up canned beans, a zippy cole slaw, and Southern-style cornbread. For dessert, I suggest Strawberry Shortcake, but peach cobbler, berry crisp, or any ice cream dessert would be just as good a choice.

DO-AHEAD PLANNING

UP TO 6 MONTHS IN ADVANCE: Make the barbecue sauce. It improves as it ages.

UP TO 1 MONTH IN ADVANCE: Make the Buttermilk Cornbread Squares and freeze them.

UP TO A DAY AHEAD: Make the cole slaw; cover and refrigerate until shortly before serving time. Prepare the beans through Step 2. Bake the shortcake biscuits.

THE MORNING OF THE PARTY: Make the Pulled Pork: Poach the ham shoulders and smoke them while they are still warm. It will probably be late afternoon by the time they are finished, but if you're serving at night, you can still plan ahead. After shredding the pork, arrange it on heatproof platters, douse the meat with a little of the barbecue sauce to keep it moist, and then reheat shortly before serving in a low oven, being careful that it doesn't dry out. Reheat the cornbread about 1 hour before serving.

JUST BEFORE SERVING: Assemble the Strawberry Corn Shortcakes.

CHEF MICKEY'S PULLED PORK

36 SERVINGS

When he was a young boy in Nashville, Michael Campbell remembers being allowed to stay up as late as he wanted on those special summer nights when the men were smoking meat. A group of buddies would volunteer to smoke the big front pork shoulders all night, up to 14 hours. The ritual that accomplished this involved drinking a lot of beer—not whisky or vodka, but beer. That's because the men would get sleepy in the early hours of the morning, and only copious quantities of beer would ensure one or another would wake up sequentially as nature called and use the opportunity to stoke the fire and add more hickory to the smoker.

As a New York City chef, with a palate piqued by travels through the Tuscan hills, burnished by stays in Rome and Florence, Chef Mickey rethought the beloved barbecue of his youth. After all those hours of smoking, the barbecued pork he cherished in retrospect was rather dried out and chewy, and it tasted a lot like wood. His technique simmers the meat first in a spicy court bouillon and then smokes it for just about 2 hours, until mahogany brown, so that it has all the hickory taste but remains moist and juicy.

3 fresh picnic shoulders, or "Callies," 7 to 8 pounds each

3 onions, quartered

9 garlic cloves, smashed

6 imported bay leaves

3 teaspoons crushed hot red pepper

3 tablespoons coarse salt

1½ quarts Poot's Secret Tennessee Barbecue Sauce (opposite page)

Hamburger or potato buns

1. Assuming you have two stockpots, one very large (4 gallons) and one large (2½ gallons): Put 2 shoulders in one pot and 1 in the other. Add 2 onions, 6 garlic cloves, 4 bay leaves, 2 teaspoons hot pepper, and 2 tablespoons coarse salt to the larger pot. Put 1 onion, 3 garlic cloves, 2 bay leaves, 1 teaspoon hot pepper, and 1 tablespoon salt in the other. Add enough cold water to cover the meat by at least 1 inch. Slowly bring to a boil. Reduce the heat slightly and simmer for 3 hours, adding water if needed to keep the pork covered.

2. After 3 hours, the pork will be very tender and almost falling off the bone. The trick is to remove the picnic shoulders from the pot without letting them fall apart. A large flat skimmer is a good tool to use along with a slotted spoon or spatula. If necessary, push the shoulders together again and let cool. They will hold their shape better when they set. While the pork cools, get your fire going.

3. In a wood smoker, get a good fire going with large chunks of hickory. If using a gas or covered charcoal grill, add soaked hickory chips to the fire. In either case, once your fire is going, carefully push it to one side so that the pork smokes indirectly. Your goal is to generate smoke, not heat. The pork is already cooked. If using a gas fire with a smoker box, turn the heat to low. Put the picnic shoulders in the smoker but not over the wood and smoke indirectly for 1½ to 2 hours, turning over once, until mahogany brown all over.

4. When the pork is cool enough to handle, pull the meat off the bones and tear it into shreds. If it is still too hot to handle, use a long fork and a knife to cut it up. Mix the meat with about 1 cup barbecue sauce per shoulder. (The recipe can be made ahead to this point. If you reheat the pulled pork, do so in a microwave or in a preheated 325°F oven, covered so that it doesn't dry out.) Heap the meat onto a large platter and put out the remaining barbecue sauce and a basket of buns on the side.

POOT'S SECRET TENNESSEE BARBECUE SAUCE

MAKES ABOUT 1 GALLON

Serve enough of this and they'll start calling you Elvis. A gallon? Yes, a gallon! And you'll need it. Well, you'll need about 1½ quarts for this party, and won't you be glad to have those other 2½ quarts squirreled away in jars for the rest of the season, anytime you need just the greatest barbecue sauce for steaks, ribs, hamburgers, chicken—you name it. This stuff keeps a very long time, and it doesn't even need refrigeration. This heirloom barbecue sauce was passed on to Chef Mickey by his father, Paul Campbell, whose nickname is Poot.

2 quarts apple cider vinegar

⅓ cup Crystal, Frank's, or Louisiana hot sauce

¼ cup Worcestershire sauce

2 tablespoons Tabasco sauce

1 cup sugar

⅓ cup coarse salt

¼ cup ground black pepper

2 tablespoons cayenne pepper

2 tablespoons chili powder

2 tablespoons celery seed

48 ounces ketchup

1. In a large nonreactive pot, combine all the ingredients except the ketchup. Bring to a boil.

2. Stir in the ketchup, reduce the heat to low, and simmer for 15 minutes. Ladle into bottles or preserving jars, cap tightly, and store in a cool, dark place. This sauce keeps for at least 6 months and improves with age.

PAULINE'S DOWN-HOME DOCTORED BEANS

36 SERVINGS

Homemade baked beans are best but cumbersome and time-consuming when you're cooking for three dozen people. These fixed-up beans from a can, from Chef Mickey's mother, Pauline Campbell, taste great, and with almost no effort, they can be on the table in little more than an hour.

½ pound bacon

2 large (#10) cans pork and beans in tomato sauce

4 medium onions, finely chopped

2 cups ketchup

2 cups yellow mustard

¾ cup molasses

1. Heat the oven to 325°F. Cut the bacon strips crosswise into thirds.

2. Combine all the remaining ingredients and stir until well mixed. Turn into a large casserole. (In a pinch, Pauline uses a disposable foil roasting pan.) Scatter the bacon strips over the top.

3. Bake for 45 minutes, until the bacon is lightly browned. Stir, turning the beans from the bottom up to the top. Continue to bake 20 to 25 minutes longer, or until the beans are piping hot and the flavors have mellowed slightly.

BUTTERMILK CORNBREAD SQUARES

MAKES 48 SQUARES

No Southerner would add a speck of sugar to his or her cornbread, so you know this is my recipe, not Chef Mickey's. A little more cornmeal than flour yields a grittier bread, which goes perfectly with butter and honey. Or enjoy it plain, to sop up those barbecued juices.

While they can be served at room temperature, I sometimes wrap the squares in foil and warm them on the edge of the grill or in the oven just before serving.

3½ cups yellow cornmeal

2½ cups all-purpose flour

⅓ cup sugar

5 teaspoons baking powder

1 teaspoon baking soda

1½ teaspoons salt

¼ teaspoon cayenne pepper

4 eggs

4 cups (1 quart) buttermilk

12 tablespoons (1½ sticks) unsalted butter, melted and cooled slightly

1. Heat the oven to 425°F. Grease two 9 × 13-inch baking dishes. Place the dishes in the oven while the oven preheats.

2. In a large bowl, combine the cornmeal, flour, sugar, baking powder, baking soda, salt, and cayenne. Whisk gently to mix.

3. In a smaller bowl, beat together the eggs and buttermilk until just blended. Mix in the melted butter. Add to the dry ingredients and stir until just blended; do not overmix.

4. Divide the batter between the two hot pans and bake for 22 to 25 minutes, or until the cornbread is golden brown on top and a tester inserted in the center comes out clean. Let cool slightly before cutting each pan of cornbread into 24 squares.

KICK-ASS COLE SLAW

MAKES ABOUT 6 QUARTS

Plenty of onion, celery seed, and black pepper distinguish this zesty cabbage salad. It is crispest the day it is made and still fine if made a day ahead, but after that, the cabbage will soften. Serve with a slotted spoon.

2 large green cabbages (3½ to 4 pounds)

5 medium carrots

2 medium red onions

2 cups cider vinegar

⅔ cup sugar

1 tablespoon coarse salt

1 teaspoon celery seed

1 teaspoon freshly ground pepper

1. Either use a large sharp knife to cut the cabbages into thin shreds or cut them into wedges and shred them on the slicing disk of a food processor.

2. Peel the carrots and onions. Shred the vegetables on the coarse holes of a box grater or in the processor with the grating disk.

3. In a very large bowl, combine the vinegar, sugar, salt, celery seed, and pepper. Stir to dissolve the sugar. Add the shredded cabbage, carrots, and onions. Toss well. Let stand, tossing occasionally, for at least 2 hours. Cover and refrigerate for up to a day before serving.

Family Reunion

FOR 36

POTLUCK HORS D'OEUVRE

OR

PESTO DEVILED EGGS (PAGE 173)

TACO BEAN DIP (PAGE 237)

RAW CLAMS AND OYSTERS
(IF YOU HAVE A DESIGNATED SHUCKER)

CHIPS AND SALSA

NUTS AND RAW VEGETABLE STICKS

OLD-FASHIONED BARBECUED CHICKEN

BACON AND BRANDY BAKED BEANS

POTATO SALAD WITH FRESH FENNEL AND TARRAGON

COOL CABBAGE SALAD WITH CARROTS
AND RED PEPPERS (PAGE 242)

DINNER ROLLS OR WHOLE-GRAIN BREAD

HEIRLOOM CHOCOLATE CAKE

FRUIT PIES

Over 95 percent of all family reunions take place in the summer. After all, if you don't have an outdoors, where do you put so many relatives? For that reason, a barbecue makes welcome sense, along with a lot of traditional sides that easily translate into large numbers. A family reunion practically screams, "Potluck!"—at least for those who live in the town where the party is taking place. Let anyone who wants bring an appetizer, a side, or a dessert. And be sure to let them know it will be greatly appreciated.

The basic menu here is modeled on the innumerable church suppers and firemen's chicken barbecues that are so popular in my rural home county. So is the salty vinegar and egg wash that yields an incomparably tender and juicy barbecued chicken. While my own town is dry, this recipe for baked beans decidedly is not, and the smoky sweetness of the brandy included complements the whole pound of bacon that's added. After its 8 hours in the oven, though, you don't have to worry about anyone getting inebriated on your baked beans. I've also included a potato salad recipe that's a little bit different—laced with crisp fresh fennel in place of the usual celery and flavored with fragrant tarragon in place of parsley. If you prefer something more traditional, you could substitute a recipe and a half of the Egg and Potato Salad with Roasted Red Peppers on page 209 or, for a lighter choice, the Parsleyed Potato Salad on page 252.

For a dessert everyone loves, whether they reside in the city or the country, a moist chocolate sheet cake, slathered with an intense fudgy frosting, can do nothing but enhance your culinary reputation, especially with the kids. Cut into roughly 2-inch squares, this cake will give you 40 pieces. It's rich enough to satisfy, and you can always add a scoop of vanilla ice cream, but there are those for whom one dessert is never enough, so let anyone who asks bring a pie.

DO-AHEAD PLANNING

UP TO 3 DAYS AHEAD: Make the Taco Bean Dip.

UP TO 2 DAYS AHEAD: Make the potato salad. Bake the cake; let it cool, then wrap well in plastic wrap and set aside at room temperature. Soak the beans overnight.

A DAY BEFORE THE PARTY: Make the Pesto Deviled Eggs, the cabbage salad, and the baked beans. Make the frosting and ice the cake.

THE MORNING OF THE PARTY: Marinate and grill the chickens. Remove the beans from the refrigerator.

SHORTLY BEFORE SERVING: Reheat the beans in the oven and the chickens on the grill or serve them at room temperature.

OLD-FASHIONED BARBECUED CHICKEN

36 SERVINGS

As with any kind of barbecue, styles of chicken vary, often from state to state. This recipe from rural Pennsylvania uses lots of vinegar and salt but no tomato. And the secret ingredient—egg—makes for a delightfully crisp skin. For this amount of chicken, either build a grill pit as described or borrow a couple of extra grills. You might want to grill the chicken early in the day or even a day in advance and reheat it either in the oven or on a grill. Because of the raw egg, which is preserved by the acid in the vinegar but still warrants care in hot weather, be sure to cook the chicken for at least 3 minutes after the last basting.

36 chicken quarters, about 18 pounds

4 cups cider vinegar

2 cups olive oil or peanut oil

¼ cup coarse salt

1½ tablespoons dried thyme leaves

1 tablespoon hot paprika

1 tablespoon coarsely cracked black pepper

3 medium onions, thickly sliced

3 garlic cloves, smashed

4 eggs, preferably organic

1. Trim any excess fat and loose skin from the chicken quarters.

2. In a food processor, combine all the remaining ingredients. Work in batches if necessary. Puree until thick and emulsified.

3. Put the chicken in a large tub or 2 large bowls. Pour the marinade over the chicken. Marinate at room temperature for about 1 hour or in the refrigerator for up to 3 hours, turning the pieces once or twice or turning the closed container upside down to be sure the pieces marinate evenly.

4. Meanwhile, prepare a barbecue pit (see sidebar) or an indirect medium-hot fire in two or three charcoal grills or preheat a gas grill on high. Turn the chicken pieces so they are coated with the marinade as you set them on the grill racks. Grill, basting with the marinade remaining in the bowls and turning the pieces every 10 to 15 minutes, until the chicken is golden brown outside and white to the bone but still juicy inside, 35 to 45 minutes on a covered gas or charcoal grill or up to 1½ hours over a glowing pit.

Building a Barbecue Pit

While it's called a pit, the construction is actually above ground. First of all, you need a cleared area, with at least 3 feet of plain dirt or gravel with no trees or bushes or anything else that is flammable. For the "pit" itself, a fair number of cinder blocks are required, so it's only worth the effort if you plan to grill in quantity frequently. Basically, you want to build a rectangular four-sided rim about 2 feet high. Then you need stainless steel wire grating stiff enough to sit well and hold 10 to 20 pounds or more of meat, extending far enough over the side to remain completely stable. A few large rocks can anchor the grate in place once the fire is all set and the food is on. Since you will want to lift the grate on and off, it's best to purchase two or three pieces, so they are easy to handle. Other equipment you'll need are silicone mitts and extra-long tongs and forks.

BACON AND BRANDY BAKED BEANS

30 TO 36 SERVINGS

Lots of smoky bacon, a good hit of brandy, and two kinds of mustard add extra kick and smoky interest to what are otherwise traditional though tasty baked beans. While I give a quick option for preparing the dried beans, do try to remember to soak them overnight. The results are far superior.

3 pounds dried small white beans, pink beans, or pinto beans

1 pound slab bacon, in 1 piece

1⅓ cups ketchup

1⅓ cups molasses

¼ cup Dijon mustard

3 tablespoons powdered mustard

4 medium onions, chopped

1½ cups brandy (I use a fruity California brandy)

2⅔ cups boiling water

1 tablespoon cider vinegar

1 teaspoon salt

1 teaspoon freshly ground pepper

½ teaspoon hot pepper sauce

1. Rinse the beans and pick them over to remove any grit. Soak the beans overnight in 3 inches of cold water to cover. Or bring them to a boil, boil for 2 minutes, and then simmer for 30 to 40 minutes, until tender but not mushy. Drain the beans.

2. Heat the oven to 250°F. Cut the rind off the bacon and reserve. Cut the bacon into 1 × ¼-inch strips, or lardons.

3. In a large bean pot or flameproof casserole, combine the beans, bacon, ketchup, molasses, Dijon mustard, powdered mustard, onions, and brandy. Stir to mix. Add the boiling water, cover, and bake for 3 hours.

4. Season the beans with the vinegar, salt, pepper, and hot sauce. Add more boiling water if they appear dry. Continue to bake, covered, for 4 to 5 hours longer, checking every hour or so and adding water, about ½ cup at a time, as needed. The beans are even better after being reheated in a low oven the next day.

POTATO SALAD WITH FRESH FENNEL AND TARRAGON

36 SERVINGS

You can't have too many recipes for potato salad. Since a family reunion is a traditional occasion, I was tempted to give an old-fashioned potato salad, loaded with mayonnaise, celery, onions, parsley, and eggs; but chances are, you already know how to do that. This more contemporary version substitutes crisp, refreshing fresh fennel for the celery and tarragon, which has a grassy flavor with anise overtones, for the parsley, imparting a springlike fragrance. If you are in a more conservative mood, just put the celery and parsley back in place of the fennel and tarragon, and you'll have a very nice traditional potato salad.

7 pounds Yukon gold potatoes

2 cups mayonnaise

⅓ cup Champagne vinegar or other white wine vinegar

⅓ cup Dijon mustard

⅓ cup chopped fresh tarragon or 1 tablespoon dried

Salt and freshly ground pepper

2 large bulbs of fresh fennel, diced

4 large shallots, minced, or 1 large white onion, finely diced

4 eggs, hard-cooked and coarsely chopped, optional

1. Put the potatoes in a large pot with cold salted water to cover by at least an inch. Bring to a boil over high heat and cook until the potatoes pierce easily to the center with the tip of a small knife. This will take 15 to 25 minutes, depending upon the size of your potatoes. Drain in a colander. Rinse the pot with cold water to cool it, then return the potatoes to the pot and fill with cold water. Pick them out one by one and peel off the skins, which will slip right off. Let the potatoes cool to room temperature, then cut them into ½-inch cubes or slice them.

2. In a large bowl, whisk together the mayonnaise, vinegar, mustard, and tarragon. Season generously with salt and pepper. Add the potatoes, fennel, and shallots and toss to coat. Taste and season again with salt and pepper. Add the eggs and toss lightly to mix.

3. If not serving within the hour, cover the potato salad and refrigerate for up to 3 days. Check the seasoning again before serving.

HEIRLOOM CHOCOLATE CAKE

MAKES ONE 11 × 16-INCH SHEET CAKE; ENOUGH TO CUT 36 ROUGHLY 2-INCH SQUARES

My good friend Peter Wynne, former food editor of the *Bergen Record,* baked this cake for my birthday, and it was so good I've decided it will be an heirloom in my family. It already is in his, since he got the cake recipe from his niece, professional pastry chef Alisa Huntsman. Peter tells me the frosting is mine, so with three good hands in it, how could it be bad! This cake is a real keeper. You can make it several days in advance and wrap it well. After frosting, store at room temperature for up to a day or refrigerate for up to 2 days, but let it return to room temperature before serving so its lightness can be appreciated.

This recipe will make enough batter for three 9-inch or four 8-inch pans or what I like to use for more than 12 people: one 11 × 16-inch pan, 2½ inches deep. The 11 × 16-inch cake will take about 40 minutes to bake. Because of the large amount of baking soda, which is needed for the cocoa, the batter will begin to bubble as soon as you combine the dry ingredients and liquid. To ensure success, do not overmix, and get the cake into the oven as soon as possible.

3 cups all-purpose flour

2½ cups sugar

1 cup unsweetened cocoa powder (5 ounces)

2½ teaspoons baking soda

1¼ teaspoons baking powder

3 eggs

1¼ cups vegetable oil

1¼ cups milk

1¼ cups brewed coffee, the stronger the better

2 teaspoons vanilla extract

Rich Chocolate Frosting (page 232)

1 cup apricot preserves

2 teaspoons Cognac or brandy

1. Heat the oven to 350°F. Grease an 11 × 16-inch metal cake pan well and line it with parchment.

2. Combine the dry ingredients and sift into a large bowl.

3. In another large bowl, beat together the eggs and oil, then beat in the milk, coffee, and vanilla. Add about half the liquid to the dry ingredients. Whisk together, then add the remaining liquid, stirring to combine. Avoid overmixing.

4. Pour the batter into the pan and spread out evenly. Bake for 40 minutes, or until the cake just begins to pull away from the sides of the pan and a tester inserted in the center comes out clean. Let the cake stand for 10 minutes, then unmold onto a rack, carefully peel off the parchment, and let cool completely.

5. While the cake is cooling, make the chocolate frosting. Warm the apricot preserves in a small saucepan until melted. Stir in the Cognac. Strain the preserves through a sieve so they are smooth.

6. Set the cake on the platter you plan to use. If you don't have a big enough platter, cut out a rectangle of heavy-duty cardboard a couple of inches larger than the cake and wrap the cardboard in foil to make a platter. First glaze the top of the cake with the apricot preserves. Then frost the sides of the cake with about half the frosting. Scoop the rest of the frosting into a pastry bag fitted with a star tip and draw a diamond-shaped lattice over the top of the cake. With the remaining frosting, pipe an edge around the top rim of the cake. If you have any frosting left, pipe little dots at the intersections of the lattice. Let the frosting set for at least 2 hours before cutting the cake.

RICH CHOCOLATE FROSTING

MAKES ABOUT 2½ CUPS

Here's the simplest chocolate icing you'll ever make . . . and possibly the most irresistible.

4 ounces German's Sweet Chocolate

4 ounces semisweet chocolate

¾ cup heavy cream

3 tablespoons unsalted butter, at room temperature

2 tablespoons Myers's dark rum

1. Chop the chocolate by pulsing it in a food processor. Bring the cream to a simmer and pour through the feed tube over the chopped chocolate while the machine is whirling.

2. Turn this "ganache" out into a bowl and whisk in the butter, 1 tablespoon at a time. Let cool a bit, then whisk in the rum. Cover and chill in the refrigerator until the frosting reaches a spreading consistency. Beat with a whisk to fluff up a bit so that it spreads easily.

Mexican Grillfest

FOR 36

BARBECUED CARNITAS
WITH PINEAPPLE-CHIPOTLE SALSA

GUACAMOLE FOR A CROWD

TACO BEAN DIP

SHRIMP AND JICAMA SALAD

MARGARITAS BY THE BATCH (PAGE 148) AND COLD BEER

CHICKEN AND BEEF FAJITAS

GRILLED PEPPER AND ONION STRIPS

WARM FLOUR TORTILLAS

COWBOY BEANS WITH BEER AND BACON

CREAMY BAKED RICE WITH CORN, CHILES, AND CHEESE

COOL CABBAGE SALAD WITH CARROTS AND RED PEPPERS

CHOCOLATE ICE CREAM CAKE ROLL WITH CINNAMON-
COFFEE ICE CREAM AND KAHLÚA FUDGE SAUCE

It's not often you'll be entertaining three dozen fun-loving friends, but on the rare occasions you do, this lively menu offers a delightful, doable plan. You don't need a poll to tell you that second only to Italian, Mexican is the favorite ethnic cuisine in America. Whether it's the mix of crunchy and velvety textures or the sprightly, piquant flavors, adults and children alike can always find something to enjoy with relish.

With this big a crowd, I'm assuming an extended stand-up socializing hour before everyone's ready to tuck into the main food. Suggested below are four appetizers that will pique your taste buds. The two dips—Taco Bean Dip and Guacamole—are so easy they're made almost in an instant. So is the Pineapple-Chipotle Salsa, which draws raves from my friends. The carnitas can be prepared two ways: barbecued or roasted and fried (which takes more effort but yields better flavor); either way, the little cubes of pork can be completely cooked a day or two in advance and reheated until hot and slightly crusty just before serving.

The Shrimp and Jicama Salad is a variation of a Mexican shrimp cocktail from Acapulco, which is in my friend Marge Poore's book *365 Easy Mexican Recipes*. While ketchup may seem an unlikely ingredient, one taste of the sauce, blended with fresh lime juice and cilantro, speaks instantly of the dish's authentic origins. The recipe is sublimely simple but does involve a bit of prep. Chopping up the shrimp and jicama lets you eat the salad on chips or in endive leaves and obviates the need for forks; it also stretches the shrimp. If you find yourself short of time, though, you can just put out a big bowl of cooked shrimp with your favorite brand of salsa for dipping.

Even though the star of the main course is your barbecue grill, with the exception of the skirt steak, which should be cooked for 3 to 4 minutes just before serving, everything else can be ready and waiting. Both the chicken and the pepper and onion strips can be grilled a day in advance and reheated, either on the top shelf of your grill or in the oven. The rice casserole will hold for at least 2 days before being reheated in the oven. Beans improve when cooked ahead and keep well for up to 5 days, though I prefer them after 3 days. And to my surprise, they even freeze well. About the only dish that's best served the same day it's made is the Cool Cabbage Salad, but that's a matter of personal taste; some people will probably prefer the more pickled quality it acquires if refrigerated for a day or two. Finally, there is dessert, a luscious ice cream roll you pull right out of the freezer.

Despite all the advance pacing you can achieve with these recipes, entertaining 36 people is a lot of work; don't think otherwise for a second. But this menu will cut your stress and effort dramatically. The day before the party, you may well be tired. But when your guests arrive the next day, you will be refreshed and ready to enjoy yourself. And just for the record, please note that it is in the nature of the recipes here to halve—or even quarter—easily, so I hope you'll use them for smaller numbers as well. It's one of my favorite parties, where the food and drink almost guarantee a rollicking good time.

DO-AHEAD PLANNING

UP TO 3 WEEKS IN ADVANCE: Make the Chocolate Ice Cream Cake Roll with Cinnamon-Coffee Ice Cream.

UP TO 3 DAYS IN ADVANCE: Make the Taco Bean Dip. Make the Cowboy Beans with Beer and Bacon.

UP TO 2 DAYS IN ADVANCE: Make the Shrimp and Jicama Salad. Marinate the pork for the carnitas and the chicken for the fajitas. Prepare the Creamy Baked Rice through Step 4.

THE DAY BEFORE THE PARTY: Grill the chicken for the fajitas. Grill the carnitas if you are barbecuing them; otherwise, roast them. Grill the Pepper and Onion Strips or prepare them using an alternate method. Marinate the beef for the Fajitas. Make the Kahlúa Fudge Sauce.

THE MORNING OF THE PARTY: Make the Guacamole for a Crowd and the Cool Cabbage Salad.

ABOUT 3 HOURS BEFORE THE PARTY: Make the Pineapple-Chipotle Salsa. Remove the beans from the refrigerator; they take a long time to reheat, and you'll reduce the risk of scorching if they are closer to room temperature when you set them over direct heat.

UP TO 2 HOURS BEFORE THE PARTY STARTS: Squeeze the lime juice for the margaritas.

ABOUT 1 HOUR BEFORE YOUR COMPANY ARRIVES: Set out the Guacamole for a Crowd, Taco Bean Dip, Shrimp and Jicama Salad, and Pineapple-Chipotle Salsa, covered with sheets of plastic wrap. Slowly reheat the beans on top of the stove, stirring often, and the creamy rice casserole in the oven.

SHORTLY BEFORE SERVING: Reheat the carnitas in a preheated 400°F oven. Reheat the chicken and the Pepper and Onion Strips. Heat the flour tortillas for the Fajitas in stacks of 8 to 12, wrapped in foil, either on the top rack of the grill or in the oven. Grill the skirt steaks for the Fajitas, let stand for a minute or two, then quickly cut crosswise on a slight angle into strips; this entire process will take no more than 10 minutes. Reheat the Kahlúa Fudge Sauce.

BARBECUED CARNITAS WITH PINEAPPLE-CHIPOTLE SALSA

30 TO 36 SERVINGS AS AN APPETIZER

Tasty little morsels of grilled marinated pork served with toothpicks and a spicy-sweet fruit salsa for dipping make a perfect summer appetizer. If you're cooking indoors, the pork cubes can be broiled or roasted in a 325°F oven for 1 to 1½ hours, until browned and crisp.

4½ pounds boneless country-style ribs

1 tablespoon coarse salt

1 teaspoon freshly ground pepper

1 tablespoon ground cumin

1½ teaspoons dried thyme

3 garlic cloves, crushed

⅓ cup fresh lemon juice

3 tablespoons olive oil or other vegetable oil

Sprigs of cilantro or parsley, for garnish

Pineapple-Chipotle Salsa (below)

1. Trim any excess fat off the pork and cut the meat into ¾-inch cubes.

2. In a large bowl, toss the pork cubes with the salt, pepper, cumin, thyme, garlic, lemon juice, and olive oil. Cover and marinate for at least 2 hours at room temperature or up to 2 days in the refrigerator.

3. Up to 6 hours before cooking, spear the pork on long metal skewers, leaving a little space between the pieces of meat. Wrap and refrigerate; let stand at room temperature for at least 1 hour before cooking.

4. Light a hot fire in a charcoal grill. Grill the skewers of carnitas, turning, until well browned outside and no longer pink in the center, 12 to 15 minutes. Slide the meat off the skewers onto a platter and garnish with sprigs of cilantro. Serve with toothpicks and a bowl of Pineapple-Chipotle Salsa.

PINEAPPLE-CHIPOTLE SALSA

MAKES ABOUT 3½ CUPS

Incredibly easy to make in a food processor, this sweet-spicy dipping sauce is a guaranteed winner. While I serve it here with crisp cubes of pork, it would also work beautifully with grilled chicken or shrimp.

1 small ripe pineapple

½ cup coarsely chopped white onion

⅓ cup cilantro sprigs

1 to 2 tablespoons hot and spicy chipotle salsa, such as Trader Joe's

Coarse salt

1. With a large, sharp stainless-steel knife, cut the top and bottom off the pineapple. With it standing up in front of you, cut off the thick skin in strips, removing all the "eyes." Cut the pineapple into large chunks, discarding the tough inner core.

2. In a food processor, finely chop the pineapple, onion, and cilantro. Stir in the spicy salsa and season with salt to taste. This salsa is best eaten when freshly made.

GUACAMOLE FOR A CROWD

MAKES ABOUT 8 CUPS

Tart Mexican green "tomatoes," or tomatillos, allow this guacamole to be made in advance without discoloring. Fresh are much more common in supermarkets than they used to be, but if you cannot find them, substitute 1 cup of prepared tomatillo salsa. Tomatillos are sold canned, but I've found the quality of the canned varies wildly.

½ pound fresh tomatillos

½ medium white onion, thickly sliced

2 garlic cloves, smashed

¾ cup packed cilantro sprigs

2 to 3 serrano chiles or 4 large jalapeño peppers, chopped

Juice of 2 lemons or 3 limes

½ teaspoon coarse salt

8 large ripe avocados

1. Peel off the outer papery husks from the tomatillos. Bring a large pot of lightly salted water to a boil. Add the tomatillos and boil for 3 minutes. Drain and rinse under cold running water to cool.

2. In a food processor, combine the tomatillos, onion, garlic, cilantro, serrano chiles, lemon juice, and salt. Puree until almost smooth.

3. Cut open the avocados, remove the pits, and scoop the meat into the processor. Pulse until the guacamole is partially smooth with some small chunks of avocado still intact. Season with additional salt to taste.

TACO BEAN DIP

MAKES ABOUT 6 CUPS

I make this easy dip even easier by buying the cheese already shredded. Keep in mind that the dip improves greatly if made a day or two, or even three, in advance. It holds up well in the refrigerator for a good week.

1 can (15 ounces) refried beans, preferably vegetarian

1 cup salsa

1 cup sour cream

8 ounces shredded Cheddar cheese

2½ tablespoons taco seasoning mix

1½ tablespoons ground cumin

1 cup thinly sliced scallion greens

2 tablespoons minced pickled jalapeños, optional

1. In a food processor, combine the beans, salsa, sour cream, Cheddar cheese, taco seasoning mix, and cumin. Puree until smooth.

2. Stir in the scallions and the pickled jalapeños, if you're adding them. Cover and refrigerate for up to 3 days before serving.

SHRIMP AND JICAMA SALAD

36 SERVINGS

Instant Acapulco, this enticing salad is designed to be scooped up with tortilla chips or endive spears. You could leave the shrimp whole, turning the salad into a sort of Mexican shrimp cocktail and serving it on small plates, with forks. Either way, the dish is simple and can be made at least a day ahead. I call for cooked shrimp to save work, but if using raw shelled shrimp, simply boil for 2 to 3 minutes, until pink and curled.

3 pounds cooked shelled shrimp

1½ pounds jicama

1 large white onion

2½ cups ketchup

1 cup fresh lime juice

1½ cups coarsely chopped cilantro

¾ cup minced fresh jalapeño peppers

Coarse salt and freshly ground pepper

1. If the shrimp you buy are flabby and barely cooked, dump them into a pot of boiling water for an extra minute. Then drain and dump into a bowl of ice and water to chill and firm up. Cut the shrimp into ½-inch dice.

2. Shave off the brown skin from the jicama and cut the white meat into ⅜-inch dice. Finely dice the onion.

3. In a large bowl, blend the ketchup and lime juice. Stir in the onion, cilantro, and jalapeños. Season with salt and pepper to taste. Add the shrimp and jicama and stir to mix evenly. Cover and refrigerate until serving time.

CHICKEN AND BEEF FAJITAS

36 SERVINGS

Because there is often a division of taste between those who eat only chicken and seafood and enthusiastic beef eaters, I designed these fajitas to give a choice of the two. Omnivores will have a great time! Of course, if it's easier for you, all chicken or all skirt steak can be used. This is an excellent marinade, which would also serve well for pork. Three hours is plenty of time to marinate both of these meats, though you could go as long as 6 hours in the refrigerator. The steak can sit overnight, but skinless, boneless chicken softens too much if left in an acid for too long. I find covered plastic containers are handy for marinating the meat. Serve the fajitas with the Grilled Pepper and Onion Strips, which follow, bowls of salsa, guacamole, and sour cream, if you like, on the side.

6 pounds skinless, boneless chicken breasts

4 medium onions, sliced

6 garlic cloves, thinly sliced

6 pounds skirt steaks

2 cups fresh orange juice

1 cup sherry vinegar

⅔ cup fresh lime juice

½ cup light olive oil or vegetable oil

2 tablespoons dried oregano, preferably Mexican

2 tablespoons ground cumin

1½ tablespoons salt

1 teaspoon freshly ground black pepper

½ teaspoon cayenne pepper

Warm flour tortillas

1. Layer the chicken with half the onions and garlic in one large plastic container or large bowl. Layer the beef with the remaining onions and garlic in a second container or bowl.

2. Whisk together the orange juice, vinegar, lime juice, oil, oregano, cumin, salt, pepper, and cayenne. Pour half over the chicken and half over the beef. *(Note: If you are preparing this recipe so that you can grill the chicken in advance, make all the marinade, pour half of it over the chicken, and store the remainder in a covered jar, to use the day you grill the beef. Do not use all the marinade for the chicken and then reuse it for the beef; bacteria could develop.)*

3. To cook the chicken, prepare a moderately hot fire in a barbecue grill. Remove the chicken from the marinade and pat dry; scrape off any onions or garlic that cling. Grill the chicken, turning occasionally, until the chicken is nicely browned outside and white inside but still juicy, 12 to 15 minutes. Transfer to a cutting board and let stand for a minute or two, then cut into strips.

4. To cook the beef, remove the skirt steaks from the marinade and pat dry; scrape off any onions or garlic. Prepare a hot fire in a barbecue grill and cook for about 2 minutes on each side; skirt steak has to be on the rare side or it will be tough. Transfer to a cutting board and let stand for a minute or two before carving crosswise on the diagonal into thin slices. Serve the chicken and beef strips with flour tortillas and your choice of garnishes.

GRILLED PEPPER AND ONION STRIPS

36 SERVINGS AS A CONDIMENT

Strips of grilled peppers—used to garnish fajitas, tacos, grilled steaks, and the like—are called *rajas* in Mexico. Poblanos are usually the dominant pepper, but here I temper their mild heat with sweet red, green, and yellow peppers, which are also very pretty, and with onions, which add sweetness when cooked.

***Rajas* can be prepared several ways. My favorite is on a very hot grill, so they pick up that nice smoky flavor; that's the technique given below. Alternatively, the peppers can be roasted under the broiler and the onions sautéed in a pan until golden, but you'll find it will have less character that way.**

6 large poblano peppers

2 large green bell peppers

2 large red bell peppers

2 large yellow bell peppers

2 large white onions

¼ cup olive oil

Coarse salt

1. Light a hot fire in a barbecue grill. Put the whole peppers on the grill and roast them, turning, until blackened all over, 10 to 15 minutes. Set aside until cool enough to handle.

2. Thickly slice the onions, brush them with a little of the olive oil, and grill them, oiled side down, until browned on the bottom, 3 to 5 minutes. Brush again with oil, turn over, and grill until the onion slices are softened but still slightly firm and browned on the second side, 3 to 5 minutes longer.

3. Rub the blackened skin off the peppers. Cut them in half and discard the stems, seeds, and watery inner membranes. Slice the pepper halves into thin strips about 1½ inches long.

4. Cut the onion rings in half to make strips. Toss the pepper and onion strips in a bowl with the remaining olive oil. Season with salt to taste. Serve at room temperature or reheat in a skillet.

COWBOY BEANS WITH BEER AND BACON

36 SERVINGS

Three pounds of dried beans cook up to a large kettleful, so you'll want to use a big stockpot for this recipe. A heavy bottom is best, because beans can scorch if the material is too thin. If you have any leftover beans at the end of the party, parcel them into covered containers or heavy-duty sealable plastic bags and freeze for future meals. They hold up surprisingly well.

3 pounds dried pinto beans

1 pound thickly sliced bacon

¼ cup vegetable oil

3 medium onions, coarsely chopped

2 bottles (12 ounces) lager beer, such as Corona Extra

1 can (28 ounces) Italian peeled tomatoes, with their juices

¼ cup packed dark brown sugar

1 tablespoon dried oregano, preferably Mexican

2 dried chipotle chiles or 1 teaspoon chipotle chile powder

1½ tablespoons coarse salt

1. Rinse the beans well and pick over to remove any grit. Either soak them overnight in enough cold water to cover by at least 2 inches or simply boil the beans in a very large pot of unsalted water until they are about half-cooked, about 30 minutes. Drain the beans into a colander.

2. Cut the bacon crosswise into short, ¼-inch-wide strips. In a large stockpot, cook the bacon in the oil over moderate heat until the strips give up most of their fat and begin to brown lightly, 5 to 7 minutes. Using a skimmer or slotted spoon, remove the bacon to a plate. If there is more than ½ cup fat in the pot, spoon out the excess; otherwise, just leave the drippings in the pot.

3. Add the onions, raise the heat to moderately high, and sauté, stirring occasionally, until golden brown, 10 to 12 minutes.

4. Pour in the beer and bring to a boil, using a wooden spatula or spoon to scrape up any browned bits from the bottom of the pan. Add the beans to the pot. Add the tomatoes with their juices, brown sugar, oregano, chipotles, and 4 quarts of water. Bring to a boil, reduce the heat to moderately low, and simmer until the beans are tender, 1 to 1¼ hours.

5. Using an old-fashioned potato masher, mash the beans in the pot to crush about one-quarter of them. Add the salt and continue to simmer until the beans are soft and the liquid surrounding them is thick.

CREAMY BAKED RICE WITH CORN, CHILES, AND CHEESE

36 SERVINGS

Every large party needs a filler, and this is it. Those who want to eat light will head for the cabbage salad; hearty eaters will dig into this substantial rice and corn dish. Because it is designed for advance preparation and last-minute reheating, I have used converted rice rather than a more traditional rice. Because the grains won't stick together, the dish will feel lighter, and the texture will hold better.

6 large ears of corn, yellow or bicolor

⅓ cup vegetable oil or olive oil

2 medium onions, finely chopped

4 garlic cloves, chopped

1 tablespoon ground cumin

6 cups converted long-grain white rice

8 cups hot chicken stock

2 teaspoons salt

2 cups sour cream

4 cups shredded Monterey Jack or sharp white Cheddar cheese (about 10 ounces)

1 cup finely diced cooked green chiles—roasted poblanos and/or canned diced green chiles

1 bunch of scallions, thinly sliced

1 cup cilantro sprigs, chopped

½ cup diced pickled jalapeño peppers

1. Shuck the corn and cook it in a large pot of boiling salted water for 2 to 3 minutes, until just tender. Rinse under cold running water and let stand until cool. Then use a large sharp knife to cut the kernels off the cob. Use the back of the knife to scrape the cobs to collect all the little inner bits and "milk."

2. In a large flameproof casserole, heat the oil over moderately high heat. Add the onions and cook, stirring occasionally, until lightly browned, 5 to 7 minutes. Add the garlic and cumin and cook, stirring often, for about 1 minute.

3. Add the rice and stir to coat with the oil. Pour in the stock and 2 cups of water and add the salt. Bring to a boil, reduce the heat to low, cover, and cook for about 15 minutes, or until the liquid is absorbed and the rice is tender but still al dente. Turn out into a very large, wide bowl or onto a sheet pan and let cool, folding the bottom up to the top to speed the process.

4. When the rice is just warm, add the sour cream and fold gently to mix. Add the corn, 3 cups of the cheese, the green chiles, scallions, chopped cilantro, and pickled jalapeños and stir gently to mix. Check to make sure there is enough salt. Turn the rice into 2 oiled large casseroles about 2½ inches deep; even a glass baking dish will work. Sprinkle ½ cup shredded cheese over the top of each. Cover and refrigerate for up to 3 days.

5. Be sure to remove the casserole from the refrigerator an hour or two before you plan to serve it. Heat the oven to 350°F.

6. Bake covered for 15 minutes. Uncover and continue to bake until the rice is hot throughout and the cheese on top is melted and lightly browned, about 10 minutes longer.

COOL CABBAGE SALAD WITH CARROTS AND RED PEPPERS

36 SERVINGS

Because this crisp salad is so simple, it benefits greatly from garden-fresh cabbage, if that is possible. Whenever cabbage tastes overly strong or "skunky," it is a sign of age. I like this best made the same day, but it will keep in a covered container or sealed plastic bags in the refrigerator overnight.

2 large green cabbages, garden fresh if possible

3 large carrots

2 large red bell peppers

⅔ cup Champagne vinegar, cider vinegar, or rice vinegar

⅓ cup sugar

Coarse salt and freshly ground pepper

1. Cut the cabbage into wedges, discarding the thick core. Shred into thin strips using the slicing disk of a food processor.

2. Peel the carrots. Shred them on the coarse holes of a box grater.

3. Stem and seed the red peppers and cut them into thin strips. You may be able to do this in the processor; I use a large knife.

4. In a large bowl, toss the cabbage with the carrots, red peppers, vinegar, and sugar. Season with salt and pepper to taste.

CHOCOLATE ICE CREAM ROLL WITH CINNAMON-COFFEE ICE CREAM AND KAHLÚA FUDGE SAUCE

16 TO 18 SERVINGS

You'll need two chocolate rolls for this party, which is not too difficult since they can be made weeks in advance, at two different times if you like, and tucked away in the freezer. Or make one ice cream roll and let a friend bring a different dessert. Notice that there is no flour in this chocolate "cake," which is really more of a fallen soufflé.

8 ounces bittersweet chocolate

¼ cup espresso or strongly brewed coffee

8 eggs, separated

½ cup sugar

1 teaspoon vanilla extract

⅛ teaspoon salt

½ gallon coffee ice cream, slightly softened

2 tablespoons ground cinnamon

Kahlúa Fudge Sauce (opposite page)

1. Heat the oven to 350°F. Butter a 13 × 18-inch half-sheet pan. Line the bottom with waxed paper or parchment, leaving some overlap at the short edges. Lightly butter the paper. Dust the bottom with flour and tap out any excess.

2. In a double boiler over simmering water or in a heavy-bottomed saucepan over low heat, melt the chocolate in the coffee. Remove from the heat and whisk until smooth. Set aside to cool slightly.

3. In a large mixing bowl, beat the egg yolks with an electric mixer until light and slightly thickened. Gradually beat in ¼ cup of the sugar, beating until the mixture holds a slowly dissolving ribbon when the beaters are lifted, about 2 minutes. Beat in the vanilla. Beat the egg yolk mixture into the melted chocolate.

4. In a large, clean bowl, beat the egg whites and salt using clean beaters until frothy. Gradually beat in the remaining ¼ cup sugar and beat until soft but definite peaks form. Stir about one-fourth of the whipped egg whites into the chocolate to lighten the mixture. Then fold the chocolate mixture into the remaining egg whites in the bowl.

5. Turn the batter into the sheet pan and bake for 18 to 20 minutes, or until the edges of the cake are just beginning to pull away from the sides of the pan and the top is firm and springs back when lightly touched.

6. Cover the cake with a kitchen towel that you have sprinkled lightly with water. Let cool in the pan on a rack for about 15 minutes. Then run a dull knife around the edges and use the paper edges to help lift the cake out of the pan. Have the long side facing you.

7. Spread the coffee ice cream evenly over the chocolate cake. An easy way to do this is to cut the ice cream into slices with a large knife (dipped in hot water and wiped dry, if necessary). Smooth gently with a spatula to fill in any large gaps but do not tear the cake. Sprinkle the cinnamon evenly over the ice cream.

8. Starting with the long side near you, roll up like a jelly roll, using the waxed paper to help you and peeling it off as you go. Wrap the chocolate roll well in plastic wrap and freeze for at least 2 hours or up to 2 months before cutting into slices about 1 inch thick. Serve with the fudge sauce.

KAHLÚA FUDGE SAUCE

MAKES ABOUT 2⅓ CUPS

Coffee-flavored Kahlúa blends smoothly with chocolate to add a subtle hint of Mexico.

Rich Chocolate Sauce (page 31)

⅓ cup Kahlúa

1. Make the chocolate sauce as directed. If it is cold, reheat in a heavy pot over very low heat, stirring. You want to get it hot without scorching the chocolate.

2. Remove from the heat and stir in the Kahlúa.

Wedding Supper

FOR 50

SMOKED SALMON RILLETTES

NIÇOISE SWORDFISH SALAD IN ENDIVE CUPS

PROVENÇAL BASIL DIP WITH CRUDITÉS

RICH LIVER MOUSSE WITH TOASTED HAZELNUTS (PAGE 110)

MUSHROOM-LEEK TURNOVERS

COLD FILLET OF BEEF WITH SHERRY WINE VINAIGRETTE

SESAME-GINGER GRILLED SALMON (PAGE 166)

PARSLEYED POTATO SALAD

GREEN BEAN SALAD WITH ROASTED RED PEPPERS

STILTON AND BRIE

ASSORTED BREADS AND CRACKERS

BASKETS OF PEARS, GRAPES, AND STRAWBERRIES

WEDDING CAKE

This is not just a hypothetical party; it is the menu I created for my own wedding, many years ago. We decided to get married at home. It was a second marriage for both of us, and we wanted the affair to be small, intimate, and very special. To make life easy, I hired an excellent caterer to supply all the hors d'oeuvre as well as the plates, silverware, glasses, napkins, trays, coffee urns, etc., and the waiters and bartender. All these things can be rented separately, but having the caterer act as general contractor made life very easy.

Since the caterer has many hands, there were six or seven canapés as well as crudités with two dips. I prepared the main-course Fillet of Beef, the Parsleyed Potato Salad, and the Green Bean Salad with Roasted Red Peppers the day before; the caterers arranged it on platters for me. A neighborhood baker duplicated one of Rose Levy Beranbaum's chocolate wedding cakes and decorated it like dotted Swiss to match my dress.

If you want to stage your own wedding, I cannot recommend this strategy highly enough. The caterers thought of all sorts of tiny details that might not have occurred to me; for example, tea and brewed decaf as well as low-calorie sweetener next to the regular coffee urn, lots of extra Champagne glasses, tiny blush rosebuds for the top of the cake. Everyone had a wonderful time, and I felt like a pampered guest in my own home. The day turned out exactly as I had hoped it would—perfect. If you do want to produce the entire event yourself, you can do it with enough time, planning, and advance preparation.

DO-AHEAD PLANNING

UP TO 2 MONTHS BEFORE THE WEDDING: Make a double recipe of the Mushroom-Leek Turnovers and freeze them unbaked.

UP TO 3 DAYS BEFORE THE WEDDING: Make a double recipe of the Rich Liver Mousse with Toasted Hazelnuts. Roast the peppers for the green bean salad, doubling the amount. Buy a wheel of ripe Brie and an impressive wedge of Stilton cheese.

UP TO 2 DAYS IN ADVANCE: Make the Smoked Salmon Rillettes and the Provençal Basil Dip.

THE DAY BEFORE THE WEDDING: Prepare the vegetables for the crudités and refrigerate them in plastic bags. Make the swordfish salad and prepare the endive. Roast the fillets, let cool, and refrigerate, well wrapped. Make the Parsleyed Potato Salad. Blanch the green beans and make the Sherry Wine Vinaigrette. Wash and dry the fruit.

THE DAY OF THE WEDDING: Don't underestimate how nervous you will be, no matter how much you're in love. Do everything as far ahead as possible and get as much help from family and friends as you're willing to accept.

UP TO 4 HOURS IN ADVANCE: Assemble the Niçoise Swordfish Salad in Endive Cups. Slice the beef and arrange the platters. Cover with plastic wrap and refrigerate. Complete a double recipe of the Green Bean Salad with Roasted Red Peppers. Remove the cheese from the refrigerator. Marinate two salmons for the Sesame-Ginger Grilled Salmon.

UP TO 2 HOURS IN ADVANCE: Grill or broil the salmon. Slice the bread early in the day and set aside in plastic bags, so the slices can be thrown into baskets when it's time. All the dips and spreads should be in serving dishes ready to be put out. The turnovers are popped frozen into the oven just before serving. If possible, set out the wedding cake a good hour or two before the ceremony. Also, remove the beef and cheese from the refrigerator at least 2 hours before serving.

SMOKED SALMON RILLETTES

MAKES ABOUT 4 CUPS

A rich hors d'oeuvre spread like this, served with toasted croutons of French bread, can be put to good use on any number of occasions. For a smaller group, this recipe can be cut in half easily.

1 pound smoked salmon, such as Norwegian or Scottish

⅓ cup finely diced red onion

3 tablespoons vodka

1½ tablespoons fresh lemon juice

¼ teaspoon freshly ground black pepper

3 or 4 dashes of cayenne pepper, to taste

¾ cup heavy cream

8 tablespoons (1 stick) unsalted butter, melted and cooled to tepid

2 tablespoons rinsed and drained tiny (nonpareil) capers

1. In a food processor, combine ¾ pound of the salmon with the onion, vodka, lemon juice, black pepper, and cayenne. Puree, scraping down the sides of the bowl once or twice, until the salmon and onion are minced.

2. With the machine on, slowly add the cream through the feed tube; scrape down the bowl. Gradually add the melted butter. Turn the mixture into a medium bowl.

3. Finely dice the remaining ¼ pound salmon. Fold the diced salmon and the capers into the puree. Pack into crocks or a serving bowl, cover, and refrigerate for at least 3 hours and up to 2 days before serving.

NIÇOISE SWORDFISH SALAD IN ENDIVE CUPS

MAKES 5 DOZEN

This wonderful hors d'oeuvre, from prolific cookbook author and former caterer Rick Rodgers, combines the lush flavors of the Mediterranean in a light package that's easy to pick up. It utilizes the natural shape of Belgian endive leaves, so there are no fussy containers to prepare. Best of all, the components can be made ahead and assembled several hours before serving. For a smaller group, halve the recipe exactly.

6 to 8 heads of Belgian endive

2 pounds swordfish steak, cut 1 inch thick

1 cup plus 2 tablespoons extra-virgin olive oil

1 cup (8 ounces) Kalamata or Mediterranean olives, pitted and coarsely chopped

6 tablespoons chopped fresh basil

6 tablespoons fresh lemon juice

Salt and freshly ground pepper

6 ounces sun-dried tomatoes packed in oil, drained and cut into thin strips, about 1½ inches long × ¼ inch wide

1. Wipe the outside of the endives with a damp paper towel. Cut off about ¼ inch of the base and separate the heads into leaves. Reserve 60 of the largest; discard the small inner leaves or reserve for salad. (The endive can be prepared a day ahead and stored in the refrigerator wrapped in moist paper towels inside a plastic bag.)

2. Heat the broiler with the rack set about 3 inches from the heat. Pat the swordfish dry and brush both sides of the fish with 2 tablespoons of the olive oil. Broil the swordfish, turning once, for about 4 minutes on each side, or until just barely opaque throughout. It will feel slightly firm to the touch; do not overcook or the fish will be dry. Let cool slightly, then remove and discard the skin and cut the fish into ⅜- to ½-inch cubes.

3. In a medium bowl, combine the swordfish, olives, and basil. In a small bowl, whisk together the remaining 1 cup olive oil and the lemon juice. Pour over the swordfish salad and toss to coat. Season with salt and pepper to taste. Cover and refrigerate until ready to assemble. (The swordfish salad can be prepared up to a day ahead.)

4. To assemble the hors d'oeuvre, scoop 1 heaping teaspoon of the swordfish salad into each endive cup, letting any excess dressing drain off as you spoon it up. Garnish each piece by laying a strip of sun-dried tomato diagonally across the salad. (The recipe can be completely assembled up to 4 hours before serving, covered with plastic wrap, and refrigerated.) Serve slightly chilled.

PROVENÇAL BASIL DIP

MAKES ABOUT 3½ CUPS

This is one of those easy all-purpose dips that can go just about anywhere. Be sure to use a fresh cheese and your best fruity olive oil. And serve it with whatever vegetables are freshest in the market—whole and cut up, raw and lightly steamed. It's also thick enough to dollop on bread or crackers.

1 log (9 ounces) soft white goat cheese, such as Coach Farm or Montrachet

1 package (8 ounces) cream cheese

1½ cups lightly packed fresh basil leaves

8 sun-dried tomato halves packed in oil, optional

1 large garlic clove, crushed

1 cup heavy cream

⅓ to ½ cup extra-virgin olive oil

Salt and freshly ground pepper

1. In a food processor, combine the goat cheese, cream cheese, half the basil, the sun-dried tomatoes, and the garlic. Puree until smooth.

2. Add the remaining basil. With the machine on, add the cream and ⅓ cup olive oil through the feed tube. If necessary, thin with a little more olive oil, 1 tablespoon at a time. Season with salt and pepper to taste. Cover and refrigerate for up to a day but be sure to let soften before serving.

MUSHROOM-LEEK TURNOVERS

MAKES ABOUT 6 DOZEN

These tasty morsels have been in my culinary repertoire for decades, and I never tire of them. Best of all for entertaining, they freeze beautifully and can be baked just before serving.

2 medium leeks (white and tender green), chopped, well rinsed, and drained

3 tablespoons unsalted butter

¾ pound mushrooms, minced

¾ teaspoon dried tarragon, crumbled

¾ teaspoon salt

½ teaspoon freshly ground black pepper

3 or 4 dashes of cayenne pepper

2 tablespoons all-purpose flour

¾ cup heavy cream

1 tablespoon fresh lemon juice

1½ ounces soft white goat cheese, such as Coach Farm

Flaky Cream Cheese Pastry (page 250)

1 egg beaten with 2 teaspoons water to make a glaze

1. In a large skillet or flameproof casserole, cook the leeks in the butter over moderate heat, stirring occasionally, until they are tender but not brown, 5 to 10 minutes.

2. Increase the heat to moderately high and add the mushrooms. Cook, stirring frequently, until the juices they give up evaporate and the mushroom pieces separate and begin to brown, about 10 minutes. Season with the tarragon, salt, black pepper, and cayenne.

3. Sprinkle on the flour and cook, stirring, for 1 to 2 minutes. Add the cream and cook, stirring, until the filling thickens to a mass. Stir in the lemon juice and goat cheese and cook, stirring, until the cheese melts and blends evenly. (The filling can be made a day ahead. Let cool, then cover and refrigerate.)

4. Roll out half the cream cheese pastry about ⅛ inch thick. Using a 2½-inch round cutter, preferably with a crinkled edge, cut out as many circles as possible. Scoop up ½ teaspoon of the mushroom-leek filling, squeeze it into a lozenge shape and set in the middle of each circle. Fold over the dough to make a semicircle and press the edges, beginning in the middle, to seal. Crimp the edges of the pastry with the tines of a fork. Prick each turnover once or twice with the fork to allow the steam to escape. Gather together the scraps of dough and set aside. Repeat with the second half of the dough. Combine all the scraps of dough, roll out, and use for more turnovers. (The recipe can be prepared to this point up to 3 months ahead. Put the turnovers on ungreased baking sheets, brush with the egg glaze, and freeze until they are hard. Then transfer to plastic bags or a covered container and freeze until you are ready to serve them.)

5. To cook, heat the oven to 350°F. Arrange the frozen turnovers on ungreased baking sheets. Bake for 12 to 15 minutes, until golden, crisp, and hot.

FLAKY CREAM CHEESE PASTRY

1½ packages (12 ounces) cream cheese, at room temperature

2 sticks (½ pound) unsalted butter, at room temperature

¾ teaspoon salt

3 cups unbleached all-purpose flour

1. In a food processor, combine the cream cheese with the butter. Process until blended and smooth. Add the salt. Gradually add the flour, processing until well blended.

2. Divide the pastry in half and form each piece into a ball, then flatten into a ½-inch-thick disk. Wrap both pieces of pastry separately in plastic bags and refrigerate for at least 30 minutes before rolling out.

COLD FILLET OF BEEF WITH SHERRY WINE VINAIGRETTE

ABOUT 50 SERVINGS

Nothing is more elegant than a rosy red, lean, and flavorful fillet of beef. How nice that it is just as good at cool room temperature as it is hot so you can easily cook it a day ahead. Here the slices of meat are garnished with pungent arugula, enlivened with colorful ripe tomatoes and red onions, and anointed with a dashing dressing made with plenty of shallots, fresh herbs, capers, and your very best aged sherry wine vinegar.

4 whole fillets of beef, about 5 pounds each, trimmed and tied

½ cup Cognac

½ cup minced shallots (about 6 large)

2 teaspoons salt

4 teaspoons coarsely cracked black pepper, preferably Tellicherry (I crush mine in a mortar)

½ cup fruity extra-virgin olive oil

6 large bunches of arugula, tough stems removed

Parsleyed Potato Salad (page 252)

8 large ripe tomatoes, sliced

6 medium red onions, thinly sliced

Sherry Wine Vinaigrette (opposite page)

1. Trim any excess external fat from the beef and place the fillets in a large roasting pan or shallow baking dishes. Rub each fillet with about 2 tablespoons of the Cognac. Sprinkle the minced shallots over the meat. Season each fillet with ½ teaspoon of the salt and 1 teaspoon of the pepper. Rub 2 tablespoons of the olive oil all over the meat. Set aside at room temperature for 30 minutes, turning once or twice.

2. Heat the oven to 450°F. Place a large ovenproof skillet or flameproof gratin dish over high heat. Add 2 of the fillets and cook, turning, until browned all over, about 5 minutes. Transfer to the roasting pan and repeat with the other 2 fillets.

3. Put the roasting pan in the oven and roast the fillets for 15 to 20 minutes, until the internal temperature reaches 125° to 130°F for rare. Let stand for at least 15 minutes. (The recipe can be prepared ahead to this point. Let stand at room temperature for several hours or wrap the meat and refrigerate overnight. Let return to room temperature before serving.)

4. Carve the fillets into slices about ½ inch thick. Arrange the arugula around the edge of 2 large platters. Mound half the potato salad in the center of each platter. Decoratively arrange rows or circles of the beef, tomatoes, and onions around the salad. Drizzle about ¼ cup of the dressing over the meat on each platter. Pour the remaining dressing into two gravy boats and set out with the platters.

SHERRY WINE VINAIGRETTE

MAKES ABOUT 4 CUPS

The quality of sherry vinegars varies hugely. For an occasion like this, it's worth splurging and buying a new bottle, if necessary, so that you have one that allows the flavor of the sherry to overtake the astringency of the vinegar. If your local market does not have one that is up to snuff, look online for specialty food purveyors: La Tienda and The Spanish Table are just two of the many places you can look for a wide assortment of high-quality oils and vinegars.

¾ cup sherry vinegar

¼ cup Dijon mustard

1½ teaspoons salt

1½ teaspoons coarsely cracked black pepper

3 cups extra-virgin olive oil

¾ cup minced shallots (about 8 large)

¾ cup minced parsley

⅓ cup tiny (nonpareil) capers, rinsed and drained

½ cup minced fresh tarragon, or 4 teaspoons dried

In a medium bowl, whisk together the vinegar, mustard, salt, and pepper. Gradually whisk in the olive oil until well blended and emulsified. Add the shallots, parsley, capers, and tarragon. Mix well.

PARSLEYED POTATO SALAD

ABOUT 50 SERVINGS

Because there's no mayonnaise in this light, flavorful potato salad, it can be set out at room temperature for hours.

12 pounds large waxy potatoes, such as Yukon gold or red-skinned

1¼ cups dry white wine

8 large shallots, minced

1 cup red wine vinegar

2 tablespoons Dijon mustard

1 tablespoon plus 1 teaspoon salt

2 teaspoons freshly ground pepper

2 cups extra-virgin olive oil

1 cup chopped parsley

1. Put the potatoes in a large stockpot of salted water, bring to a boil, and cook until the potatoes are tender, about 25 minutes from the time the water boils; drain.

2. As soon as the potatoes are cool enough to handle, peel off the skins and slice the potatoes. Put them in a large bowl and toss with the wine while they are still warm. Add the shallots and toss to mix.

3. In a medium bowl, whisk together the vinegar, mustard, salt, and pepper until blended. Gradually whisk in the olive oil until emulsified.

4. Pour the vinaigrette over the potatoes and toss to coat. (The recipe can be prepared ahead to this point and set aside at room temperature for several hours or refrigerated overnight.) Toss with the parsley shortly before serving.

GREEN BEAN SALAD WITH ROASTED RED PEPPERS

24 SERVINGS

Whether guests discern that this dish reflects all the colors of the Italian flag or not, they can't help but notice its vibrant color. If you can obtain an affordable quantity of narrow French green beans, called *haricots verts*, their flavor and texture are superior, and I recommend them highly. If you do cook the thinner beans, simply cut off the stem ends and leave them whole.

Make a double recipe for this party.

4 pounds green beans, trimmed and broken in half

1 large white onion, thinly sliced

2 large red bell peppers, roasted, peeled, seeded, and cut into very thin strips about 1½ inches long

¼ cup sherry vinegar

¾ cup extra-virgin olive oil

Salt and freshly ground pepper

1. In a large stockpot of boiling salted water, cook the beans until they are tender, 4 to 6 minutes. Drain in a colander and rinse with cold running water; drain well.

2. In a large salad bowl, combine the green beans, onion, and roasted red peppers. Drizzle on the vinegar and oil. Toss well. Season with salt and pepper to taste and toss again. Serve at room temperature.

Afternoon Open House

FOR 50 OR MORE

ROMESCO SAUCE (PAGE 39) WITH CRUDITÉS AND PITA TRIANGLES

THINLY SLICED PEPPERONI AND/OR SOPPRESSATA

WHEEL OF AGED CHEDDAR CHEESE OR LARGE CHUNK OF FRESH PARMESAN

NUTS AND OLIVES

MEAT LOAF FROM THE WALDORF

TURKEY TONNATO (PAGE 67)

TRIPLE-MUSTARD POTATO SALAD

DILLED PASTA SALAD WITH SCALLOPS AND SMOKED SALMON

LYDIE MARSHALL'S RATATOUILLE WITH GOAT CHEESE

TOSSED GREEN SALAD

ASSORTED PASTRIES AND COOKIES

RED AND WHITE WINE AND BEER

NONALCOHOLIC PARTY PUNCH

When I was married and living in student housing at the University of Chicago many years ago, our neighbors down the hall threw a huge open house, just as I was cooking my way through Julia Child's *Mastering the Art of French Cooking*. I had fallen in love with cooking—permanently, as it turned out—and I knew this couple had spent a year in France. Seeing how they entertained was going to be like finding the Holy Grail.

To my surprise, the spread she put out, though delicious, was quite casual. There were pâtés and cold meats, wheels of cheese, and big bowls of assorted salads. The house glowed with the soft light of thick tallow candles, and everyone had a wonderful time. Our hostess remained relaxed and quick to smile all evening.

She had learned something important. Even if you're a fabulous cook, entertaining 50-odd guests dropping in at unexpected intervals during the day will keep you busy enough—greeting everyone, taking coats, making introductions, steering people to the food and drink. The kitchen is the last thing you should have to worry about on the day of the party. That's why I tried to keep this buffet as simple as possible.

For an open house, you really don't need any formal appetizers. Place some bowls of nuts and olives around the room. All the buffet food is served chilled or at room temperature, which means it can all be prepared in advance and only needs to be arranged on platters the day of the party and refreshed. While I've given you a whole list of recipes to make, keep in mind you can substitute bought food for any one of them. For example, while I love homemade meat loaf, you could just as easily put out a spiral-cut baked ham, which needs nothing more than heating in the oven.

Tasty and pâté-like, the meat loaf can be prepared up to 3 days in advance; its flavor will actually improve upon sitting. Wait until it's cold to slice it: Cut it lengthwise in half and then into ½-inch slices. You should end up with at least 46 pieces. Arrange them attractively on a platter and garnish with fresh herbs or olives and cherry tomatoes.

Though I happen to love my potato salad freshly made, this one stands up nicely for a day or two in the refrigerator. The ratatouille improves if made a day in advance, but let it return to room temperature before serving. The seafood pasta salad can be completely assembled the night before, but it will be tastier if you prepare all the components in advance and wait to toss them with the dressing until shortly before serving. If you do so, you may have a little extra dressing. Set it aside, in case you need it later.

Get everything ready for the punch but mix only half of it just before the first guests arrive and refill the bowl later as needed. That way, it will stay chilled without getting watered down by melting ice.

As with any buffet, try to set out different dishes in different places, so you don't get any traffic jams in one spot. With a big, all-day affair like this, if you don't have enough plates and glasses and prefer not to rent, buy good-quality paper plates and napkins, sturdy plastic utensils, and plastic cups. This way you can enjoy the party as much as your guests, which will guarantee its success.

DO-AHEAD PLANNING

UP TO 3 DAYS BEFORE THE PARTY: Make the meat loaf and the Romesco sauce.

UP TO 2 DAYS IN ADVANCE: Make the Ratatouille with Goat Cheese. Poach the turkey breast for the Turkey Tonnato; let it cool, then refrigerate it in its poaching liquid.

THE DAY BEFORE THE PARTY: Prepare the crudités. Make the Triple-Mustard Potato Salad. Boil the pasta, poach the scallops, and make the dressing for the Dilled Pasta Salad with Scallops and Smoked Salmon. Make the sauce for the Turkey Tonnato.

THE MORNING OF THE OPEN HOUSE: Remove the cheese and the ratatouille from the refrigerator. Complete the Dilled Pasta Salad. Assemble the Turkey Tonnato. Make the Nonalcoholic Party Punch.

MEAT LOAF FROM THE WALDORF

MAKES 2 LARGE LOAVES; 46 TO 50 SERVINGS

Chef John Dougherty made this meat loaf for his visiting aunts because he knew it was the kind of honest home-style food they enjoyed. It turned out so well that he decided to put it on the menu at Oscar's of the Waldorf-Astoria. I like it cold even more than hot, especially in a sandwich with spicy Dijon mustard.

14 slices of firm-textured white bread

1½ cups milk

1½ cups tomato puree

2½ tablespoons vegetable oil

4 medium onions, chopped

1 small red bell pepper, finely diced

1 large green bell pepper, finely diced

4 large garlic cloves, minced

4 pounds lean ground beef

3 pounds lean ground pork

3 pounds ground veal

2 cups ketchup

½ cup Dijon mustard

¼ cup Worcestershire sauce

1 teaspoon hot pepper sauce

6 eggs

½ cup chopped fresh basil, or 2 tablespoons dried

1 tablespoon salt

2 teaspoons freshly ground pepper

1 pound sliced bacon

1. Trim the crusts from the bread and cut the slices into ½-inch dice. Put in a large bowl and add the milk and tomato puree. Let soften while you prepare the vegetables.

2. In a large heavy skillet, heat the oil. Add the onions and cook over moderately low heat until softened, about 3 minutes. Add the bell peppers and garlic, increase the heat to moderately high, and sauté until the peppers are softened but still bright colored and the onions are golden, 3 to 5 minutes longer.

3. Mash the softened bread in the bowl. Add the sautéed vegetables, the beef, pork, veal, ketchup, mustard, Worcestershire sauce, hot sauce, eggs, basil, salt, and pepper. Roll up your sleeves and mix very well with your hands. (The recipe can be prepared to this point up to a day ahead. Cover the meat loaf mixture and refrigerate.)

4. Heat the oven to 375°F. Form the meat mixture into 2 free-form loaf shapes on 2 large greased baking sheets (with edges to catch the drips). Arrange half the bacon slices crosswise over each meat loaf, tucking in the edges underneath.

5. Bake for 1 hour 10 minutes, switching the 2 sheets for even cooking halfway through, or until the internal temperature measures 180°F. Remove from the oven and pour off the fat from the baking sheet. Let stand for at least 10 minutes before slicing. For a buffet, it's often best to cut the loaves in half lengthwise and then crosswise into ½-inch-thick slices.

TRIPLE-MUSTARD POTATO SALAD

40 TO 50 SERVINGS AS PART OF A BUFFET

There are a million recipes for potato salad, and this one makes it a million and one. Toasted mustard seeds impart a lovely nutty flavor and surprising crunch. If you prefer, you can skip them and call it Double-Mustard Potato Salad. Needless to say, the better the mustard you use, the better this salad will be.

8 pounds red-skinned potatoes

2⅔ cups mayonnaise

⅓ cup grainy mustard, such as Pommery

⅓ cup sharp Dijon mustard, preferably imported

⅓ cup fresh lemon juice

⅓ cup mustard seeds

⅓ cup olive oil

Salt and freshly ground pepper

1. Put the potatoes in a large pot of cold salted water to cover. Bring to a boil and cook for 20 to 25 minutes, or until tender; the potato will slip off a knife inserted into the center when it's done. Drain and let stand until cool enough to handle. Peel the potatoes and cut them into 1-inch chunks.

2. In a small bowl, combine the mayonnaise, grainy mustard, Dijon mustard, and lemon juice; mix well.

3. In a large serving bowl, combine the potatoes and mustard dressing. Toss to coat.

4. Combine the mustard seeds and olive oil in a medium covered skillet. Cook over moderate heat with the lid on, shaking the pan, until the seeds start to pop, 1 to 2 minutes (you'll hear them). Immediately remove from the heat and keep shaking the pan with the lid on until they stop popping. Scrape the seeds and oil over the potato salad and fold gently to mix them in. Season with salt and pepper to taste. (The potato salad can be made up to 2 days in advance. Cover and refrigerate.)

DILLED PASTA SALAD WITH SCALLOPS AND SMOKED SALMON

24 SINGLE SERVINGS; 48 TO 50 SERVINGS AS PART OF A BUFFET

Everything for this salad can be prepared ahead and refrigerated overnight, but the pasta, seafood, and sauce should be tossed together shortly before serving to preserve the creamy consistency. If you prefer, shelled shrimp can be substituted for the scallops.

2 pounds bay scallops or halved sea scallops

3 pounds fusilli, shells, or penne

2 tablespoons olive oil

2 cups sour cream

⅔ cup honey mustard

½ cup fresh lemon juice

1¼ cups chopped fresh dill (do not substitute dried)

1 cup minced scallions

2 garlic cloves, crushed through a press

1 pound smoked salmon, preferably Norwegian, cut into thin slivers about 1½ inches long

1. Poach the scallops in a large saucepan of simmering salted water until just white throughout, 2 to 3 minutes. Drain in a colander.

2. In a large stockpot of boiling salted water, cook the fusilli until just tender, 10 to 12 minutes. Drain and rinse under cold running water; drain well. In a large bowl, toss the pasta with the olive oil. Cover and refrigerate for up to a day.

3. In a small bowl, blend together the sour cream, honey mustard, and lemon juice. Stir in the dill, scallions, and garlic. Cover and set aside for up to 1 hour or refrigerate for up to 24 hours before serving.

4. To assemble the salad, add the sauce to the pasta and toss to coat lightly. Add the scallops and smoked salmon and toss to distribute the seafood throughout. Serve slightly chilled or at room temperature.

LYDIE MARSHALL'S RATATOUILLE WITH GOAT CHEESE

40 TO 50 SERVINGS

Cookbook author Lydie Marshall was a celebrated New York cooking teacher until she left to open a culinary school in a chateau in her native France. Her food always has a special twist that makes it her own, as you'll find when you try this ratatouille made with sweet red and yellow peppers and goat cheese.

4 pounds eggplant, unpeeled, cut into ½-inch dice

3 tablespoons coarse salt

About ⅔ cup extra-virgin olive oil

6 medium onions, sliced

3 pounds red bell peppers, cut into ½-inch squares

3 pounds yellow bell peppers, cut into ½-inch squares

8 medium tomatoes, peeled, seeded, and cut into ½-inch dice

4 medium zucchini, cut into ½-inch dice

6 garlic cloves, minced

¼ cup minced fresh tarragon or basil

½ teaspoon freshly ground black pepper

¼ teaspoon cayenne pepper

10 ounces fresh white goat cheese

1. Put the eggplant in a colander and sprinkle with 2 tablespoons of the salt; toss. Let drain for 30 minutes. Rinse the eggplant under cold running water, drain, and pat dry.

2. Heat ⅔ cup olive oil in a very large (preferably 9-quart) nonreactive flameproof casserole. Add the onions and sauté over moderately high heat until just beginning to color, 5 to 10 minutes.

3. Add the red and yellow peppers to the onions and cook, stirring frequently, until they are slightly softened, 5 to 10 minutes.

4. Add the eggplant and cook, tossing and adding additional oil if the eggplant begins to stick, until it is translucent on the outside, about 15 minutes.

5. Finally, add the tomatoes, zucchini, garlic, and tarragon. Season with the remaining 1 tablespoon salt, the black pepper, and the cayenne. Cover and cook for 40 minutes, stirring frequently to prevent sticking.

6. Uncover the pan and cook until the liquid is reduced to a syrupy consistency, about 15 minutes. Remove the pan from the heat. (The recipe can be prepared ahead to this point. Refrigerate, covered. Reheat before proceeding.)

7. Crumble half the goat cheese into the vegetables and stir to mix. Crumble the remaining cheese over the top of the ratatouille, cover the pan, and let stand for 5 minutes to let the cheese melt. Serve warm or let cool to room temperature.

NONALCOHOLIC PARTY PUNCH

MAKES ABOUT 3 GALLONS

So many different flavors blend together in this delightful tropical mix that the resulting drink is sophisticated and refreshing, and the lack of alcohol is not apparent.

2 bottles (1½ quarts each) Mauna La'i guava/passion-fruit drink or other tropical beverage

2 bottles (1½ quarts each) cranberry juice cocktail

2 quarts grapefruit juice, preferably from the refrigerated section of the supermarket

3 bottles (1 liter each) ginger ale

2 trays of ice cubes plus a big bag of cubes for individual drinks

4 or 5 limes, halved lengthwise and cut into thin slices

1. In a large punch bowl or in several large pitchers, blend together the Mauna La'i, cranberry juice, grapefruit juice, and ginger ale. Add the 2 trays of ice cubes and the lime slices. Put the remaining ice in an ice bucket.

2. To serve, put 2 or 3 ice cubes in an old-fashioned glass or punch cup and ladle on the punch, making sure everyone gets a slice of lime.

Party Punch with a Wallop

Make the punch as above but omit the ginger ale. Instead add 1 bottle (750 ml) vodka and 1 bottle (750 ml) golden rum, such as Mount Gay or Bacardi Gold Reserve. Serve smaller portions.

Help

I wrote this book to guide you through a big party or dinner for a large crowd without any additional help. However, there's no question your job will be easier if you have an extra pair of hands. Straightening the kitchen in between courses makes a large sit-down dinner much more manageable. Getting rid of dirty dishes and glasses at a buffet or open house keeps the room attractive and the party fresh. And there are special occasions, such as a wedding or graduation in the home, when you really want to be a guest at your own party.

Remember that help doesn't always wear a uniform. If you have a child or close relative of appropriate age, try recruiting him or her for a favor or nominal fee. Teenagers and older people are often happy to work for a reasonable hourly rate. Some high schools and colleges have programs that train young people for exactly this kind of work: serving and cleaning up, though not, of course, bartending. Someone—a friend or spouse—should be assigned to tend bar, whether that means mixing drinks or just making sure bottles are opened, there's enough ice, and the punch bowl is full.

If you decide to hire help for a special occasion, be sure to check references. Unless you know of someone through a personal recommendation, go through an agency that specializes in household personnel. Be sure the duties of any outside help are clearly defined beforehand and check if fees include a tip or not. They usually don't, and a cash tip at your discretion is expected; 15 percent is the norm. Don't be shy about setting up your own rules—such as no smoking—for anyone who works for you for the evening. And make it clear to anyone hired to serve that he or she will be expected to double—taking coats, bussing dirty ashtrays and dishes, and helping to clean up in the kitchen, as well as passing food. Try to allow time for a dry run or at least a few moments to show them where everything is. If you're going to have a stranger working in your kitchen, it's best to have all serving pieces out and marked with what they're to be used for.

A professional caterer will tell you that you need one server for every 10 guests at a buffet, or three waiters for every 20 guests at a sit-down dinner, plus kitchen help and a bartender. Since most of us cannot afford that kind of help, I'd say that at a big open house or buffet, a bartender is nice to have, but one person to clean up in the kitchen, keep the room in order, and help serve can make all the difference in the world.

Cocktails and Hors d'Oeuvre

FOR 50 OR MORE

The cocktail party is so versatile, and the number of people invited can vary so much, that it's difficult to talk about it in just one way. That's why I've chosen the "one from column A, one from column B" approach. Given your guest list and the tone you wish to set, you can design your own menu from the choices listed below. Begin with at least five items: for example, purchased assorted cheeses and olives, a spread, a dip with crudités, and one individual hors d'oeuvre that will be served hot or cold. Add another item for every five more guests up to 32; then add another dish for every eight guests.

Allow one ounce of cheese, smoked salmon, or cured or smoked meat per person. Depending on which recipes you choose, you may have to double recipes. There should be at least two, and preferably three, of any one hors d'oeuvre and about one-quarter cup of a spread for each guest. This varies, of course, depending on the number of choices and total amount of food available. Whenever you are in doubt, remember that cheese, nuts, and chips can take up the slack. An invitation to a cocktail party implies drinks and nibbles, not a filling supper.

Don't try to do too much. Only a few hot hors d'oeuvre are given in this book because, without help, I think it is very difficult even just to reheat and pass around a tray. There's nothing wrong with having all the food chilled or at room temperature. Set out anything you can ahead. Get platters prepared and the spreads and dips put in bowls. Prepare crudités a day ahead and refrigerate them in a bowl of cold water or in plastic bags with a damp paper towel. If you have the time to cook, prepare the bulk of the food yourself. If you don't, buy plenty of cheese and cured meats, smoked salmon, olives, and nuts. The few dishes you do pass around will stand out as stars.

When choosing the menu for a cocktail party, keep in mind that spicy, salty foods are pleasant with drinks, but offer a nice mix of flavors and textures. Balance creamy and spicy, smooth and crunchy, seafood, vegetables, and meats. An eclectic blend of tastes is highly desirable with this kind of piecemeal sampling of foods and makes for a great party.

MENU IDEAS

BUY

- Nuts
- Olives
- Cheese
- Smoked salmon
- Prosciutto or Serrano ham, thinly sliced
- Pepperoni
- Caviar
- Crudités
- Tortilla chips
- Crackers, Melba toast, cocktail rye, and pumpernickel bread and/or baguettes

DIPS AND SPREADS

- Provençal Basil Dip (page 248)
- Gingered Eggplant Spread (page 190)
- Hummus (page 54)
- Rich Liver Mousse with Toasted Hazelnuts (page 110)
- Smoked Salmon Rillettes (page 246)
- Romesco Sauce (page 39)
- Sour Cream and Two-Caviar Dip (page 191)
- Fresh Tomato Salsa (page 149)

COLD OR ROOM-TEMPERATURE CANAPÉS AND HORS D'OEUVRE

- Cheese Straws (page 174)
- Niçoise Swordfish Salad in Endive Cups (page 247)
- Pesto Deviled Eggs (page 173)
- Caviar Nachos (page 146)
- Marinated Black Olives (page 106)
- Spiced Nuts (page 147)
- Shrimp and Jicama Salad (page 238)

HOT HORS D'OEUVRE

- Grilled Stuffed Grape Leaves (page 96)
- Coriander Chicken Rolls (page 165)
- Mushroom-Leek Turnovers (page 249)
- Barbecued Carnitas with Pineapple-Chipotle Salsa (page 236)
- Crispy Cheese Puffs (page 158)
- Sweet and Tangy Shrimp Kebabs (page 96)

BAR

- Cosmopolitans (page 264)
- Mojitos (page 264)
- Margaritas by the Batch (page 148)
- Chilled white wine
- Red wine
- Assortment of hard liquor, if you wish: gin, vodka, Scotch, bourbon, rum, and sweet and dry vermouth
- Plenty of mixers and nonalcoholic beverages: club soda, cola (regular and diet), orange juice, and tonic

COSMOPOLITANS

MAKES 8 DRINKS

If you're going to offer a house cocktail, these pink martini-like drinks are popular. For a professional touch, stick the cocktail glasses in the freezer before the party starts, so that they are chilled when you pour.

Ice cubes

2 cups lemon-flavored vodka

1 cup Cointreau or Triple Sec

½ cup fresh lime juice

½ cup cranberry juice

Fill a pitcher at least one-third full with ice cubes. Add the vodka, Cointreau, lime juice, and cranberry juice. Stir for 30 seconds. Strain into cocktail glasses.

MOJITOS

MAKES 8 DRINKS

If you want to see your most reserved guests learn the tango, this is the drink to serve them. With the surge in nuevo-Latino flavors in restaurants across the country, this mint-flavored potion, happily, was not left behind. Only drawback: Fresh mint is a must. This drink calls for a simple syrup, which, as the name implies, is incredibly simple to make. However, it must chill before being used, so you have to remember to make it a day, or a week, ahead of time. In case you want to make more mojitos, or lemonade—which it is great for, too—I suggest you make a double or triple batch of the syrup in Step 1. It will keep in the refrigerator for months.

½ cup sugar

½ cup water

½ cup fresh mint leaves

5 limes—4 cut into 3 or 4 wedges each, 1 thinly sliced

1 cup light rum

1 cup club soda

Crushed ice or ice cubes

1. In a small saucepan, combine the sugar and water. Bring to a boil, stirring to dissolve the sugar. Remove from the heat and let the syrup cool; then pour into a jar, cover, and refrigerate until cold.

2. Pour the cold syrup into a pitcher. Add the mint leaves and lime wedges. Using a wooden spoon, press on the mint and lime to press out a lot of the juice and crush the mint. Pour in the rum and club soda. Stir to mix.

3. Fill 8 highball glasses with crushed ice or ice cubes. Pour the mojitos over the ice. Garnish each with a slice of lime.

INDEX

Underscored page references indicate boxed text.

C

E

F

R

S

T

Conversion Chart

These equivalents have been slightly rounded to make measuring easier.

Volume Measurements

U.S.	*Imperial*	*Metric*
¼ tsp	–	1 ml
½ tsp	–	2 ml
1 tsp	–	5 ml
1 Tbsp	–	15 ml
2 Tbsp (1 oz)	1 fl oz	30 ml
¼ cup (2 oz)	2 fl oz	60 ml
⅓ cup (3 oz)	3 fl oz	80 ml
½ cup (4 oz)	4 fl oz	120 ml
⅔ cup (5 oz)	5 fl oz	160 ml
¾ cup (6 oz)	6 fl oz	180 ml
1 cup (8 oz)	8 fl oz	240 ml

Weight Measurements

U.S.	*Metric*
1 oz	30 g
2 oz	60 g
4 oz (¼ lb)	115 g
5 oz (⅓ lb)	145 g
6 oz	170 g
7 oz	200 g
8 oz (½ lb)	230 g
10 oz	285 g
12 oz (¾ lb)	340 g
14 oz	400 g
16 oz (1 lb)	455 g
2.2 lb	1 kg

Length Measurements

U.S.	*Metric*
¼"	0.6 cm
½"	1.25 cm
1"	2.5 cm
2"	5 cm
4"	11 cm
6"	15 cm
8"	20 cm
10"	25 cm
12" (1')	30 cm

Pan Sizes

U.S.	*Metric*
8" cake pan	20 × 4 cm sandwich or cake tin
9" cake pan	23 × 3.5 cm sandwich or cake tin
11" × 7" baking pan	28 × 18 cm baking tin
13" × 9" baking pan	32.5 × 23 cm baking tin
15" × 10" baking pan	38 × 25.5 cm baking tin (Swiss roll tin)
1½ qt baking dish	1.5 liter baking dish
2 qt baking dish	2 liter baking dish
2 qt rectangular baking dish	30 × 19 cm baking dish
9" pie plate	22 × 4 or 23 × 4 cm pie plate
7" or 8" springform pan	18 or 20 cm springform or loose-bottom cake tin
9" × 5" loaf pan	23 × 13 cm or 2 lb narrow loaf tin or pâté tin

Temperatures

Fahrenheit	*Centigrade*	*Gas*
140°	60°	–
160°	70°	–
180°	80°	–
225°	105°	¼
250°	120°	½
275°	135°	1
300°	150°	2
325°	160°	3
350°	180°	4
375°	190°	5
400°	200°	6
425°	220°	7
450°	230°	8
475°	245°	9
500°	260°	–